The FILMS *of*
WIILLIAM HOLDEN

The FILMS *of* WILLIAM HOLDEN

by LAWRENCE J. QUIRK

THE CITADEL PRESS   •   SECAUCUS, NEW JERSEY

Dedication

for MICHAEL RITZER
and the coming generations of film writers,
scholars and buffs

Acknowledgments

Mark Ricci and The Memory Shop, New York; Ernest
D. Burns and Cinemabilia, New York; Movie Star
News, New York; Kenneth G. Lawrence and The Movie
Memorabilia Shop of Hollywood; The Staff of the New
York Public Library's Theatre and Film Collection,
Library & Museum of Performing Arts, New York; War-
ner Bros. Pictures, Wynn Loewenthal; Columbia Pic-
tures Corp., Hortense Schorr; Metro-Goldwyn-Mayer,
Paramount, United Artists, Universal Pictures, National
General Pictures.

And James E. Runyan, Fredric March, Rouben Ma-
moulian, Bosley Crowther, Doug McClelland, Michael
Ritzer, John Cocchi, Paul and Helen Denis, Fredda
Dudley Balling, Albert B. Manski, Gene Ringgold, Don
Koll, and Edward Z. Epstein.

First edition
Copyright ©1973 by Lawrence J. Quirk
All rights reserved
Published by Citadel Press
A division of Lyle Stuart, Inc.
120 Enterprise Avenue, Secaucus, N. J. 07094
Printed in the United States of America by
Noble Offset Printers, New York
Designed by William Meinhardt
Library of Congress catalog card number: 73–84150
ISBN 0–8065–0375–0

Contents

WILLIAM HOLDEN:
His Life and Work

William Holden at age sixteen, 1934

WILLIAM HOLDEN:
His Life and Work

William Holden is fifty-five years old, he has been a film star for thirty-four years, and he has made close to sixty films.

He started out as a wide-eyed, idealistic, All-American smiling-Jim type—the nice, well-brought-up middle-class boy from Pasadena, replete with limited, straitlaced, Congregationalist views inculcated by cautious parents whose approval he craved and earned—the bright new Golden Boy of 1939, and the world of Hollywood lay before him like a land of dreams.

Now, in 1973, in a world far different from the world of his youth, a world that changed relentlessly and radically as he himself changed, he is a weary, life-battered, hypersophisticated middle-aged man of broad human experience who has traveled and lived all over the world, maintains homes in far-flung places like Kenya, Switzerland, and Hong Kong—and has finally been divorced, after a number of separations, by the wife he married thirty-two years ago.

Over those thirty-four years he has won one Academy Award and has savored the variegated rewards, prestigious and monetary, of a superstar who could command large slices of his picture grosses. He has won a fortune and largely lost it. He has seen his two sons grow to manhood and follow him into acting. His adopted daughter has made him a grandfather several times over. And he has experienced several disillusioning and impermanent extramarital romances with women who, in time, went their way as he went his way.

His interests are widespread. He calls his acting his "vocation" and does one picture a year. He calls his business pursuits, his involvements with bird and game conservation, and his safari club and game preserve in Africa, his "avocations" and pursues them with greater relish than the film career he retains, parttime, primarily for the money to finance "the other things."

It has been a long, hard, life-straining road for this complex man whom the world long regarded as the

9

personification of simplistic extroversion, this man who took many years to break finally and completely out of the conservative, solid-citizen shell that was slowly asphyxiating him spiritually and esthetically—to become, at last, truly himself.

Today he adopts toward life and people a tolerant detachment tinged with a cordial but intellectually abstract enthusiasm for projects in which he believes. Throughout his career the most unactorish of actors, he is the first to admit that his talent was a limited and constricted one, confined in the main to playing versions and ramifications of William Holden—usually the William Holden he wants the world to see. The real William Holden, even at fifty-five, seems to surface more in his lifestyle than in his cinematic images.

The thoughts of such a man, alone in hotel rooms in Hollywood, London, Paris, Rome, or wherever he happens to be while away from his three bases, must be long, long thoughts, the memories deep and piercing.

And at times he must think back to when and where and how it all began . . .

He was born William Franklin Beedle, Jr., in O'Fallon, Illinois, a small town near St. Louis, on April 17, 1918. His father, William Franklin Beedle, Sr., was an industrial chemist who later became head of the George W. Gooch Laboratories. His mother was a schoolteacher. He was one of three sons. His brother Robert, a Navy pilot, died in action in World War II. His brother Richard later went into business with his father.

Of mixed Irish, Dutch, and English stock, he was collaterally descended from George Washington on his mother's side (years later the National Society of the Sons of the American Revolution gave him Washington's family coat-of-arms as a present, and he hung it on the wall of his office at Paramount).

In 1921, when Holden was three, the family moved to Pasadena, California, where his father went into the chemical and fertilizer-analysis business. His mother taught English in the schools of Pasadena and Monrovia for many years, and after retiring she became active in church and charitable groups. She had strict ideas about personal standards and deportment, and she found Holden, even at an early age, a willing adherent to her ideas. She made him sing in church choirs, which he rather enjoyed. He pleased her mightily, she said years later, by doing his homework, accepting chores without complaint, sitting straight at the table, and keeping out of serious trouble, while remaining always a regular boy. He got equal attention from his father, a talented amateur gymnast, who taught him tumbling and grounded him in the health-imparting principles of physical education that he was always to retain. At eight he could tumble as well as any circus kid. He also got on well with his brothers and seemed to prize, even in childhood, all the standard virtues of middle-class respectability as they were practiced in conventional American homes of the 1920s and 1930s. While some who knew him in childhood and adoles-

William Holden at age sixteen, 1934, with two friends

10

cence said of Holden that "He was almost too good," his mother described him in his early years as "an angel, an absolute angel, the kind of well-behaved and courteous, yet normal and regular boy, that every mother hopes to raise."

But just so no one would doubt that he was all-boy despite his "goodness," Holden went on rare binges. His family for years told the one about his throwing a straw dummy on a highway in front of a speeding automobile, then hiding in the bushes with a friend while they roared with laughter. However, the car that screeched to a halt turned out to be a police cruiser. That took the grins off their faces, and they spent the next six weeks at a neighborhood station house memorizing traffic rules.

While attending grade school at Monrovia and South Pasadena, Holden found time for primitive experiences with the dramatic muse. At age ten, in 1928, he played Rip Van Winkle in a sixth-grade play. This experience did not inspire immediate urges along acting lines, but it stayed in his subconscious, he later recalled, and in his conscious for that matter, as an enjoyable experience.

As he went through his teens, Holden did all the things expected of a well-brought-up boy of the starchy, spit-and-polish Pasadena middle class. He rough-housed with his brothers, he went out for athletics, he dated girls. "He worshipped his family," one of his friends said years later. "Always Bill wanted to be on the right sleigh, do the right thing; he was human, sure, and normal; those young male urges and fierce animalism were always there, just beneath the surface, but even though he got in a few relatively harmless escapades

as young kids will, his teen years were straight and clean even by nineteen-thirties standards."

Holden decided for a while to follow in his dad's footsteps and at Pasadena Junior College studied chemistry—but found he disliked it. Nonetheless, everyone expected he would go into business with his father and brother Dick. For a while he thought so, too. "His mother was always pounding into him that it was important to be safe, secure, disciplined, and sensible," a family friend has recalled. "He swallowed wholesale her ideas about keeping life neat, pigeonholed, and straight-and-narrow, replete with personal decency, a job, saving money, the right girl, kids, owning a house and property, joining the correct organizations, being a factor in community life. He was so serious about building that kind of lifestyle, he took it all so literally, he was so intent on doing the right thing, that at nineteen he was like an old man in some ways."

Perhaps in an effort to compensate, to prove he was a redblooded all-American boy lest people get him pegged wrong, Holden would go on "danger-kicks" from time to time. When other boys dared him to jump over a four-and-one-half-foot fence from a standing position, he was always ready to oblige, especially if bets were made. At age sixteen he indulged his streak of derring-do exhibitionism by walking along the outer rail of a Pasadena structure known as "Suicide Bridge," coolly oblivious of the 190-foot drop below. About this time his father gave him a motorcycle, and he thought for a time of trying out for Victor McLaglen's trick motorcycle-riders. He was often seen on the Pasadena streets standing on the seat of his cycle. His father, hoping he would follow a career in natural sciences,

Messmore Kendall, President General of the National Society of the American Revolution, presents a scroll of the coat of arms of the Washington family to William Holden, a collateral descendant of George Washington on the maternal side, in 1939. The presentation took place on the steps of Washington Hall at the World's Fair, which celebrated "Golden Boy Day" with Holden as guest of honor. In costume are members of the Daughters of the American Revolution and of the National Society of the Sons of the American Revolution.

put him to work in a chemical laboratory during summer vacations.

For a while he toyed with becoming a musician, became fairly adept on the piano and clarinet, and played a mean drum. He also sang in the Oneonta Congregational Church choir.

Thanks to a naturally robust physique and his father's physical-education training, he developed exceptional timing and coordination, which helped him later as an actor. In his teens he also became an expert horseman and rifle shot.

In 1937, age nineteen, he and a friend decided to gratify their curiosity about New York City. During the course of a several-month crosscountry auto-trip, they

With Gladys Niesen of St. Louis, who won a luncheon guest lottery tendered by the World's Fair, 1939. Her hosts: Holden and Adolphe Menjou

wound up in the Big Town, where they lingered for some time. The Broadway ambience intrigued him. He went to plays and became stagestruck. He told his friend he wanted to go back to New York after he had graduated from college, and study acting. But this he never did.

At Pasadena Junior College in 1938 he took a course in radio drama and was selected to act in several radio plays for station KECA. He became involved with the Pasadena Workshop Theater and appeared in that group's *Manya*, a play about Marie Curie, in which Holden played eighty-year-old Eugène Curie, her father-in-law. It happened that Milton Lewis, a Paramount talent scout, was in the audience on opening night. He couldn't make out much of Holden behind

Clowning with Ellen Drew on the set of THE REMARKABLE ANDREW, *1942*

The Golden Circle (a group of promising Paramount players being groomed for stardom) on personal appearance tour for Cecil B. DeMille's UNION PACIFIC, *1939. Top row, left to right: Louise Campbell, Betty Field, Joseph Allen, Ellen Drew and Judith Barrett; Center row: Robert Preston, Patricia Morison, Susan Hayward, William Henry. Bottom row: Joyce Matthews, Janice Logan, William Holden and Evelyn Keyes.*

13

the whiskers, makeup and voluminous clothing, but he liked the voice, and something about the manner intrigued him. Lewis went backstage later to talk to him, and as he later recalled, "Underneath, it was all there." He invited Holden to Paramount the next day, but the young man surprised him with his cool independence and fundamental indifference to the beckoning glories of a film career. "Sorry, I have to take an exam tomorrow," he replied.

When Holden finally showed up at the studio several days later, he was tested, then put under contract at fifty dollars a week. "Beedle! It sounds like an insect!" one Paramount executive scoffed, and renamed him William Holden, after a newspaperman acquaintance.

Soon Holden found himself assigned to a group of promising young players being groomed for stardom at the Paramount of 1938. They were called "The Golden Circle" and they included Louise Campbell, Betty Field, Joseph Allen, Ellen Drew, Judith Barrett, Robert Preston, Patricia Morison, Susan Hayward, William Henry, Joyce Matthews, Janice Logan, and Evelyn Keyes. Of these twelve hopefuls of 1938, two—Holden and Hayward—were to emerge, in time, as top stars; two others, Field and Preston, were to enjoy solidly respectable careers; Campbell, Drew, Keyes, Morison, and Henry were to do fairly well, sometimes as leads and sometimes as character players; the rest were to be consigned, in time, to cinematic oblivion. The group were sent out on personal-appearance tours such as that for Cecil B. DeMille's *Union Pacific.*

Of this period Holden said later, "I wanted to be the best motion-picture actor in the world. My heroes were Fredric March and Spencer Tracy. They were my ideals. I used them as a kind of goal for myself. I had enough of the extrovert in me to want that kind of recognition."

Meanwhile he did bit parts. He pounded rocks for a brief flash in *Prison Farm.* He was one of hundreds of graduates who said "Thank you" while receiving his diploma in *Million Dollar Legs.*

Over at Columbia in early 1939 the search was on for a new face to play the lead in *Golden Boy,* the film version of Clifford Odets's 1937 Broadway play. Barbara Stanwyck and Adolphe Menjou were to play two of the leads. Director Rouben Mamoulian came upon Holden's Paramount test while sifting through dozens of prospects, and after running it several times, decided that was the boy he wanted. Mamoulian recently recalled that he "had found in this twenty-one-year-old

Fingerprinted by Tech. Sgt. D. S. Anderson during induction as a private at the U.S. Army enlisting station, Los Angeles, April 20, 1942

In the Army Air Corps Officer Candidate School, Miami Beach, 1943.

an indefinable quality which I felt was necessary to make believable a role in which a young man suffers conflicts over giving up a musical career, for which his family had made sacrifices, to further a boxing talent professionally."

Mamoulian made a test of Holden at Columbia, just to be sure, but Harry Cohn wanted John Garfield. Warners refused to lend Garfield (Cohn and Jack Warner were feuding at the time) and though Cohn was less than enthusiastic about Holden, he finally allowed Mamoulian to use him.

Mamoulian found the inexperienced Holden difficult to work with, and claims he never worked harder to achieve a performance that met professional standards. "Chemistry, looks, that mysterious quality—and iron determination, carried him through," Mamoulian says. "Also the will to work—and Barbara Stanwyck." Shooting did not proceed smoothly. Cohn looked at the early rushes in grim silence. Holden tried to tell Mamoulian how to direct. Several times, caught between grumbling Harry Cohn and the occasionally exasperated Mamoulian, he was nearly taken off the picture. Holden began working seventeen hours a day, studied minutely the fingering of the violin, and trained in a gym to get the required realism into his ring work.

Stopping off at the Stork Club during a bond-selling tour for the Army Air Corps, 1944

With his children West (Peter) and Scott in the mid-fifties.

He got to calling his mother in Pasadena half a dozen times a day, grew ever more tense, and stumbled through complicated emotional scenes with the spirit, if not the grace, of a young colt. Soon he gave signs of an imminent nervous collapse.

Barbara Stanwyck came to the rescue. She worked with Holden for long hours at night, Mamoulian recalls with admiration, went over the next day's scenes with him patiently, cued him in on nuances of speech and movement. The callow but determined twenty-one-year-old boy and the experienced superstar of thirty-two kept up this routine night after night for weeks. According to Mamoulian, Stanwyck even let takes get printed that did not display her own performance to best advantage if they happened to be the best takes Holden could achieve. Holden never forgot her unselfishness and her giving spirit, and to this day he sends Stanwyck red roses on the anniversary of *Golden Boy*'s starting date.

When the picture opened in the late summer of 1939, critical reaction was mixed, but it was conceded that Holden's was a promising talent. There was argument over the picture itself, with some reviewers maintaining that the Odets play had been diluted and bowdlerized, with the ending changed from a tragic to a happy one, and the sociopolitical elements largely excised to concentrate on character conflicts. Nonetheless, it was an auspicious debut for a newcomer, and Harry Cohn, aware at last that he had a potential star on his hands, bought half of Holden's contract from Paramount. Holden later said, "When Cohn bought half of me, he paid me half of the fifty dollars Paramount paid me. I was doing pictures for twenty-five dollars a week!"

But in 1972 Holden told Merv Griffin, "Studio heads like Harry Cohn created an esprit-de-corps morale

Playing around with guitar on the set of DEAR WIFE, *1950*

through discipline, which, right or wrong, was still there, and you knew it. Cohn provided a tough but smooth-running organization of the kind that is missed today. You ran scared, but you did what had to be done."

Taking his two boys to the rifle range, about 1954

Christmas, 1951. Hollywood Women's Press Club Golden Apples were awarded to Anne Baxter, as most cooperative female star of the year, and to William Holden and John Derek, who tied for male honors. Fredda Dudley Balling, club president, presents the awards.

Though proud of his Hollywood success, his parents worried about its effect on his conduct. Mrs. Beedle informed him that there was "an abyss" between the moral standards of Pasadena and those of Hollywood. Holden tried to live it up for a while, but found that his "Congregationalist conscience" gave him too hard a time, and elected for conservatism.

He was next borrowed by Warners to appear with George Raft in *Invisible Stripes*, a typical Burbank melodrama about an ex-convict (Raft) trying to go straight. Holden played the younger brother that Raft wanted to keep "clean." But before landing the part, Holden again had to face the doubts of those who thought him unsuitable. Director Lloyd Bacon wanted Warner player Wayne Morris for the role. To prove to Bacon that he could show up well with Raft, Holden took a bit part in a Raft film, *Each Dawn I Die*, that was made back-to-back with *Invisible Stripes*. He was in the earlier film no more than a minute, but it was sufficient to convince Bacon. Which gives some idea of Holden's determination.

Invisible Stripes was standard fare, and did little to solidify the beginning Holden had made with *Golden Boy*. He was better cast on loanout to United Artists for *Our Town* (1940) in which, under Sam Wood's perceptive direction, he ably delineated the character of George Gibbs, one of those who live, love, and sorrow in the Grovers Corners, New Hampshire, ambience of the Pulitzer Prize–winning Thornton Wilder play, written by Wilder for the screen with Frank Craven and Harry Chandlee. The boy with the "Congregationalist conscience" understood this boy of an earlier, gentler era, and he delivered a workmanlike performance.

With this "prestige" success to his credit, Holden found himself billed over the title in another period drama, *Those Were The Days*, in which he played a 1904-style college mischiefmaker redeemed by love. He was well-photographed, and the fan mail began coming into Paramount.

Then it was back to Columbia and Jean Arthur, then at her zenith, for his first Western, in a role tailored for Gary Cooper, who had declined it. *Arizona* opened in February, 1941, to mixed reviews. At twenty-

Lined up for a shot with Joan Caulfield, Billy De Wolfe, Edward Arnold, Mary Philips, Mona Freeman, and Raymond Roe, 1950

Kidding with a coworker (note painted shoe) on set of SUBMARINE COMMAND, *1951*

With his Oscar for STALAG 17

two Holden was playing opposite thirty-three-year-old Arthur in a story about a frontier tomboy who falls in love with a romance-'em-and-leave-'em type (Holden) who eventually returns from California to rescue her from crooks. Director Wesley Ruggles got a manly and forthright performance out of him.

Holden began showing his mettle at this time about parts he disapproved of, went on suspension, and for a time was idle for eight months. "It was a whirl of pressure and strain in Hollywood at that time [1940]," he said years later. "Studio heads, publicity people, the press—I guess my youth and energy kept me going."

He next went into *I Wanted Wings* at Paramount, in which Veronica Lake of the blond peek-a-boo hairdo also figured. An air drama with distractingly banal love angles, the film did little to advance Holden's fortunes, though some reviewers called his work "excellent." Miss Lake was dismissed by one scribe as "displaying chiefly a talent for wearing extreme décolletage."

Then it was back to Columbia for another Western, *Texas*, with his friend Glenn Ford. The boys had started out at Columbia at roughly the same time, and director George Marshall elicited competent performances from them, with Ford the good boy and Holden the bad boy who go in for cattle-rustling, Ford later becoming a rancher and Holden dying for his misdeeds. Claire Trevor was the gal both guys love.

Holden had for some time been heeding the family admonitions to "find that nice girl and settle down and raise some kids." He had met a young actress named Brenda Marshall, an erstwhile Errol Flynn leading lady at Warners who had changed her name from Ardis Ankerson. Brenda (or Ardis, as Holden always called her) was an attractive brunette with natural acting talent. She also had an air of breeding and refinement that Holden liked. They flew to Las Vegas on July 13, 1941, and tied the knot. Holden remembers that both came down with appendicitis at the time. They settled into a comfortable but unpretentious home in the Toluca Lake section of the San Fernando Valley and lived quietly. "It's a steady, constructive life and I like being married," he told an interviewer at the time.

Mrs. Holden had a three-year-old daughter, Virginia, from a previous marriage, and Holden legally adopted her. Their son Peter Westfield Holden (known as West) was born in 1944 while his father was in the service, and another son, Scott, in 1946.

Holden was well-suited to his next Paramount part, in *The Remarkable Andrew*, in which he played a young municipal bookkeeper who is falsely accused of embezzlement and who calls on the ghost of his idol Andrew Jackson (he is a history buff) to rescue him.

Typical of his reviews for this was the one that called him "the most talented of the younger acting contingent."

Next he was a sailor in *The Fleet's In,* got the girl (Dorothy Lamour), but found himself lost in a welter of overproduced acts and musical numbers.

During this period he was swinging yoyo-style between the two studios that shared his contract, Columbia and Paramount, and while he gained experience from a variety of roles, they tended to be lightweight.

The last two he did before going into the service were prime examples.

In *Meet The Stewarts,* which opened in New York on the second half of a double bill, he was a young husband coping with an extravagant wife from a wealthy background (Frances Dee). In *Young and Willing* with Susan Hayward (his Golden Circle teammate of 1938) which also opened in New York on the lower rung of a double bill, he was a young actor struggling for New York success.

In 1942 Holden enlisted in the Army, serving until 1945. He graduated from the Army Air Force Officer Candidate School at Miami Beach, Florida, and for the next three years did stateside public relations and entertainment duty. He also made training films, serving

With Richard Erdman, left, and Neville Brand, right, during a relaxed moment on the set of STALAG 17, *1953*

in Connecticut and Texas. He managed occasional leaves home, and even managed to be on hand for the birth of his son in 1944. In 1943 he legally changed his name to William Holden.

When he reported back to the studio in September, 1945, he found that he had almost been forgotten. When he left for the Service, Harry Cohn had said, "I hope this makes a man out of you." The boy of twenty-four was now a man of twenty-seven, with a wife and three children to support. He sat around for eight months waiting for an assignment.

His looks had matured, and when he revisited Paramount the gateman didn't even recognize him and wouldn't let him in. In the inner sanctums he was still remembered as Smiling Jim. There was no hurry to find parts for him. He later recalled this period of enforced inactivity as one of the most miserable and stagnant of his life.

When the new picture came, it was something of a disappointment, and hardly the kind of thing calculated to put him back with a bang. This was *Blaze of Noon,* a John Farrow–directed opus about pioneer airmail carriers. He found himself awash amid the competition of Ray Milland, Sterling Hayden, and Sonny Tufts, and was outacted by the flamboyant Anne Baxter, who had just won an Oscar for her supporting role in *The*

With his wife in Rome, 1954

Razor's Edge. Some reviews called his work "highly personable" and "well-played."

Realizing that he needed maximum exposure, Holden took any parts offered in the next few years, a minority of them good, the majority lightweight. His two remaining 1947 apearances were in *Dear Ruth,* about a lieutenant who falls in love with pen-pal Joan Caulfield (whose sister Mona Freeman has really written the letters), and *Variety Girl,* in which he made a brief song-and-dance appearance amidst a welter of song-and-dance acts even more cluttered than those he had endured in *The Fleet's In.* One critic noted that in his *Dear Ruth* performance he had achieved a new, easy naturalism in his acting style.

The year 1948 brought Holden better luck. He registered strongly in *Rachel and the Stranger,* on loan to RKO, in which he played a pioneer widower who gradually falls in love with his bondswoman (Loretta Young) and weathers an Indian attack, and *Apartment for Peggy,* on loan-out to 20th-Fox, in which he appeared to advantage as the GI student husband of Jeanne Crain who weathers assorted problems in regaining a civilian footing. Typical review: "Jeanne Crain and William Holden make a thoroughly believable and ingratiating young couple."

For his first picture at Columbia since the war, he was handed *The Dark Past,* a remake of a Chester Morris–Ralph Bellamy thriller of 1939. Reunited with his *Golden Boy* father, Lee J. Cobb, he gave his best performance to date, as a convict escapee with mental problems who holes up in the home of a psychiatrist (Cobb) who tries to help him unravel them.

With wife Brenda Marshall at the Academy Awards, 1954

He was next reunited with his friend Glenn Ford for their first picture together since *Texas* seven years before. This was *The Man From Colorado*, and it depicted the sadistic complexities of a post–Civil War judge (Ford) with Holden as his stalwart friend who tries to counter his evil-doing. Though it got a mild reaction from the reviewers, its handsome color and action sequences drew some praise.

Then it was back to Paramount for still another Western, *Streets of Laredo*, a remake of two earlier films about the Texas Rangers. A Mélange of action and romance, the critics found it exciting if unmemorable, with Holden as the bandit who turns Texas ranger to find a pal and finds he likes the right side of the law.

At Columbia he made a brightly amusing comedy with Lucille Ball, *Miss Grant Takes Richmond*. Holden was Richmond, a bookie–gang head masquerading as a real-estate entrepreneur who turns honest when not-so-dumb secretary Ball gives him a prod.

Dear Wife, a sort of sequel to *Dear Ruth*, was next on his 1950 list, with Holden as the serviceman-turned-husband who runs into his share of in-law trouble and even finds himself, through a fluke, running against his father-in-law for public office. Joan Caulfield, Mona Freeman, and Edward Arnold repeated their original roles. It was generally considered an anemic reworking of the by-then-tired *Dear Ruth* formula.

Offscreen he had settled down to raising his family, but blew off steam with hotrodding, doing his own picture stunts, and hanging by one arm from the ledges of upper-story windows. Billy Wilder recalls Holden remaining at the bottom of a pool for over a half hour in an aqualung on a cold winter night, just to prove his endurance. Wilder has described Holden as of that period as "an inhibited boy who feels very uncomfortable to act. He is the exact opposite of the ham. He was sort of pushed into acting. He drifted into the profession slightly against his own will. He would rather, in my opinion, have been a racing driver. He loves fast cars."

At Columbia Holden did the second of his 1950 clinkers, *Father Is A Bachelor*. The story of a ne'er-do-well former carnival-entertainer who for no good reason adopts a slew of orphans, probably represents his nadir in picture fare. One review summed it up: "a complete waste of money and talent."

Of this 1947–1950 period Holden has said, "I got into the rut of playing all kinds of nice-guy, meaningless roles in meaningless movies in which I found neither interest nor enjoyment. By 1950 I had appeared in eleven movies that, for me, added up to one big static blur." Higher-ups kept informing him that he "had no sex appeal" and about 1947 one bigwig had even informed him that he had a face "that looked like a baby's behind" (an analogy Holden finds puzzling to this day).

"I always felt I was an individual," he has said,

With his wife Brenda Marshall in the game room of their San Fernando Valley home, 1954

*Going over pictures of friends with
his wife, 1954*

"different from anyone else, as all of us are, really.
I was waiting, and hoping for, and struggling toward,
that particular movie that would demonstrate just how
individual I could be, as actor and as man, and finally
I found it."

That picture was *Sunset Boulevard*, and on its release it made him an important star. As the down-and-
out Hollywood writer-turned-gigolo who humors a
half-mad silent star (Gloria Swanson) who falls in
love with, and later murders, him, Holden not only
exhibited the sex-appeal producers had said he didn't
have, but offered a subtle command of characterization,
a deeper comprehension of human nature, than he had
previously been credited with.

There were now to be no further repetitions of supermarket incidents such as that in which an old lady had
come up to him (while he was shopping, about 1949)
and said, "Young man, you ought to be in pictures;
you look like Alan Ladd." Now he was to the world

and to himself, definitely and unequivocally, William
Holden: Film Star. There were to be greater glories
ahead, but the year 1950 is one which Holden looks
back on as the turning point in his career, and *Sunset
Boulevard* is his favorite film. It won him his first
Academy Award nomination.

He was next seen—again with Nancy Olson, who had
formed one corner of the Swanson-Holden-Olson romantic triangle in *Sunset Boulevard*—in *Union Station*,
a forgettable melodrama about railway police tracking
down a kidnapper, with cop Holden heading the hunt.
It was a slight setback for him, but his next, *Born
Yesterday* at Columbia was a Class-A comedy, a film
remake of the stage success that had made Judy Holliday a star. Holliday repeated on film her role of the
ex-chorine mistress of junk tycoon Broderick Crawford
who is educated to a new awareness by intellectual-
minded journalist Holden. Harry Cohn wanted Holden
for the part, but Holden had been concerned lest he be

With his son, Peter Westfield Holden, on the Paramount lot, 1955

George Seaton directs Holden and Grace Kelly in a scene from THE COUNTRY GIRL, *1954*

vice president. Shortly afterward he was wrangling with studio execs over better conditions for his fellow actors. He won much admiration by demonstrating that he was willing to fight for others as well as himself. The more he became involved with Hollywood the better he understood its problems. He also came to understand the executive mind, and though he clashed with Cohn and others over money and parts, he drew by osmosis an increasing understanding of their problems which his analytical mind stored away for future use.

At this time he also became an officer of the Academy of Motion Picture Arts and Sciences and was named guild delegate to the Hollywood Coordinating Committee, which arranged entertainment tours for troop audiences overseas. He also joined the Motion Picture Industry Council, the Permanent Charities Committee, the Parent-Teachers Association of his home community, and the Motion Picture Relief Fund. He managed to sandwich in regular visits to veterans hospitals, an activity he had initiated shortly after World War II. In 1951 he received the Golden Globe Award from the Hollywood Women's Press Club as most cooperative actor.

Meanwhile he continued his upward progress as an

overshadowed by the other, more colorful roles. Billy Wilder and Garson Kanin, however, who had written the play, pointed out to him that he couldn't help profiting from association with a surefire smash. In this they proved right.

Holden was meanwhile evolving into one of Hollywood's most solid citizens. His private life was notably staid and responsible at this time; no night life for him. His marriage, then ten years old, was regarded as stable and happy, and he was a devoted father to his sons, teaching them to swim and shoot. Their Toluca Lake home was gradually expanding, and filling up with trophies and mementos, but the atmosphere was homey and unpretentious.

Taking his responsibilities seriously on the civic as well as domestic front, Holden became active in the Screen Actors Guild and eventually was elected its first

Holden envies assistant director Carter De Haven's sandwich during 1955 shooting of PICNIC.

actor with *Force of Arms*, a 1951 World War II romantic melodrama with lots of action. Nancy Olson appeared with him for the third time as his WAC girlfriend, and reviewers commented on the pleasing chemistry they displayed as a team. Miss Olson was with him for the fourth and last time in *Submarine Command* (1952), in which Holden played a sub commander who must live with the guilt of having caused his commanding officer's death in line of duty. Olson was the wife who waits and worries at home.

Boots Malone, back at Columbia (his last two had been at Warners and Paramount respectively) displayed him as a jockey's agent in a racetrack drama in which he befriended a teenager who wants to be a jockey and is later forced to defend him against crooks who want the boy to throw the race. While the picture was a pleasant-enough little item, some of Holden's admirers felt it lacked the Class-A gloss that their hero deserved. The same could be said of his Paramount melodrama, *The Turning Point*, in which he was a crusading crime reporter who dies for his efforts.

Billy Wilder, who had given the Holden career a giant boost with *Sunset Boulevard,* and who had promised him at the time of *Born Yesterday* that he would find something truly worthy of his abilities at the first

Discussing a scene with director Joshua Logan on the PICNIC *location at Halstead, Kansas, 1955*

opportunity, kept his promise in 1953 with *Stalag 17*. This time not just a nomination but the Oscar itself went to Holden for his crisp delineation of a ratty opportunist in an American prisoner-of-war camp in World War II Germany. For the first time he ceased altogether to be William Holden playing William Holden, and lost himself in the character. This sacrifice of personality to characterization in depth, was to prove the exception rather than the rule in the Holden career.

As he himself has described it:

I never think of myself as an actor the way Alec Guinness is an actor. He can do anything. He's completely devoted to acting. He can act anywhere. I can act only in films, and even there I'm limited. I'm best at playing someone relevant to our lives today. Rarely have I stepped into a period film. I've just never felt qualified to do it. I've made a good living out of acting, but I'm not dedicated to it. I can see how men like John Gielgud and Alec Guinness, who give their work their complete devotion, must get a deeper satisfaction out of it than I do.

Asked about the art of acting as he saw it, he replied:

Movie acting may not have a certain kind of glory as a true art, but it's damn hard work. I'm not like some movie actors who feel that they must pretend they're just dying to act in the theater. I've been tempted by it only once, when I briefly

thought about doing *Mister Roberts*. Henry Fonda was in it then and he had some kind of knee trouble. But I didn't replace him and it was just as well with me. I've never pretended I could be an Alec Guinness in the theater.

He thinks movie acting can be "a terrible emotional drain. It's devastating. You have to keep up the level of your performance. The way I do it is to think of myself as a reporter. My job is to portray the character and bring it to the audience in a way that will enable them to involve themselves emotionally. I read a script and analyze it. I find that if you develop an attitude toward the character, the mannerisms will come later. You attempt to stay as detached as possible. Then there's a kind of final melting in your mind about a week before the picture is supposed to start."

Earlier in his career, Holden said, he would ask himself, "What would Fredric March do with this character? What would Gary Cooper do?" As he had achieved Joe Gillis in *Sunset Boulevard* through sympathy for the character, he had achieved Sefton in his Oscar-winning performance through observation. "I've seen men like Sefton. I know what they're like. I don't know what you'd call the talent or whatever it is that makes

On a personal appearance tour for Toward the Unknown, *1956*

Sporting a leg splint for a make-believe wound during the filming of The Proud and the Profane, *1956.*

it possible for me to act by using that approach. Maybe it's just knowing a little more than the next guy."

As the middle 1950s approached, Holden acquired increasingly a reputation for holding ultraconservative views, not only on his own conduct but the conduct of others. "Garfield represented the odd-man-out in the Roosevelt era," one scribe cracked, "and Holden is the Eisenhower Republican type." He disapproved of the Bogart Rat Pack and said so. He felt that it gave the wrong image of Hollywood to the world.

He had meanwhile become a member of the Los Angeles Park and Recreation Commission. He began traveling abroad on behalf of Paramount and the movie industry in general, an informal ambassador of good will. He told reporters, "I feel that as an actor I have a job to do. Like anybody I go to work." He added that in his opinion no actor or actress need be recognized on Fifth Avenue unless they wanted to be. "It's your manner," he said. "If you're flamboyant and show-offy, you will get attention. If you keep your coat-collar up and quietly windowshop, people will leave you alone."

Associates noted that he handled his career like a business executive, sans temperament. One said, "He's detached, he runs the commodity known as William Holden like an investment. He's diplomatic, shrewd and alert. He's sort of outside his career image, not in it—analyzing it, keeping it smooth-running, well-oiled."

This, then, was the William Holden the world knew around 1954, when he was on top of the world with the Oscar and, at age thirty-six, had his life, his mar-

Holding a trophy presented to him by the Theatre Owners of America for "Outstanding Service to the Motion Picture Industry, The Community and the Country at Large," 1956

riage, his kids, his career, and his assorted activities in apple-pie order. His variegated business interests by this time included partnerships in exporting and importing, radio stations, and aviation. "I was young then," he said recently. "The world was my oyster. Seventeen-hour days were nothing to me. I wanted to see it all and get it all. I wanted to miss nothing."

In 1953–1954, at a time when television was making catastrophic inroads on the Hollywood market, it was noted that Holden films such as *Stalag 17*, *The Moon Is Blue*, *Escape From Fort Bravo*, and *Executive Suite* were making all kinds of money. Holden began to think of the day when he could go into business for himself as a star-corporation.

Myron N. Blank, President of the Theatre Owners of America, Inc., presents the organization's 1956 Star of the Year Award to William Holden at the TOA's President's Banquet at the Waldorf-Astoria. At right is Ernest G. Stelling, TOA President who succeeded Mr. Blank.

In *Escape From Fort Bravo* he was a strict Union captain commanding a stockade of Confederate prisoners in the West. The film featured Indian attacks and other Western heroics. While competently directed and played, it did nothing for Holden. Yet it made money, as did his MGM picture, *Executive Suite*, in which he appeared for the first time with his idol Fredric March. The two played rivals for the presidency of a furniture company, with March the sly opportunist who plumps for rampantly commercial approaches and Holden the idealist electing for quality products. A solid cast included Barbara Stanwyck (her first with Holden since *Golden Boy*), June Allyson, Paul Douglas, and Walter Pidgeon.

Next he did *Forever Female* at Paramount and scored as the young playwright trapped between two enamored women, one (Ginger Rogers) an aging stage star, the other (Pat Crowley) an ambitious young hopeful.

Teamed with fellow Oscar winners Humphrey Bogart and Audrey Hepburn in *Sabrina*, again under Billy Wilder's direction, Holden attempted a light performance as an irresponsible society playboy. It was not up his alley, and Hepburn and Bogart outplayed him in the story of a Long Island chauffeur's daughter with chic who aspires to one son of a wealthy family and wins the other instead. Holden drew third billing in this, as he did in *The Country Girl*. Under director-writer George Seaton's aegis, he did extremely well as the stage director who gradually falls in love with the wife of an actor struggling to make a comeback. Again

Chumming with an elephant in Ceylon, 1957, during shooting of Bridge on the River Kwai

His presence in the controversial (for 1953) *The Moon Is Blue* has always been something of a puzzle, for one wonders how he squared this with his public pronouncements about "Hollywood's image." At the time the Motion Picture Production Code made much fuss about its allegedly frank approach to sex. Today it seems a harmless bit of fluff about a girl who is determined to remain a virgin until marriage and puts off the wolves with hyperfrank questions. David Niven proved adept enough with such farce (Maggie McNamara played the girl), but Holden seemed, in the words of one critic, "slightly labored."

Photographing Ceylonese children during shooting of Bridge on the River Kwai, *1957*

With the mayor of San Juan, Puerto Rico, Felisa Rinçon de Gautier, 1958

he was teamed with two Oscar winners, Bing Crosby and Grace Kelly (she won hers for this film). This was one of Holden's more solid performances, portraying as he did the multishaded role of a man who comes to realize the true and genuine qualities of a woman he at first despises, then comes to respect, and finally to adore. Grace Kelly, in her expert handling of the embittered wife, proved herself as successful at muting her standard Hollywood image as Holden had been, in *Stalag 17,* in muting his.

Reunited with March and Grace Kelly in *The Bridges at Toko-Ri,* in which he was an aircraft-carrier-based Korean War pilot who dies heroically, he followed this up with the remarkably popular *Love Is A Many-Splendored Thing,* with Jennifer Jones. While the picture for all its exotic settings and handsome mounting, has a soapy, dated look today, it featured fine performances from the principals, playing an Eura-

sian doctor and a correspondent who love, then lose, each other.

This was followed by Columbia's screen version of the William Inge play *Picnic* with Holden in the role Ralph Meeker had originated on Broadway. At thirty-seven Holden seemed a little old for the role of the sexy drifter who visits a college chum in a little Kansas town and wreaks emotional havoc with several women. Nor did he seem suited by temperament to the character of Hal Carter, who was as alien to Holden's actual personality as one could get.

He then returned to Paramount for *The Proud and the Profane,* a rather turgid World War II melodrama in which he was crudely forthright as a tough, mustached Marine officer romancing a sensitive Red Cross worker, Deborah Kerr. The publicists' much-vaunted "Holden-Kerr" chemistry didn't seem to come off, in a picture which drew distinctly mixed reviews.

At home with his primitive art collection, 1958

Holden then embarked on his first independent venture, under Warners auspices, *Toward The Unknown.* It was made under the banner of his Toluca Productions (named for his home district in the San Fernando Valley). The mid-fifties saw the full-strength advent of the actor-producer. Stars like James Stewart, Burt Lancaster, John Wayne, and Gary Cooper were assuming financial and creative control of their own pictures, with tax gains, profit-sharing and freedom from front-office interference among the benefits sought. This time

Lunching with France Nuyen and Clifton Webb during shooting of Satan Never Sleeps, *1961*

With director Leo McCarey during shooting of
SATAN NEVER SLEEPS, *1961*

Holden was a jet pilot testing untried craft despite the initial disapproval of commanding officer Lloyd Nolan, who distrusts Holden's ability to keep his cool since he was once a Korean brainwashee who cracked under pressure. Producer-director Mervyn LeRoy kept things moving at a fast clip, but the critics wrote that the plane stuff and special effects were superior to the romantics (a tired triangle involving Holden, Virginia Leith, and Nolan).

Holden has said of this film, "I was an actor by day, and by night a caster, a cutter, and a producer. I'll never do anything like that again."

In 1957 he decided to accept a role in Columbia's *The Bridge On The River Kwai*, under the producing aegis of Sam Spiegel. For this he was paid $250,000 against 10 percent of the gross, and his contract specified that his share be paid him in annual installments of $50,000. The film went on to gross, by the early 1960s, some $30,000,000 worldwide, Holden's share at that time coming to some $3,000,000. It is estimated that he and his heirs will be benefiting from that contract for the next half-century. At a later point Holden sued to enjoin the film from being shown on TV, claiming that such exposure would cut into theatrical profits.

In the film, shot in Ceylon at a cost of $2,700,000, Holden was involved in World War II action heroics as an American sailor passing himself off as a commander who is cajoled into joining a British raiding party assigned to blow up a bridge being constructed by the Japanese with conscript British labor under the command of Alec Guinness, who gave—as the martinet commander who lives by the book—a performance so brilliant that he won the 1957 Academy Award. Guinness dominated the picture, with Holden's role and performance overshadowed, but he could take consolation from the financial gain.

He next undertook *The Key*, again on a percentage basis, with Sophia Loren and Trevor Howard. A British production, it was released in the United States by Columbia. The film proved popular. It dealt with a

With France Nuyen and friend during shooting of SATAN NEVER SLEEPS

woman (Loren) who consoles a succession of World War II seamen, each of whom bequeaths the key to her apartment to his successor when he senses he will be killed. Holden plays the officer who tries to break the pattern. The Consensus of critical opinion was that the picture did better on the high seas than in the boudoir.

During this period, the late 1950s, Holden was appearing regularly on the top ten lists of exhibitors who gauged stars' box-office appeal. When he succeeded John Wayne as top man one year, Wayne sent him a kidding telegram with one word in it: "Sneak!" He and Wayne were paired in 1959 in *The Horse Soldiers*, with each receiving $750,000 against 20 percent of the gross. This was the heyday of big-star salary demands; Holden proved as adept at lining his purse as the next man. Though the story was a standard Civil War–heroics yarn about a Union commander and a military doctor (Wayne and Holden) who figure with an outfit assigned to raid Confederate territory to cut off supplies to a crucial terminal point, the film had the benefit of John Ford's warmth and humanity set off against action values.

Holden had been traveling extensively in the preceding years, and in 1959 he moved lock, stock, and barrel to Switzerland with his wife and children. He also announced, "My blueprint is to make one very important picture a year that is not only artistically satisfying to me but successful at the boxoffice. Ideally I'd like to spend six or seven months on my vocation, and five or six months on my avocational activities."

Soon the Holdens had three homes: an apartment in Hong Kong; the base domicile in Switzerland, where Mrs. Holden and the children held forth; and the Mount Kenya Safari Club in Africa, one of the "avocational" projects Holden had mentioned, which he had founded with Carl Hirschmann, a Swiss banker, and Ray Ryan, an Indiana oil man. Holden in 1962 described this Shangri-La as being "on the slopes of Mount Kenya outside the town of Nanyuki. We've got sixty acres, with fruit and vegetable gardens, tennis courts, swimming pools, trout streams, 120 servants, and 500 adjacent acres, complete with an African village and the prize rose garden on the continent. Our members have included John Wayne and Winston Churchill. We're about 12,000 miles from Hollywood, and about 6,000 miles from my home in St. Prex, Switzerland. From the club, you can get to Hollywood in one full day. These are, after all, times of galloping transportation. I take care of a million things in my export-import business—importing electronic equipment from Tokyo and things like that. After all that avocational activity I get back to acting and I feel refreshed."

By the time of *The World of Suzie Wong*, released

Holden watches as Leo McCarey cues in Clifton Webb for a scene in Satan Never Sleeps, *1961*

in late 1960, critics were hinting that he was paying too much attention to matters other than the acting that had provided the original wherewithal for his variegated projects. The film drew severe critical censure as a comic-strip travesty about an American artist, Holden, and a Hong Kong prostitute, who as played by Nancy Kwan came through as a lollipop version of a good-time girl as compared, one critic pointed out, to the sordid and grim realities of prostitution as actually practiced in Hong Kong, replete with its rampant disease and brutal exploitation. Another reviewer said Holden was too old for his role, looked "like an aging bellhop," and was "a bit worn for such moonshining."

About this time the rumors that Holden was drinking heavily accelerated, though in point of fact he had always imbibed to relieve on-set tensions, his favorite phrase, even back in the early 1950s, being, "Warm up the ice-cubes." Reporters had pointed out as early as 1956 that beneath his assured exterior Holden was actually very tense and inhibited, and that he needed a few shots in order to relax sufficiently for the all-pervading camera eye. Paramount President Y. Frank Freeman, who had tie-ins with Coca-Cola, was opposed to hard liquor on the lot, so as a result Holden had the only dressing room with a bar. The once-smiling-

Jim-All-American-Boy face by 1962—age forty-four—was growing ever more lined and puffy, and rumor had it that this was the result not only of the increased drinking but of the increasing marital squabbles.

Meanwhile Holden gave out testy interviews, in one of which he said, "Actors' salary figures are misunderstood and misinterpreted. There are 212 millionaires in Shreveport but you're not asking them about the money they earn. Compared to them I'm in Sunday school. Do you know what I'm looking forward to right now? The martini I can have on Sunday afternoon. I'm working all week for that martini. Monday I work for my lawyers, Tuesday for my agent, the other four days for government. Sunday if I'm lucky I may have the afternoon off and I'll have the martini."

When asked if, taxes being so high, it might not be better to work less and still keep as much money, he snapped, "What do you want me to do? Not work, or go back under contract to a major studio and be a sucker for a corporation and let them keep the money? I have a corporation of my own. It's the least active in the world. I'm trying desperately to stay in the art side of the business rather than in the business side of the art, because if you mix them it's a disaster. You show me a successful businessman in Hollywood and I'll show you a man who knows nothing about motion pictures." In the same interview he said of Barney Balaban of Paramount: "He once told me he hadn't read a script in twenty-five years but that doesn't mean he hasn't hired good talent for the art side of the business."

He also waxed defensive about the mounting criticism in the United States of his establishing residence in Switzerland. There had been attacks in Congress on his expatriate leanings, with the implication that he was seeking a tax haven and had become indifferent to things American. He was also criticized for raising his children in Europe. He rebutted that he wanted them to have the broadening influences of European culture, and that America did not contain too large a share of the world's culture. His fellow workers in Hollywood, and the actors' union he had once ably served, scored him for making movies around the world, "thus aiding runaway production." He defiantly rejoined, "I'm living the kind of life that I think is best for me and my family. I'll continue to do so no matter what laws are changed or what anybody says."

In the early 1960s the Kennedy Administration recommended the elimination of tax havens overseas for well-to-do actors. The Screen Actors Guild backed this approach. While admitting that there were certain tax advantages in a Swiss residence, Holden reminded his critics that he still had residual payments on pictures like *The Bridge on the River Kwai* and *The Key* on which he paid American taxes in the 90 percent bracket, that this situation would continue for fifteen years or more, and that he also paid taxes in the countries where he worked.

In 1962 he told a reporter, "It seems to me that Americans have always been noted for moving around, for being unafraid of new challenges, new frontiers. Now certain people are trying to tell us to stay at home and not work abroad. It's a form of isolationism. Why did President Kennedy institute the Peace Corps, if not to encourage Americans to live and work in foreign lands?" He added that the U.S. government "can change the laws any way they like. That won't make things any different for me. Living in Switzerland has been the most rewarding experience of my life."

Holden's old Hollywood friends, noting reports of his increased drinking, his marital estrangement, his dalliance with lovely actresses, his restless peregrinations around the world, said that Holden was weathering "the mid-forties blues," and "the seven-year itch." In 1963 there were reports that Holden was seeing very little of his wife and had fallen in love with Capucine, his co-star in *The Lion.* At one point he and Capucine were reported cruising the seas in a luxury yacht. All this was a far cry from the "solid citizen," "homebody" image he had assiduously cultivated ten years before, and it was not helpful to his public relations.

His screen performances from 1962 on seemed ever more tired; his appearance steadily deteriorated. Critics commented on the listless, empty look in his eyes as he walked through roles with what seemed a preoccupied air. His movies, like his performances, became perfunctory, mechanical contrivances. Nor did he choose wisely such 1962-vintage fare as *Satan Never Sleeps,* an equally tired Leo McCarey rehash of the *Going My Way* theme, with Holden inappropriately cast (for more reasons than one) as a priest who did missionary work in China with fellow-priest Clifton Webb (also inappropriately cast). France Nuyen was on hand to provoke balcony snickers as an oriental who hankers after Holden, who finally gets her wed to a fellow Oriental after rape, Communist terrorism, and other extraneous ingredients had run their course.

The Counterfeit Traitor was still another anti-Nazi spy yarn, of which there had already been a cinematic oversupply, with Holden as an American-born Swedish national who does espionage work for British intelligence in Nazi Germany. *The Lion* was about a young girl whose closest friend is a lion; the locale is Africa, and the shots of wild life are the best things in the film. Holden plays her father, who visits his ex-wife (Capucine) and her current husband (Trevor Howard) in Africa and takes both ex-wife and child back to Connecticut after the lion is killed.

In 1963 Brenda Marshall Holden decided she had had it with her twenty-two-year marriage and separated from her husband. Holden told the press, "We are living apart. It has been that way since I went to Malaya to do my last film, but there has been no discussion about signing any papers or any court action. I hope it won't come to that. I just want to be on my own for

On the set of ALVAREZ KELLY, *1965*

a while to think things out." He claimed that his long location trips in recent years had contributed to the estrangement by limiting their time together. Nothing was said about Capucine, but she was on all the reporters' minds. Meanwhile Mrs. Holden's daughter Virginia, who had married, made her a grandmother.

Holden was off the screen for two years. His next, released in 1964, turned out to be a silly, tasteless comedy with Audrey Hepburn called *Paris When It*

Sizzles. It concerned a writer and his secretary who live in a dream world while writing a movie script in Paris, acting out the projected scenes together. Judith Crist's succinct analysis was "Strictly Hollywood—when it fizzles." Next came a turgid action romance, *The Seventh Dawn,* laid in Malaya, in which Holden starred with Capucine and Susannah York. One critic said, "Bill Holden at forty-six seems a trifle old for this."

He was seen in no films in 1965. The year 1966 brought one picture, *Alvarez Kelly,* still another Civil War action drama with Holden an Irish-Mexican rascal who plays North and South against each other while he trades in cattle that both armies need for food. The film got mixed reviews. *Casino Royale,* an all-star international jape with a confused plot-line, was his sole credit for 1967.

In a 1967 interview he admitted that *Alvarez Kelly* and other films had been bad, adding, "Over the years I try to keep a standard but nobody bats 1,000. But I haven't made that many pictures recently. I have too many other interests. The chief ones are game conservation and exploration in Africa."

His most important headlines of the 1966-1967 period came from Italy, where on October 27, 1967, he was convicted by an Italian court of manslaughter after his sports car, in which he had been accompanied by two American girls, had collided with a small Italian car, killing its occupant. The prosecution had asked for a year's sentence but the court, admitting extenuating circumstances (the Italian driver had failed to make sufficient room on the highway after Holden had signaled he wanted to pass), sentenced Holden to eight months in jail, then suspended sentence. Holden was not present for the verdict, telephoning for the result from his Swiss home.

The threatened end of his marriage in 1963 did not in fact take place and as the Capucine involvement (and presumably other attachments) receded in time, Mrs. Holden attempted a reconciliation, which was only partially successful. But by the summer of 1966, shortly after the Holdens' silver anniversary, Sheilah Graham was telling her readers, "Mrs. Holden, the former actress Brenda Marshall, is packing her personal belongings to take to California, where she will file suit for divorce. They tried a reconciliation during the past year but it did not work out." The divorce action, at least for that year, was later forestalled.

During the 1960s Holden made a few TV appearances as the narrator of such documentaries as *William Holden's Untamed World* (Africa) and *Report On Hong Kong.* Television did not seem to suit him, and Holden made no effort to press his ambition in that medium until 1973.

In 1968 Holden made *The Devil's Brigade,* which was partially filmed in Italy. The story of a World War II commando group that is specially trained to give the Germans hell (and does) was attacked by reviewers for its attempts to imitate the formula of *The Dirty Dozen,* and *The New York Times* critic said, "There is hardly a character, a situation, or a line of dialogue that has not served a useful purpose in some other film."

Meanwhile, in his private life Holden was amply bearing out an analysis made of him twenty years before by a Hollywood friend:

> Holden is in constant revolt against authority and his family and against everything. Bill's living in a straitjacket manufactured in Pasadena. He is the typical American boy who wanted to be a slob—but never did. He really wants to be a sort of intellectual beachcomber. He is the original displaced person. Bill would be the happiest person in the world as a fugitive from society. He has a deep yearning to be let alone and not have to prove anything. He detests the challenges and trappings of society. That's why he loves Hong Kong. This is one reason why he travels abroad so much. Hong Kong is a long way from both the movies and his father's chemical analysis business.

At fifty William Holden was spelling out—in spades—the insights expressed by his pal when he was only thirty. Time, as it usually does, had brought him answers—and results.

Some reviewers said he was losing his perspective when he did *The Wild Bunch* in 1969. A brutal and ultraviolent film about a Holden-led gang that roamed around inciting mayhem, it drew added bad publicity when Holden let it be known that he thought violence on the screen produced certain psychic benefits for audiences. Judith Crist retorted, "Quotes attributed to Mr. Holden that this sort of violence is a healthy purgative for viewers [are] just about as sick" as "the bloodiest and most sickening display of slaughter that I can ever recall in a theatrical film."

Possibly to make points he thought valid, Holden next elected to do *The Christmas Tree,* about a boy poisoned by atomic radiation who dies by his Christmas tree. Holden played the grieving widower-father and Virna Lisi, looking much too young for him, was around to provide romantic interest. One critic summed this effort up with the words, "[It] treats a searching problem with a mere evasive whimper."

Holden returned to the screen in 1971 in *Wild Rovers,* co-starring with Ryan O'Neal. A confused, murky story, replete with pointless symbolisms, it traced the lives of two cowpokes of fifty and twenty-five who rob a bank to escape what they conceive to be a humdrum existence, are pursued by a posse, and finally perish. Critics said that Blake Edwards, who seemed to have a point in mind but lacked the artistic integrity to articulate it with forthright courage, had, in his writing and direction of the film, settled for hide-and-seek abstractions, the result being the most boringly indecipherable film of the year.

The year 1972 found Holden in an also-ran Western, *The Revengers*, in which he was a man seeking the murderer of his family who enlists the aid of some ne'er-do-wells to track his man across the Western wastes to Mexico, then decides to let his enemy off and goes back to Susan Hayward, a farm woman who had nursed him when he was wounded. It was the first joint Holden-Hayward film appearance since 1943; both had come a long way since then, personally and careerwise. Holden's twenty-six-year-old son Scott, who like his brother West, nurses acting ambitions, appeared in the film as an Army lieutenant.

Holden made, for 1973 release, a picture for Universal called *Breezy*, in which he has a romance with a younger woman. It has been described as "a story that both shows the generation gap and makes entertainment out of it." Clint Eastwood took a sabbatical from acting to direct. More film projects are forthcoming for Holden, who gives no indication he wishes to retire.

"I can't," he told a recent interviewer. "I need the money from my vocation to finance my avocations." Pressed further, he admitted he wasn't that well off any more, having made some investments that didn't take. He added that his divorce settlement (Mrs. Holden had finally gone through with it in 1971) "had cost me a small fortune." Rumors that he planned to marry Pat Stauffer, ex-wife of Hollywood restaurateur Ted Stauffer, fizzled when the pair broke up.

One of his current "avocations" (a word he seems to favor) is a project at Wuvulu, near New Guinea in the South Pacific. Here he and associates plan to study and research endangered bird species and primates, along with the sponsorship of a marine biology laboratory run by Jacques Cousteau, the eminent marine scientist. His Mount Kenya Safari Club over the years has mushroomed into the Mount Kenya game ranch, which specializes in game conservation, one of Holden's prime enthusiasms.

In 1973 Holden made his TV debut, starring in *The Blue Knight*, a four-part miniseries based on Joseph Wambaugh's best-selling novel. Adapted by Rod Serling, the NBC-TV presentation offered Holden as Bumper Morgan, a Los Angeles policeman who is nearing retirement from the force.

After informing a recent journalist that he had been off the hard liquor for some years, he added that he no longer needed marriage; as he put it, "For me marriage was just a phase—and I grew out of it. It was just a natural ending of a way of life that society dictated. Don't get me wrong—I approve of the institution of marriage when it suits a time and a need: raising a family, building a life. But we've done that. It's over."

On the Mike Douglas Show, *1972*

And he had never looked more tired, more life-battered, as he gave the interviewer a parting sally, one that made his current philosophy as understandable as anything about this complex, chameleonlike man can ever be:

"When I was a little boy, I thought life was made up of two parts: youth and old age. As I got older, I added a middle part called work. Then I came around to thinking there were four divisions because middle age was there, too. And now, at fifty-five—well, now I kind of hate to think about dividing it into any more pieces..."

The FILMS of
WIILLIAM HOLDEN

With Lee J. Cobb, Adolphe Menjou, Joseph Calleia, Edward Brophy, Frank Jenks, Don Beddoe

Golden Boy

1939   Columbia

CAST:

BARBARA STANWYCK *(Lorna Moon)*; ADOLPHE MENJOU *(Tom Moody)*; WILLIAM HOLDEN *(Joe Bonaparte)*; LEE J. COBB *(Mr. Bonaparte)*; JOSEPH CALLEIA *(Eddie Fuseli)*; SAM LEVENE *(Siggie)*; EDWARD S. BROPHY *(Roxy Lewis)*; BEATRICE BLINN *(Anna)*; WILLIAM H. STRAUSS *(Mr. Carp)*; DON BEDDOE *(Borneo)*; FRANK JENKS *(Boxer)*; CHARLES HALTON *(Newspaperman)*; JOHN WRAY, CLINTON ROSEMOND.

CREDITS:

WILLIAM PERLBERG *(Producer)*; ROUBEN MAMOULIAN *(Director)*; LEWIS MELTZER, DANIEL TARADASH, SARAH Y. MASON, VICTOR HEERMAN *(Screenplay); based on the play by* CLIFFORD ODETS; NICK MUSURACA, KARL FREUND *(Directors of Photography)*; VICTOR YOUNG *(Music)*; MORRIS W. STOLOFF *(Musical Director)*; LEO SHUKEN *(Orchestrations)*; LIONEL BANKS *(Art Director)*; OTTO MEYER *(Editor)*; GEORGE COOPER *(Sound)*; DONALD W. STARLING *(Montage Effects)*; EUGENE ANDERSON *(Assistant Director)*.

Opened at Radio City Music Hall, New York, September 15, 1939. Running time, 99 minutes.

THE PICTURE:

Golden Boy, Holden's first substantial part, and the film that made him a name overnight, holds up extremely well when seen on TV thirty-three years after it was made. The quality it reflects in all departments—acting, direction, production-mounting, music—make it a film worthy of that vintage year 1939—the year of *Wuthering Heights*, *Gone With The Wind*, *Mr. Smith Goes to Washington*, and *Dark Victory*. Though critical reactions at the time of its initial showings were not uniformly favorable, they seem in the main to have been shortsighted and unfair regarding a film which shines like a beacon of sincere craftsmanship when preceded and followed on the boob tube by current mediocre fare. A further indication that the critics of 1939 had trouble making up their minds: *The New York Times'* reviewer, Frank Nugent, asserted that the

With Lee J. Cobb

With Adolphe Menjou, Barbara Stanwyck

changed ending of the film (in which the hero lives rather than dies) had done no harm to the theme, while the *Herald Tribune* critic, Howard Barnes, insisted the opposite. With other 1939 reviewers pro-ing and con-ing along these lines, I decided to rely for my judgment, as I usually do, on my own impressions past and present, on my memory of my delight in the film in 1939 at age sixteen, and on what I saw in the recent telecast. I was glad to note that my impression of the

film was the same on both occasions. Genuine art never dates, is a truism I am happy to pass along. Holden gave a remarkable performance, considering that he was a boy of twenty-one at the time. There are, to be sure, minor awkwardnesses and an occasional callowness in gestures and dialogue nuances, but on the whole he is believable and suitably intense (especially in the fine love scenes with Barbara Stanwyck), and he projects a variety of emotions with a surprisingly

With Edward Brophy, Barbara Stanwyck, Adolphe Menjou.

mature grasp of technique. Director Rouben Mamoulian reportedly overruled Harry Cohn's objections to give the unknown Holden the role. At that point he was a bit player at Paramount. Mamoulian recently recalled that he had found in Holden an indefinable quality that made his projection of the young would-be violinist who sacrifices his burgeoning talent for exploits in the prize ring, an honest and living thing. Time has borne out Mamoulian's judgment. The director has also recalled that he was impressed with Holden's anxiety to excel, and remembers that he worked hard at his boxing, memorized the correct fingering for the violin, and studied phrases and even words meticulously with a dialogue coach. He was, moreover, always ready to repeat a take over and over. Mamoulian commended Stanwyck highly for her patience with Holden, noting that she would let a take stand, even if it wasn't her best one, if it displayed the fledgling actor to maximum advantage. There was a lot of pro-and-con argument in 1939 as to how faithfully Clifford Odets's play had been transcribed for the screen (since Odets himself was not available, though Mamoulian wanted him, he let four screenwriters do the best they could). While the aforementioned tragic stage ending was changed, and some of Odets's capital-labor arguments excised, the result was a relatively faithful rendition of Odets's theme of the corruption of integrity and esthetics by a variety of crass and demeaning expediencies. Moreover, the film opens up the fight scenes as the stage never could. These action-filled sequences showcased Odets's consummate cinematic sense tellingly. Stanwyck was excellent as Lorna Moon, "the dame from Newark," who hopes to wed her boss, fight manager Adolphe Menjou,

after his divorce. Her transition from hard cynic to tender romantic after she falls in love with Holden, Menjou's new ring find, is brought across with all the sincerity and absence of bathos that has always been a Stanwyck trademark. Menjou was realistic as the hard-bitten manager and Joseph Calleia was right as rain as the crass, pin-striped racketeer. Lee J. Cobb was moving and eloquent as the loving Italian father who wants his son to stick to the violin. After Menjou takes on the boy, it becomes apparent that he is pulling his punches in the ring so as not to hurt his hands; Stanwyck is delegated by Menjou to urge him to give up music and fight like a champ, meanwhile pretending a romantic interest in him. When the boy discovers the deception, he reacts to her taunts by fighting his way to near the top. Stanwyck meanwhile reverts to Menjou, though by now sincerely in love with Holden, but when he kills an opponent in the ring and breaks his hand, the shattering realization of what he has done to his life and his ideals proves too much for him. Stanwyck then returns to him and gives loving assurance that life can yet be good for them both, and together they return to his father. This altogether impressive debut for a twenty-one-year-old set Holden firmly in an onward-and-upward groove that in following years would route him to top stardom and an eventual Academy Award.

REVIEWS:

Frank S. Nugent in *The New York Times:*

An interesting, entertaining, dramatic but scarcely first-rate motion picture. While it has changed the ending of the Odets allegory, it remains on the whole a sincere, adult and faithful translation of his work. Per-

With Lee J. Cobb

With Barbara Stanwyck

With Adolphe Menjou and Barbara Stanwyck

The romance between the middleweight and his manager's girl has been accented, while the neurotic aspects of a study in frustration have been muted. The acting leaves a good deal to be desired. William Holden, in his first screen appearance, demonstrates unquestioned ability, but he is not felicitously cast as the twisted youth who is conned into giving up a musical career ... he rarely achieves the hysterical intensity which the high, emotional moments of the production demand ... in directing the production Rouben Mamoulian has been eminently successful in creating an intriguing atmosphere, as, for example, his shooting of the spectators rather than the fighters in the ring sequences, but he hasn't built up much cumulative suspense, I am quite aware that this is what is known as a yes and no review, but to my mind [the film] is a yes and no show.

haps that fidelity is the picture's chief fault, or there is such a thing as being too true to an original, too conscious of a drama's stage-bound pattern. There is an over-supply of dialogue, much of it repetitious. It has a tendency to hysterics when the drama might better have been served by the intensity of understatement. ... it has been well-played on the whole, although William Holden, the newcomer in the title role, has been guilty, in scattered scenes, of the exaggerated recoils, lip-bitings and hand-clenchings one associates with the old-time melodramatic school. In sum, however, it has been a good interpretation of an unusual role. As the "dame from Newark," Barbara Stanwyck has supplied just the proper note of cynicism and frankness. [The other actors] are thoroughly in character and in the best interests of the show. It is the sort of film we can endorse heartily in spite of its shortcomings.

Howard Barnes in the *New York Herald Tribune:*
Even those who considered the play sprawling and spotty are apt to find the screen version disappointing. The story of a youngster torn between love of fiddling and a talent for fisticuffs follows the Odets original, barring the climax, but it has lost much of its sting. The vital thrust of the drama's best passages is missing.

With Barbara Stanwyck and Lee J. Cobb

With George Raft and Humphrey Bogart

Invisible Stripes

1940   Warners

CAST:

GEORGE RAFT *(Cliff Taylor);* JANE BRYAN *(Peggy);* WILLIAM HOLDEN *(Tim Taylor);* HUMPHREY BOGART *(Chuck Martin);* FLORA ROBSON *(Mrs. Taylor);* PAUL KELLY *(Ed Kruger);* LEE PATRICK *(Molly);* HENRY O'NEILL *(Parole Officer Masters);* FRANKIE THOMAS *(Tommy);* MORONI OLSEN *(Warden);* MARGOT STEVENSON *(Sue);* MARC LAWRENCE *(Lefty);* JOSEPH DOWNING *(Johnny);* LEO GORCEY *(Jimmy);* WILLIAM HAADE *(Shrank);* TULLY MARSHALL *(Old Peter).*

CREDITS:

HAL B. WALLIS *(Executive Producer);* LLOYD BACON *(Director);* LOUIS F. EDELMAN *(Associate Producer);* WARREN DUFF *(Screenplay);* JONATHAN FINN *(Original Story); based on the book by* WARDEN LEWIS E. LAWES; ERNEST HALLER *(Director of Photography);* HEINZ ROEMHELD *(Music);* IRVING RAPPER *(Dialogue Director);* MAX PARKER *(Art Director);* RAY HEINDORF *(Orchestrations);* JAMES GIBBON *(Editor);* DOLPH THOMAS *(Sound);* ELMER DECKER *(Assistant Director);* MILO ANDERSON *(Gowns);* PERC WESTMORE *(Makeup);* BYRON HASKIN *(Special Effects).*

Opened at the Strand Theater, New York, January 15, 1940. Running time, 82 minutes.

THE PICTURE:

In his follow-up to *Golden Boy,* Holden found himself on loan to Warners, where he played the rambunctious, hot-tempered kid brother of George Raft in a standard gangster melodrama. Jane Bryan was on hand as Holden's romance. About all that could fairly be said for *Invisible Stripes* was that it ably maintained the tradition of fast-moving, shoot-'em-up gangster epics in which Warners had been specializing for a decade. Raft was the star, got most of the footage, and Holden and Jane Bryan divided what was left, with distinguished British character actress Flora Robson, who had given a fine account of herself in *Wuthering Heights* a few months before, inexplicably relegated to the role of Raft's long-suffering mother, and in a jazzed-up American milieu foreign to her temperament and image (a casting mystery that has yet to be elucidated by film historians). Humphrey Bogart, who had yet to make major stardom despite a slew of pre-1940 vivid

43

With George Raft

performances (though he was fast getting there, and would the following year), was on hand for typical Bogartisms as Raft's criminal pal. The story directed by Lloyd Bacon (an old hand by then at such material) and based, more-than-somewhat loosely, on a Warden Lewis E. Lawes book, opens with Raft's release from prison along with his pal Bogart. Raft decides to go straight; Bogart returns to his outlaw ways. An ex-convict who must report regularly to parole authorities, Raft finds it difficult to get work—"invisible stripes" and all that. He is anxious to provide for Ma Robson's future, and to keep kid brother Holden, an impetuous, aggressive kid, from getting into trouble. Holden frets because he can't make enough money to marry Bryan and give her the life he wants for her, so he goes into criminal activity, to his brother's chagrin. Raft runs afoul of the law again when he is picked up on suspicion after his place of employment is burglarized. Anxious to buy a garage as a legitimate business for Holden, Raft joins Bogart and gang in some bank robberies. When he gets enough money, he tries to quit the gang. The gang implicates Holden when it uses his garage for getaway purposes. In a blaze of complicated melodrama Holden identifies the gangsters;

Bogart gets wounded; Raft tries to help him, is suspected by the other outlaws as an informer, and dies with Bogart in a hail of bullets. Presumably a chastened Holden would find a life of quiet, right-side-of-the-law respectability with Bryan, though considering his reckless, hot-tempered nature, the audience is left to wonder. Holden was callow and awkward at times under Lloyd Bacon's direction (Bacon had his hands full keeping the action percolating), but considering that he was at an unfamiliar studio, without Mamoulian and Miss Stanwyck to guide him, he succeeded (and at the tender age of twenty-one to boot) in giving a reasonably vital performance.

REVIEWS:

Variety:

Script is slightly thin in spots, but these passages are overcome sufficiently by fast tempo and direction... it's a familiar cinematic yarn but strengthened by a zippy pace, excellent performances and direction. Raft makes the most of a meaty role, playing with effective restraint. William Holden extends himself as the hot-tempered brother who is prevented from stepping outside the law by Raft's fists.

Wanda Hale in the *New York Daily News:*

George Raft makes his Cliff Taylor so sympathetic and real that you hate to think of what is obviously coming to him. William Holden is Raft's brother and Jane Bryan is his girl friend. Holden's arguments against marriage because he can't give Jane yachts and silver lamé evening dresses is downright silly, even though it strives to reveal the feelings of small-salaried people.

Elizabeth Copeland in the *Richmond* (Va.) *News-Leader:*

William Holden is excellent as Raft's younger brother who takes a long time to learn all the lessons that seem like copy-book stuff to most of us.... It is good stuff of the type and although it is very much the same kind of thing that is done again and again, it has enough merit, both technically and morally, to be absorbing and gratifying entertainment.

The New York *Sun:*

Familiar as the Warner underworld and its denizens may be, there are still thrills and excitements in the picture. That studio knows all the tricks for this kind of film.

With Flora Robson, George Raft, and Jane Bryan

With Guy Kibbee

Our Town

1940   United Artists

CAST:

FRANK CRAVEN *(Mr. Morgan, The Narrator)*; WILLIAM HOLDEN *(George Gibbs)*; MARTHA SCOTT *(Emily Webb)*; FAY BAINTER *(Mrs. Gibbs)*; BUELAH BONDI *(Mrs. Webb)*; THOMAS MITCHELL *(Dr. Gibbs)*; GUY KIBBEE *(Editor Webb)*; STUART ERWIN *(Howie Newsome)*; PHILLIP WOOD *(Simon Stinson)*; DORO MERANDE *(Mrs. Soames)*; RUTH TOBY *(Rebecca Gibbs)*; DOUGLAS GARDINER *(Wally Webb)*; ARTHUR ALLEN *(Professor Willett)*; SPENCER CHARTERS *(The Constable)*; TIM DAVIS *(Joe Crowell)*; DIX DAVIS *(Si Crowell)*; DON WHITE *(Wedding Guest)*.

CREDITS:

SOL LESSER *(Producer)*; SAM WOOD *(Director)*; *A Principal Artists Production; from the Pulitzer Prize play by Thornton Wilder;* THORNTON WILDER, FRANK CRAVEN *and* HARRY CHANDLEE *(Screenplay)*; AARON COPLAND *(Music)*; IRVIN TALBOT *(Orchestral Direction)*; WILLIAM CAMERON MENZIES *(Production Designer)*; HARRY HORNER *(Associate)*; BERT GLENNON *(Photography)*; SHERMAN TODD *(Editor)*.

Opened at Radio City Music Hall, New York, June 13, 1940. Running time, 90 minutes.

THE PICTURE:

Our Town by Thornton Wilder had been a Pulitzer Prize play in 1938, and in 1940 it was brought to the screen with Sam Wood directing, and with Wilder, Frank Craven, and Harry Chandlee doing the screenplay. In understated but deeply affecting terms, it gives a simple dramatic account of what goes on in the lives of people in a small New England town, their regimens depicted on a progression from childhood to courtship to age to death. Fragile in its imagery, deeply tender in its regard for the hearts and minds of simple folk, and penetrating in its revelations of their quiet heroisms, *Our Town* proved an ornament to the 1940 screen, setting forth as it did the importance and validity of simple lives and elemental emotions. Martha Scott repeated her performance as the editor's daughter in her first motion-picture appearance, and it led to a number of outstanding film parts for her in ensuing years. Holden played the doctor's son who loves her, courts and marries her, and eventually and prematurely, loses her to the one rival who always has the last word: Death. Life in Grover's Corners is covered from 1901 to 1913, and the compelling details of humdrum lives are set forth with loving attention to the elements that

45

With Martha Scott

and sincerity. His presence in the film version of a play so prestigious and well-loved, helped his stock substantially during this his first year of film prominence. A slew of fine character actors gave prime support, including Thomas Mitchell as the doctor; Guy Kibbee as the editor; Fay Bainter and Beulah Bondi as their wives; Spencer Charters as the constable, and Stuart Erwin as the milkman. Frank Craven was as splendid as he was in the play, as the Narrator who comments on the action and serves as a Greek chorus for a genuine and deeply moving slice of authentic Americana seen through a poetically selective prism.

REVIEWS:

Bosley Crowther in *The New York Times:*

This is not an ordinary picture, not a straight-away plotted-story film. This is a picture which utilizes the fullest prerogatives of the camera to participate as a recognized witness to a simple, dramatic account of people's lives, not just to spy on someone's fictitious emotions. On the stage there was a character known as the stage manager, who conducted the action of the play; on the screen a small-town druggist acts as guide and Narrator on a leisurely tour of a little New Hampshire town . . . because of the technique employed we are permitted to see these people in their entirety; we see them in their normal daily tasks; we hear the thoughts which run through their minds and at the end, we behold the dream of death and survival of the soul which is dreamed by the girl who is soon to become a mother. It is, in short, a comprehensive penetration of the hearts of these good people, an external glance at the toils and humors of their humdrum lives and an internal revelation of their sorrows which brings, as Matthew Arnold said, "the eternal note of sadness in." . . . Martha Scott, as the young girl, is lovely and vibrant with emotion, and William Holden plays the boy with a clean and refreshing youthfulness

illuminate human character. There is humor here, hurt, and also much love. There is resilience and quiet strength in the face of adversity. The screen medium fleshes out the physical setting that was only suggested in the play, which was done without scenery or props and consequently depended for its effects entirely upon its performers. The screen of course permits ample opportunity for interesting photographic ambiences, creatively inspired dissolves, montages, and splendid atmospheric details of camera and setting that enhance the mood and get across the film's essential character and intent. Holden, in appearance and manner the idealized yet true image of the decent young American of the century's first decade, traced the stages of a life over a twelve-year period with unaffected naturalness

With Martha Scott

Guy Kibbee and Martha Scott

... Sam Wood has caught in his direction all the flavor of smalltown life, with exciting visual elaborations upon the theme ... it captures on film the simple beauties and truths of humble folks as very few pictures ever do; it is rich and ennobling in its plain philosophy.

The *New York Herald Tribune:*

A record of human experience which is as broad in its scope as our national heritage and as sensitively and honestly realized as any material that has made its way to the screen for a long time ... there are times when the film is deeply moving or tremendously funny. What is most important is the fact that it is always real and always fascinating. It is a photoplay in which the impact of living and feeling is recreated so intensely and persuasively that you are sure to want to see it more than once.... Mr. Craven is magnificent ... Miss Scott gives him his most valuable assistance, playing with grave sincerity and intensity ... William Holden, impersonating the doctor's son who falls in love with and marries the editor's daughter, is the only player I found wanting, and he doesn't seriously hurt any scene, although he makes the courtship less simply moving than it was behind footlights.

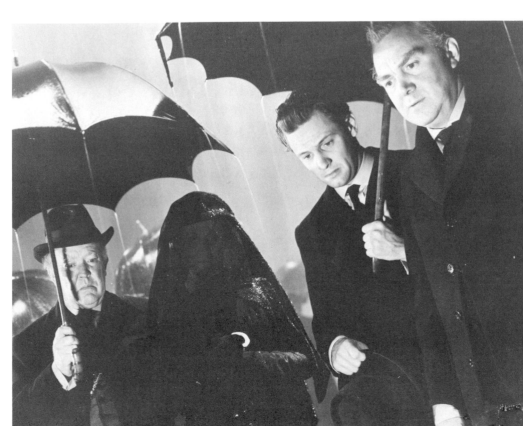

With Guy Kibbee, Beulah Bondi, and Thomas Mitchell

Those Were the Days

1940   Paramount

CAST:

WILLIAM HOLDEN *(P. J. "Petey" Simmons)*; BONITA GRANVILLE *(Martha Scroggs)*; EZRA STONE *(Alexander "Allie" Bangs)*; JUDITH BARRETT *(Mirabel Allstairs)*; VAUGHAN GLASER *(Judge Malachi Scroggs)*; LUCIEN LITTLEFIELD *(Professor Sillicocks)*; RICHARD DENNING *(Briggs)*; TOM RUTHERFORD *(Ranson)*; PHILLIP TERRY *(Sam Byers)*; ALDRICH BOWKER *(Judge Squire Jennings)*; JAMES SEAY *(Andrews)*; DOUGLAS KENNEDY *(Allen)*; JOHN LAIRD *(Saunders)*; JOHN HARTLEY *(Whipple)*; ROBERT SCOTT *(Allison)* GAYLORD PENDLETON *(Connie Mathews)*; ALAN LADD *(Keg Rearich)*; JAMES DODD *(Evans)*; WILDA BENNET *(Miss Chickering)*.

CREDITS:

J. THEODORE REED *(Producer and Director)*; DON HARTMAN *(Screenplay)*; *based on the Siwash Stories by* GEORGE FITCH; VICTOR MILNER *(Photography)*; WILLIAM SHEA *(Editor)*; GEORGE HIPPARD *(Assistant Director)*.

Opened at Loew's Criterion, New York, July 14, 1940. Running time, 74 minutes.

THE PICTURE:

With three pictures under his belt by mid-1940, Holden was billed over the title of his fourth, *Those Were The Days*, with Bonita Granville and Ezra Stone in support. His poise and assurance before the camera were improving noticeably, and it was apparent with this film that Holden was a naturally talented actor who could deliver a characterization in fine style despite limited technical experience. Considering that he was only twenty-two when he made *Those Were The Days*, his performance in it is all the more remarkable. He dominates the footage, ambles with ease through a variety of moods from love to gaiety to anger to hurt. The story, based on the popular Siwash stories by George Fitch, opens about 1940 with a gathering of folk celebrating a wedding anniversary. Holden and Granville are the middle-aged couple honored, and her father, Vaughan Glaser, proceeds to amuse the assembled guests with a humorous recounting of Holden's courtship of Granville when both were students at Old Siwash back in 1904. Holden is a brash boy on campus, a lion with the ladies but disliked by all but his faithful

With Judith Barrett

though previously he had alienated her with his tactless, cocky behavior. Within a week the girl is in love with him, but her disillusion is keen indeed when she learns from her father the real cause of his sudden interest. Despite a broken heart, she intercedes on his behalf, and the judge puts him on probation with the condition that he never contact Granville again. As is usual in such situations (at least in the cinema) Holden has meanwhile fallen in love with the girl, and finds it impossible to keep away from her. Though she snubs him consistently, he finally manages to tie her to a chair, then convinces his captive audience that he really is in love. The father finds them, calls the police, and orders him to jail. But when their fellow-students find out about all this, they stage a riot in front of the jail-house where Granville has joined Holden, and the father is forced to give way. The film ends amusingly with an epilogue in which Holden finds out his own son has gotten into hot water and is kidded by the anniversary-party guests with a like-father-like-son reminder. The movie is filled with authentic 1904 period atmosphere, and is smoothly directed by J. Theodore Reed, who also produced. Seen recently on TV, the film holds up better than the original 1940 reviews would indicate (at that time it was fobbed off as lightweight, inconsequential froth) and turns out to be a rather charming romantic comedy.

There are some amusing plot twists. When Holden fears that roommate Stone can't pass his impending exam, he tries to redeem Stone's accusations of his self-centeredness by sneaking into the examining professor's bedroom the night before and changing his alarm clock so he will be late for class. He also changes the hall clock and even tampers with the college bell-tower

roommate, Ezra Stone, because of his jaunty self-centeredness, constant mischiefmaking, and insensitivity to the feelings and needs of others. When one of his larkish pranks lands him in court before Judge Glaser, he weasels his way out of an immediate six-month sentence by requesting a week's continuance, during which he is to round up witnesses and show cause why he shouldn't be packed off to jail. When he learns that Granville is the judge's daughter, he slyly proceeds to court her,

With Ezra Stone, Judith Barrett, and Bonita Granville

clock, ending up with a chase in which he derails a streetcar and endangers a woman passenger—all of which bring about his original jail sentence. There is some snappy badinage, 1904-style, at college dances, and Holden does some fancy footwork jumping from trees to porches with college chums out to razz him hot in pursuit. The picture is high-spirited—distinctly lightweight at times, to be sure, but nonetheless appealing—and Holden carries all of it off very well with Granville, Stone, and Glaser lending able support (Granville in four short years, 1936–1940, had developed from the brattish Mary Tilford of *These Three* into a competent and likable young romantic lead.) Holden's good looks were well-highlighted by photographer Victor Milner, and the film reportedly brought about a significant increase in his fan mail at Paramount. Scenes purportedly at the midwest mythical Siwash College were shot in part on the campus of Knox College, Galesburg, Illinois. (The film was originally titled *At Good Old Siwash*).

With Bonita Granville

REVIEWS:

William Boehnel in the *New York World-Telegram:*
This amiable little charade about undergraduate pranks and petting is at best a good two-reeler. But its one pleasant little episode is so endlessly repeated that it loses all its charm, spontaneity and entertainment... parts of [the story] seem sparkling, more because of fresh and imaginative treatment than because of any inventiveness in incident. But most of it is dull and repetitious with the cast trying gamely to save the day with its competent performances... the dialogue and clothes should give modern jitterbugs plenty of laughs, make elders in the audience chuckle reminiscently.

Rose Pelswick in the *New York Journal-American:*
A comedy of college life at the turn of the century, [the film] is an amiably entertaining piece. It may not have the speedy tempo of present-day collegiate films but, on the other hand, neither has it the inevitable last-minute-to-play football finish that winds up every modern campus concoction... good performances by young Mr. Holden, by Ezra Stone, and by Vaughan Glaser keep the film moving brightly even though it becomes a bit thin toward the end. Its leisurely and nostalgic humor should appeal especially to the greying alumni.

Eileen Creelman in the New York *Sun:*
[The film] is usually rather likable, and always rather slight... it chuckles, but sympathetically, at the whole period, back around 1900, or a little later. The costumes, the hair-dos, the fancy hats, the manners, and the slang are all presented.... William Holden and Ezra Stone are good, going in for the comedy with a relish. *Those Were The Days* is far from sentimental about the good old days. It laughs at them, but it seems to think them rather nice too.

Walt. in *Variety:*
Collegiate capers and customs of the period are antiquated and as unfolded decidedly sophomoric in comparison to modern college life. Story is as much a relic as the old-fashioned automobile that is inserted in several scene backgrounds, with a linen-dustered driver tinkering from underneath. Cast is handicapped by the material at hand. Holden lightens up considerably over previous assignments as the mischievous student.

With Bonita Granville and Vaughan Glaser

William Holden

Arizona

1941   Columbia

CAST:

JEAN ARTHUR *(Phoebe Titus);* WILLIAM HOLDEN *(Peter Muncie);* WARREN WILLIAM *(Jefferson Carteret);* PORTER HALL *(Lazarus Ward);* PAUL HARVEY *(Solomon Warner);* GEORGE CHANDLER *(Haley);* BYRON FOULGER *(Pete Kitchen);* REGIS TOOMEY *(Grant Oury);* PAUL LOPEZ *(Estevan Ochoa);* COLIN TAPLEY *(Bart Massey);* UVALDO VARELA *(Hilario Gallego);* EDGAR BUCHANAN *(Judge Bogardus);* EARL CRAWFORD *(Joe Briggs);* GRIFF BARNETTE *(Sam Hughes);* LUDWIG HARDT *(Meyer);* PATRICK MORIARTY *(Terry);* FRANK DARIEN *(Joe);* SYD SAYLOR *(Timmins);* WADE CROSBY *(Longstreet);* FRANK HILL *(Mono);* NINA CAMPANA *(Teresa);* ADDISON RICHARDS *(Captain Hunter).*

CREDITS:

WESLEY RUGGLES *(Producer and Director);* CLAUDE BINYON *(Screenplay); based on a story by* CLARENCE BUDINGTON KELLAND; JOSEPH WALKER, HARRY HOLLEN-BERGER *and* FAYTE BROWN *(Photography);* OTTO MEYER *and* WILLIAM LYON *(Editors);* VICTOR YOUNG *(Music);* M. W. SOLOFF *(Musical Director);* NORMAN DEMING *(Assistant Director).*

Opened at Radio City Music Hall, New York, February 6, 1941. Running time, 125 minutes.

THE PICTURE:

Holden next found himself in his first Western, *Arizona,* opposite Jean Arthur, then one of Columbia's biggest female stars. While the picture is built around her, Holden came in for his share of attention, giving at age twenty-two (Miss Arthur was thirty-two at the time) a surprisingly mature performance in a part that had been intended for Gary Cooper. Critical reaction was mixed, complaints ranging from dislike of the film's deliberate pace to impatience with its numerous

William Holden

subplots and historical expositions that interfered with the sweep and action such a Western theme demanded. The film cost a reported $2 million, not a sum to sneeze at in 1941, and there was some disappointment in the higher Columbia echelons when the picture's reception was not all that was hoped. Miss Arthur, for all her forceful ways and sure authority on screen, did not overshadow young Holden, and the picture proved a plus for him.

Arthur plays Phoebe Titus, swaggering hellcat of Tucson in the 1860s, a pioneer gal in a pioneer town. She wears breeches, she swaggers, she beats the males at their own game and on their own terms, until Missourian Holden shows up en route to California. Then it's crinolines and feminine manners for the smitten Miss Arthur, but Holden loves-her-and-leaves-her (seems that California beckons him irresistibly). Soon our heroine has other things to occupy her mind, however, for villains Warren William and Porter Hall are up to no good. Seems Arthur has set up a freighter supply train to Yuma and the bad boys stop her every way they can: setting Indians against her wagon trains, stealing her funds, and anything else they can think

up. But as good Westerns will have it, Holden returns with Union infantry from California, turns a cattle herd on the attacking Indians in a rousing action sequence (the film could have used more of such), and then it's a ranch and marriage for the reunited lovers.

REVIEWS:

Archer Winsten in the *New York Post:*

At regular intervals, or at least whenever the cash hangs heavy, the movie companies decide that if a cheap Western is as sure-fire as it is, a super-Western ought to burn a groove to the boxoffice. Then, over a period of months stretching into years of fertile publicity, the greater project takes shape. Occasionally it lives up to the advance hysteria . . . but more often it loses the vitality of the crude Western pattern in the attempt to improve dialogue and characterizations. This is the weakness of *Arizona.* . . . They had two strikes when they accepted the handicap of Jean Arthur as Phoebe Titus, a frontier heroine and gun-slinger . . . Jean may be the very proud possessor of Hollywood's most noticeable drawl but she still misses out on that kind of task by no small margin. She's nice, clean-cut, wholesome.

With Jean Arthur

With Jean Arthur

The same goes for gentle William Holden, her hero with two whole guns. He's too pleasant even to squeeze out so much as a mean glint in one corner of one eye.

Walt. in *Variety:*
William Holden comes out best in the role of Peter Muncie. He gives a good, honest, masculine performance. ... Partly because the approach seems to have been superficial, partly because the action is sporadic and frequently interrupted, *Arizona* lacks the sweep and dramatic impulse that would have made it a great picture. Even so, it is a romantic episode with fine camerawork, great scenery, interesting details and a

With Jean Arthur

With Jean Arthur

sufficient amount of action to give it general popularity.

Kate Cameron in the *New York Daily News:*
The story has its moments of excitement but it moves a little too deliberately across the screen to create the suspense needed to hold audience interest taut through a two-hour film. . . . Young William Holden plays a bearded and booted pioneer convincingly.

Walt. in *Variety:*
Unreeling at slower tempo than is general policy for lusty western of epic proportions, picture devotes much footage to exposition of characters and incidental sidelights that veer from direct story telling. This procedure in both script and direction results in bogging down of audience interest in several instances, and prevents sustained drive of picture through the period depicted. . . . Jean Arthur dominates throughout with strongly convincing performance. . . . Holden clicks as the hero, and rates more Western assignments needing he-man zing.

With Jean Arthur

With Constance Moore and Ray Milland

I Wanted Wings

1941   Paramount

CAST:

RAY MILLAND *(Jeff Young);* WILLIAM HOLDEN *(Al Ludlow;* WAYNE MORRIS *(Tom Cassidy);* BRIAN DONLEVY *(Captain Mercer);* CONSTANCE MOORE *(Carolyn Bartlett);* VERONICA LAKE *(Sally Vaughn);* HARRY DAVENPORT *("Sandbags" Riley);* PHIL BROWN *(Jimmy Masters);* EDWARD FIELDING *(President of the Court);* WILLIAM ROBERTSON *(Judge Advocate);* RICHARD LANE *(Flight Commander);* ADDISON RICHARDS *(Flight Surgeon);* HOBART CAVANAUGH *(Mickey);* DOUGLAS AYLESWORTH *(Lieut. Hopkins);* JOHN TRENT *(Lieut. Ronson);* ARCHIE TWITCHELL *(Lt. Clankton);* RICHARD WEBB *(Cadet Captain);* JOHN HEISTAND *(Radio Announcer).*

CREDITS:

ARTHUR HORNBLOW JR. *(Producer);* MITCHELL LEISEN *(Director);* RICHARD MAIBAUM, LIEUT. BEIRNE LAY JR. *and* SID HERZIG *(Screenplay); based on a story by* ELEANOR GRIFFIN *and* FRANK WEAD; *from the book* I Wanted Wings *by* LT. BEIRNE LAY JR.; LEO TOVER, A.S.C. *(Director of Photography);* ELMER DYER, A.S.C. *(Aerial Photography);* FARCIOT EDOUART, A.S.C. *(Process Photography);* GORDON JENNINGS, A.S.C. *(Special Pho-*

tographic Effects); Songs: "Born to Love," Lyrics by NED WASHINGTON, *Music by* VICTOR YOUNG; *"Spirit of the Air Corps" by* CAPT. WILLIAM J. CLINCH; HANS DREIER *and* ROBERT USHER *(Art Direction);* HUGH BENNETT *(Editor);* GENE MERRITT *and* RICHARD OLSEN *(Sound Recording); (Western Electric Mirrophonic Recording). Filmed partially at Randolph, Kelly and March Fields, with cooperation of U.S. Army Air Corps.*

Opened at the Astor Theatre, New York, March 26, 1941. Running time, 131 minutes.

THE PICTURE:

I Wanted Wings, a cinematic salute to the Army Air Corps (as it was called in 1941), won a measure of critical praise that year for its exciting aerial shots, special-effects wizardry, and forthright male performances, but its two actresses, Constance Moore and the much-touted newcomer with the hairdo over one eye, (Miss Veronica Lake, to be sure), did not fare so well, at least with the critics, their presence being regarded as superfluous and their performances banal. The nadir

With Ray Milland and Constance Moore

of Miss Lake's critical trouncing was reached when one reviewer commented that she chiefly demonstrated "a talent for wearing low-cut gowns." But the air stuff (much of which, naturally, looks primitive and tame to a viewer today, was exciting for 1941 audiences, and it was neatly integrated into a story of three typical air cadets who go through the tough training routine (Milland, Holden, and Wayne Morris were the boys). In civilian life they had been a Long Island playboy, a garage mechanic, and a college athlete. With Brian Donlevy on hand as their commanding instructor, guide, and mentor, the students go through the usual harrowing paces of a strict regimen, try their wings at last, encounter the psychological tensions implicit in a "washout" threat if their performances should be adjudged not up to par by the higher-ups. Eventually, of course, they develop the assurance of guys who know their business. The film tends to bog down in its detours along Romance Road, with Siren Lake and Lady-Photographer Moore managing to make nuisances of themselves, Miss Moore being the "respectable" girl and Miss Lake the biggest tramp around. Mitchell Leisen directed the film with obvious respect for Air Corps traditions, and he does succeed in catching the majesty and beauty of planes aloft, the dedication to their calling that landsmen turned airmen feel. Holden, though he tended to get lost in all the fuss over the Lake hairdo, to say nothing of plane activity, mock air wars, and the like, managed to come through pleasingly enough when called upon.

REVIEWS:

Howard Barnes in the *New York Herald Tribune:*

Far more a poster than a drama. Its shots of winged dynamos flashing across the sky make a pattern of superb pictorial imagery. Its celebration of a mock air raid on Los Angeles has been devised to hasten every extension of our aerial defenses. At the same time, it presents such a patchwork of conventional situations when it comes to the human drama that it can scarcely be taken seriously. When it sticks to the air, [the film] is tremendously effective. After having seen countless aerial epics, from the classic *Wings* on, I can remember no such stunning shots of take-offs, flying pyrotechnics or the suggested terror of war in the clouds, as those which Mitchell Leisen has screened for this offering. One is inducted into all the mysteries of becoming a first-rate flyer, with the substantial equipment of several Army flying fields on frequent and spectacular parade. Pictorially, the film wants for little in the way of crafts-

With Veronica Lake

manship, production or showmanship. The players in the offering are conditioned throughout by their assignments of the moment. Ray Milland, William Holden, Brian Donlevy and even Wayne Morris are splendid when they are celebrating the arduous transformation of a landsman into a crack airman. When they are making a series of gallant and unnecessary gestures about a blonde tramp, played with rare lack of persuasion by Veronica Lake, they can be excused for stumbling. Even with a good actress in the role, the romance of (the film) would be far from palatable.

Bosley Crowther in *The New York Times:*
In spite of a thread of Class B story which gets snarled in its whirling propellers before the end, this cinematic salute to the Army Air Corps and to the young men who are entering it today is a vastly exciting motion picture and a dependable inspiration to the youth of the land.... While going down the line [the leads] do become romantically involved, and this phase of the picture, we are sorry to say, is painful indeed. For it drags into the story a lady photographer to whom [one lead] becomes attached, and likewise a lurid siren who sort of cuts across the paths of the three. It is this latter lady who is responsible for the plot's most incredible complication, the presence of herself in a "flying fortress" during critical night maneuvers. Whether this could happen is beside the point. As plain fiction it is rank melodrama in an otherwise solid and credible film ... Ray Milland, Wayne Morris and William Holden give uniformly excellent performances as the three cadets and Brian Donlevy makes a tower of strength as

With Ray Milland, Constance Moore, and Veronica Lake

a commanding instructor.... Miss Moore is inclined to artless posturing while Miss Lake, of whom much has been foretold, manages to show little more than a talent for wearing low-cut gowns.

With Ray Milland (right foreground)

With Glenn Ford

Texas

1941   Columbia

CAST:

WILLIAM HOLDEN (Dan Thomas); GLENN FORD (Tod Ramsey); CLAIRE TREVOR ("Mike" King); GEORGE BANCROFT (Windy Miller); EDGAR BUCHANAN (Doc Thorpe); DON BEDDOE (Sheriff); ANDREW TOMBES (Tennessee); ADDISON RICHARDS (Matt Laskan); EDMUND MAC-DONALD (Comstock); JOSEPH CREHAN (Dusty King); WILLARD ROBERTSON (Wilson); PATRICK MORIARTY (Matthews); EDWARD COBB (Blout).

CREDITS:

SAM BISCHOFF (Producer); GEORGE MARSHALL (Director); HORACE MC COY, LEWIS MELTZER and MICHAEL BLANKFORT (Screenplay); based on a story by LEWIS MELTZER and MICHAEL BLANKFORT; GEORGE MEEHAN (Photography); Photographed in Sepia; WILLIAM LYON (Editor); NORMAN DEMING (Assistant Director).

Opened at Loew's State Theater, New York, October 16, 1941. Running time, 94 minutes.

With George Bancroft and Glenn Ford

THE PICTURE:

Having had his share of kicks in the wide blue yonder with *I Wanted Wings*, Holden went back to horses again—and back to Columbia from Paramount. This time he had as co-star young Glenn Ford, who was also fast on the rise. Ford's career had been almost exactly contemporaneous with Holden's, and Ford at twenty-

With Claire Trevor

five and Holden at twenty-three proved to have the right co-starring chemistry. (They were to do another Western together seven years later, *The Man From Colorado*, and it is interesting, on viewing both films, to note what war service and the passage of those relatively few years had done to both boys-become-men's manner and appearance). In *Texas*, Ford and Holden were buddies, fellow veterans of the Confederate Army. They journey to Texas via Kansas to go into the cattle business. They witness a stagecoach holdup and turn the tables by robbing the bandits, but Ford is basically an honest fellow who decides to go to work for rancher Claire Trevor and raise cattle while Holden is the larcenous one who winds up a cattle rustler. This puts them on opposite sides of the law, and when both fall in love with Trevor (who has relatively little to do but does it well), things really heat up. Ford then decides to take a herd through to Abi-

With Glenn Ford

William Holden in center

lene, the rail center. Holden is assigned to head him off, but Holden doublecrosses his crooked bosses and Ford gets his seven thousand head to their destination. Then trouble ensues, Holden is killed, and Ford wins the woman, who finally appreciates that he was all along the better man anyway.

All the usual Western ingredients are very much on hand from the stagecoach holdups to cattle rustling and plenty of shooting. Talented character actor Edgar Buchanan (a shining light of many a film in this period) almost steals the show with his sharp por-

trayal of the dentist who doubles in banditry and who is always ready to check a cavity even in the midst of a shootout.

REVIEWS:

Edith Werner in the New York *Daily Mirror:*

The time of *Texas* is 1866, when it was a babe weaning on shootin' and killin'. Those were raw, vigorous days, pardner, and admirably caught in spirit and action by George Marshall. . . . Holden and Ford are excellent as the friends.

With Addison Richards (center)

*With Edgar Buchanan and
Don Beddoe*

Leo Mishkin in the *New York Morning Telegraph:*
Something very rare in a Western movie seems to have
crept into [the film's] making . . . and the result is a
surprisingly attractive picture. The something rare is
nothing less than a sense of humor, humor about the
principal characters, humor concerning the customarily
fair heroine, humor even about the dastardly deeds of
the villains . . . it's all light and carefree and happy-go-
lucky, and even if the plot is a routine business, the
approach to same helps out enormously. Mr. Holden
and Mr. Ford make a couple of likely-looking cowpokes.

The *Christian Science Monitor:*
While spoofing a little along the way, it observes the
etiquette and tradition of an accepted cinema form. It

has rough riding, cattle rustling, shooting and a story
that leaves out only the Indian raid and a rescue by
the U.S. Cavalry. . . . George Marshall's direction mixes
action, character study and burlesque . . . there are suitable performances by William Holden, Claire Trevor
and Glenn Ford.

Henry T. Murdock in the *Philadelphia Evening Ledger:*
Whenever the circumstances warrant, Director Marshall jams vigorous comedy into the plot. . . . Oddly
enough, while some of the action isn't far from slapstick, it never interferes with a really exciting tale of
the cattle country. Both young men acquit themselves
well. They are spirited, personable and resourceful.
However, the playing honors really go to Edgar Buchanan . . . George Bancroft adds to the color.

*Addison Richards, Edgar Buchanan,
and George Bancroft*

With Brian Donlevy

The Remarkable Andrew

1942   Paramount

CAST:

WILLIAM HOLDEN *(Andrew Long)*; ELLEN DREW *(Peggy Tobin)*; BRIAN DONLEVY *(General Andrew Jackson)*; ROD CAMERON *(Jesse James)*; RICHARD WEBB *(Randall Stevens)*; PORTER HALL *(Art Slocumb)*; FRANCES GIFFORD *(Halsey)*; NYDIA WESTMAN *(Miss Van Buren)*; MONTAGU LOVE *(George Washington)*; GEORGE WATTS *(Benjamin Franklin)*; BRANDON HURST *(Justice Marshall)*; GILBERT EMERY *(Thomas Jefferson)*; JIMMY CONLIN *(Henry Smith)*; SPENCER CHARTERS *(Dr. Upjohn)*; WALLIS CLARK *(R. R. McCall)*; TOM FADDEN *(Jake Pearl)*; MINOR WATSON *(Orville Beamish)*; MILTON PARSONS *(Sam Savage)*; THOMAS W. ROSS *(Judge Krebbs)*.

CREDITS:

RICHARD BLUMENTHAL *(Producer)*; STUART HEISLER *(Director)*; DALTON TRUMBO *(Screenplay)*; adapted by MR. TRUMBO *from his own novel of the same name*; THEODOR SPARKUHL, A.S.C. *(Photography)*; ARCHIE MARSHEK *(Editor)*; ARTHUR BLACK *(Assistant Director)*.

Opened at Loew's State Theater, New York, March 5, 1942. Running time, 80 minutes.

THE PICTURE:

Dalton Trumbo, on a whimsical binge, wrote a book, *The Remarkable Andrew*, after Paramount producer Arthur Hornblow offered him twice the price of his original story on the same subject if he put it first between covers. Stuart Heisler did his best to inject fluffy insouciance and dynamic satire into some heavy-handed histrionics and some awkward historical-allegorical interpolations. The result was not entirely successful, but Trumbo got his fantasies, such as they were, off his chest, and Holden got a nice part for himself as the honest young municipal bookkeeper who is falsely accused of diverting funds after he is framed by some unscrupulous city hall characters. Enter Brian Donlevy as the ghost of General Andrew Jackson. It seems our young hero's name is Andrew, he is secretary of the Andrew Jackson Society and he has an autographed poster from one of Old Hickory's campaigns, plus a plethora of scholarly tomes on the President. All this adulation is enough to raise the dead—and does—especially when the living is in trouble—and what trouble! Then there is the complication of the present-day Andrew's romantic problems with fiancée

62

With Ellen Drew

With Brian Donlevy

Ellen Drew, who finds her financially cautious swain's marriage-delays irritating. It also seems that young Andrew's ancestor had saved the old general's life in the long-ago. Donlevy-Jackson then shows up to clear this worthy young man. He drags along Ben Franklin, George Washington, Jesse James, and everyone else he can dredge up, with the possible exception of the Ghost of Christmas Past. Young Andrew can see these spirits, and so announces. He is promptly incarcerated, after being declared nuts. The old ghosts argue politics with energetic glee between attempts to save Holden. Save him they do, what with Jesse trying to spring him from jail and the other spirits messing around the city hall records to nail the bad guys. The kids are set to get married—only Donlevy wants to move in with them. When Drew threatens to leave, the old ghost departs,

then for the first time young Andrew's gal herself sees the spirit. Cute? In a way, we suppose, but the mixed reaction and the uneasy critical reports from some quarters indicated that in literal-minded, war-concerned 1942 such whimsy mixed in with historical allegory and invisible ghosts (invisible to all but the hero, that is) were a bit much. *Variety* had sounded a nervous note with "It's all pretty involved. It's going to be a little bewildering for the average audience." We would guess it was.

REVIEWS:

Pic:

William Holden, as the hero, gives an excellent performance and will no doubt give many a heart-throb to his feminine fans. Stuart Heisler, the director, de-

With Rod Cameron, Brian Donlevy, George Watts, Brandon Hurst, Ellen Drew, Montague Love, Jimmy Conlin, and Gilbert Emery.

With Eddie Bracken and Dorothy Lamour

With Dorothy Lamour and Eddie Bracken

orchestra, Bob Eberly and Helen O'Connell, and Miss Hutton singing such tuneful items as "Arthur Murray Taught Me Dancing In A Hurry" and "Build a Better Mousetrap." And then there is Cass Daley popping in and out, Gil Lamb mugging at the slightest provocation, vaudeville team Lorraine and Rognan spoofing ballroom dancers, and a windup that is little more than a collection of single acts and vaudeville sketches. Holden was frankly lost in this mishmash, but he managed to be boyishly ingratiating whenever he was seen, which wasn't all that often. When he finally got to kiss Lamour, he delivered in fine style. After the film's

release there was a flurry of Paramount fan mail carrying the message that Holden had the perfect figure for a sailor suit. Considering some of the pictures he was forced to make in this period, Holden doubtless agreed that all tangible assets helped put him over—and why not?

REVIEWS:

Herbert Cohn in the *Brooklyn Eagle:*

A breezy affair, transparent and slapstick, but funny and with songs that are easy to listen to. There's a spontaneity about it, too.... It has hardly any story

*With Betty Hutton, Eddie Bracken,
and Dorothy Lamour*

With Eddie Bracken (front center),
Dorothy Lamour (right) and sailor
pals

and even what little it has is severed midway to slip in an assortment of variety acts. But somehow the flimsiness of the plot doesn't matter this time, what with the songs and wisecracks and shenanigans that substitute for it . . . there's plenty of fun, and a lot, both comic and melodious to listen to. And it's all fast enough to hide the fact that it's a helter-skelter movie.

Leo Mishkin in the *New York Morning Telegraph:*

[The film] features such attractive people as Dorothy Lamour, William Holden and Eddie Bracken . . . but the plot, the stars and the incidentals are all subordinate to the circumstance that it's just another Paramount stage show being unreeled on the screen . . . it's all exceedingly lightweight and unimportant.

Eileen Creelman in the New York *Sun:*

A slim and obvious comedy with some good tunes. Much of the film is a roughhouse. Several reels toward the close are turned over to straight vaudeville. These final sequences are like a collection of short subjects, each devoted to one entertainer . . . perhaps the plot seems so minute because the music overwhelms it. At any rate, such an actor as William Holden is almost lost in the shuffle, although he plays a young sailor more likably than most Hollywood juveniles.

Louise Levitas in *PM:*

Specialty numbers engulf *The Fleet's In* like a tidal wave . . . the gobs who saw [the film] on opening day, however, said it was fine. And if they're not carping, why should any of us?

With Dorothy Lamour

With Frances Dee

Meet the Stewarts

1942   Columbia

CAST:

WILLIAM HOLDEN *(Michael Stewart);* FRANCES DEE *(Candace Goodwin);* GRANT MITCHELL *(Mr. Goodwin);* MARJORIE GATESON *(Mrs. Goodwin);* ANNE REVERE *(Geraldine Stewart);* ROGER CLARK *(Ted Graham);* DANNY MUMMERT *(John Goodwin);* ANN GILLIS *(Jane Goodwin);* MARGARET HAMILTON *(Williametta);* DON BEDDOE *(Taxi Driver);* MARY GORDON *(Mrs. Stewart);* EDWARD GARGAN *and* TOM DUGAN *(Moving Men).*

CREDITS:

ALFRED E. GREEN *(Director);* KAREN DE WOLF *(Screenplay); based on* ELIZABETH DUNN'S *Candy and Mike Stewart magazine stories; produced by* ROBERT SPARKS; HENRY FREULICH *(Camera);* AL CLARK *(Editor);* ABBY BERLIN *(Assistant Director).*

Opened at the Brooklyn Paramount, May 21, 1942, on second half of double bill. Running time, 73 minutes.

THE PICTURE:

Meet The Stewarts opened in Brooklyn on the second half of a double bill (with Bette Davis in *In This Our Life*) and was forthwith damned with faint praise by whatever reviewers bothered to sit through its seventy-three minutes. Not that the film was that bad, but it was one of those eminently forgettable, albeit pleasant, little domestic comedies that the best actors have had to weather—and struggle through—at various points in their early careers. Holden did his duty cheerfully enough in this potboiler about a spoiled rich girl who marries a young man with an average income and makes an effort to live within her husband's means (and how many Hollywood movies had used *that* plot up to 1942?). Based on Elizabeth Dunn's Candy and Mike Stewart magazine tales, it is replete with honeymoon quarrels, the bride's attempts to cook appetizing meals for hubby, maneuvers to make a slim budget stretch and the like. Pretty Frances Dee, back from one of her occasional screen retirements, does her best to help the then-less-experienced Holden register ease and the light touch before the cameras. The plot, such as it is, contains such elements as Holden's insistence that he will marry the rich girl only if they live on his salary. Of course the bride chafes at the monetary re-

With Tom Dugan, Edward Gargan and Frances Dee

With Frances Dee

strictions. There are domestic misunderstandings galore, but in the end she elects for a tight budget and a mightily relieved husband. Solid character actors such as Marjorie Gateson, Grant Mitchell, Anne Revere, and Margaret Hamilton worked overtime to add some bite and pertinence to the proceedings. They almost succeeded. Holden at twenty-four was likable and boyish, Miss Dee was warm and womanly, the production values—such as they were—were solid, and the direction adequate. The patrons of the Brooklyn Paramount had come to see Bette Davis in the other picture anyway, so no harm was done.

REVIEWS:

Wanda Hale in the New York *Daily News:*

Spruced up with good production and fresh, natural dialogue, if not entirely fresh situations, it serves as a vehicle for two ingratiating players, William Holden and Frances Dee . . . one of those little comedies which doesn't mean much but which you enjoy a lot while seeing it . . . William Holden, putting the serious look on his sensitive face, is a fine choice for Mike Stewart . . . Miss Dee, making one of her periodic returns to the screen, is efficient and charming . . . an acceptable little comedy.

Irene Thirer in the *New York Post:*

A synthetic bit of marital fluffilmery. A hectic time is had by all. Quarrels, separation, reunion, and the happy ending. Just a fair-to-middling summer dish, which is okay on a double bill but can hardly stand alone.

With Frances Dee

Walt. in *Variety:*

A smartly sparkling marital comedy parading the problems of a newly-wed couple combining love with a budget . . . an expert and compact script with deft direction and fine performances by William Holden and Frances Dee. Spontaneous audience reaction is obtained in the neat and intimate telling of the basic tale itself, which has been displayed on the screen many times before . . . newlywed problems are paraded throughout with amusing brightness . . . all in all, picture vividly displays that life is full of explosive complications for a young husband.

With Martha O'Driscoll

Young and Willing

1943   United Artists–Cinema Guild

CAST:

WILLIAM HOLDEN *(Norman Reese);* EDDIE BRACKEN *(George Bodell);* ROBERT BENCHLEY *(Arthur Kenny);* SUSAN HAYWARD *(Katie Benson);* MARTHA O'DRISCOLL *(Dottie Coburn);* BARBARA BRITTON *(Marge Benson);* JAMES BROWN *(Tony Dennison);* FLORENCE MAC-MICHAEL *(Muriel Foster);* MABEL PAIGE *(Mrs. Garnet);* JAY FASSETT *(Mr. Coburn);* PAUL HURST *(First Cop);* OLIN HOWLIN *(Second Cop);* BILLY BEVAN *(Phillips).*

CREDITS:

EDWARD H. GRIFFITH *(Producer and Director);* VIRGINIA VAN UPP *(Screenplay); adapted from a play by* FRANCIS SWANN; LEO TOVER *(Photography);* EDA WARREN *(Editor);* HANS DREIER, ERNEST FEGTE, *(Art Directors);* EDITH HEAD *(Costumes);* WALLY WESTMORE *(Makeup).*

Opened at Loew's Metropolitan Theater, Brooklyn, on second half of double bill, October 21, 1943. Running time, 83 minutes.

THE PICTURE:

Young and Willing was the last picture Holden made before going into the service. It was shot in 1942 but not shown in the New York area until October, 1943, and then on the second half of a double bill (with James Cagney's *Johnny Come Lately*) at Loew's Metropolitan Theater in Brooklyn. Since Holden was not to appear on the screen again until 1947, it was perhaps as well that the release of his last preservice picture was delayed. Even so, there was that three-and-a-half-year gap for a burgeoning career that had not solidly established itself. *Young and Willing* was one of a series of Paramount films produced in 1942 that wound up sold for release to United Artists, among them the Fredric March–Veronica Lake *I Married A Witch* and *The Crystal Ball.* It was a piece of fluff, haphazardly directed by Edward H. Griffith and indifferently written by the usually competent Virginia Van Upp, not that the original play by Francis Swann gave her much to work with. The thin plot had to do with a group of impecunious young actors living in Mabel Paige's Manhattan boarding house. Holden is the energetic, dedicated neophyte eager to get ahead; Eddie Bracken the clown and mimic. Susan Hayward is around as a vivacious young thing, and Martha O'Driscoll and Barbara Britton are also stage-struck types sharing a large apartment with the boys. O'Driscoll is in love with Holden, who can take her or leave her; Britton is in love with stalwart James Brown, to whom she is secretly wed against the troupe's unwritten law. Added complications: They are expecting a baby and he is about to enter the service. Paige keeps demanding the rent, which never seems to get paid. Holden and Bracken hold informal rehearsals and experiment with material. When Paige hands them the manuscript of a play that their downstairs neighbor, producer Robert Benchley, had left in a trunk in less prosperous days, the boys decide it would make a great vehicle. Benchley, an amateur chef, has been hunting his missing manuscript for years. Meanwhile O'Driscoll's stuffy father (Jay Fassett) disapproves of his daughter's "career," and she worries that he will learn that she has been footing the bills for the unconventional boy-girl menage with his money. When Benchley discovers that the youngsters have his old play, he demands it back, but they pretend the manuscript is lost and proceed to act it from memory to his tape recorder. In the windup, the young marrieds are forgiven for violating the code, Benchley is so delighted with the kids' performance that he signs them to do the play, and Holden discovers he loves O'Driscoll after she defies her father, who has tried to drag her home, and returns to the boarding house. Holden at twenty-four seemed somewhat callow and ill-at-ease in light comedy, not that direction or script worked to his benefit. His gestures and timing were awkward, his reactions too emphatic, his expressions hammy, and he didn't seem to know what to do with his hands. Bracken, unfazed by poor material, clowned and mugged as Napoleon, Othello, and a few other characters. The girls gave out in a variety of mediocre

With Eddie Bracken, Martha O'Driscoll, and Susan Hayward

ingenue styles—all except Hayward, whose fine voice, evident class, and acting aplomb were in clear evidence even at twenty-three. Benchley was—Benchley, and Miss Paige, a solid old character-type, almost stole the show as the landlady. All in all, *Young and Willing* was hardly the vehicle to preface a long absence from the screen. Holden had *not* given his fans something to remember him by.

With Barbara Britton, Susan Hayward, Martha O'Driscoll, Eddie Bracken, Robert Benchley, Billy Bevan, and James Brown.

71

With Robert Benchley, Susan Hay-
ward, Martha O'Driscoll, Eddie
Bracken, Barbara Britton, and
James Brown

REVIEWS:

Kahn in *Variety:*

The bromide that two can live as cheaply as one has been enlarged in its scope for the purposes of this United Artists release, a weak comedy that achieved mild success on Broadway two seasons ago as *Out of the Frying Pan.* The film version only emphasizes what was all too apparent in the play—it's bound to get lost among the heftier competition. Strictly for the duals, with its young names possibly enhancing its boxoffice values where the adolescent draw is concerned . . . the difficulties that arise in [the young folks'] efforts to interest the gourmet-producer afford only mild diversion in a comedy that's too intent on action and too little concerned with dialogue and original situations. The four stars, William Holden, Eddie Bracken, Robert Benchley and Susan Hayward . . . do as well as can be expected with the lame script. Florence MacMichael, with a squeaky voice that achieves a few laughs, rounds out the better performances. Direction by Edward Griffith, who also produced, is up to par, while the production indicates a limited budget.

With James Brown, Martha O'Dris-
coll, Susan Hayward, Eddie Brack-
en, and Barbara Britton

72

With Anne Baxter

Blaze of Noon

1947   Paramount

CAST:

ANNE BAXTER *(Lucille Stewart)*; WILLIAM HOLDEN *(Colin McDonald)*; WILLIAM BENDIX *(Porkie)*; SONNY TUFTS *(Roland McDonald)*; STERLING HAYDEN *(Tad McDonald)*; HOWARD DA SILVA *(Gafferty)*; JOHNNY SANDS *(Keith McDonald)*; JEAN WALLACE *(Poppy)*; EDITH KING *(Mrs. Murphy)*; LLOYD CORRIGAN *(Reverend Polly)*; DICK HOGAN *(Sydney)*; WILL WRIGHT *(Mr. Thomas)*.

CREDITS:

ROBERT FELLOWS *(Producer)*; JOHN FARROW *(Director)*; FRANK WEAD, ARTHUR SHEEKMAN *(Screenplay); based on the novel by* ERNEST K. GANN; WILLIAM C. MELLOR *(Camera)*; THOMAS TUTWILER *(Aerial Photography)*; GORDON *and* DEVEREUX JENNINGS *(Special Effects)*; ADOLPH DEUTSCH *(Music)*; SALLY FORREST *(Editor)*; PAUL MANTZ *(Chief Pilot and Aerial Unit Supervision)*.

Opened at the Rivoli Theater, New York, March 4, 1947. Running time, 90 minutes.

THE PICTURE:

Holden returned to Paramount in 1946 after four years in the Army Air Force—and found that his whole-wheat, smiling Jim, All-American boy image was a distinctly faded commodity, not only with the studio overlords but, it seemed, with the public also. Many young actors had returned from the war that year, and while such topliners as Gable, Taylor, and Stewart had no trouble resuming, almost as if they had never been away, the lesser lights like Holden found it rough going. He sat around Paramount for months waiting for a part, and though he had matured from a boyish twenty-four to a manly twenty-eight, and was a married man with several children in 1946, he found it difficult to convince producers and directors that he had what the public wanted. Finally he accepted a part in *Blaze of Noon*, and though he was technically the romantic lead, he did tend to get lost amid the likes of Anne Baxter, Sterling Hayden, Sonny Tufts, and scene-stealer William Bendix. The picture dealt with the early days of airmail flying, and was replete with 1920s atmosphere, vintage planes, fidelity to technical details, and some fancy stunt flying by famed pilot Paul Mantz, who doubled up front for the boys. Paramount sent Mantz on a six-hour-seven-minute coast-to-coast flight to publicize the film, and he set a transcontinental record in the year of the film's release.

The reviewers were divided in their opinions, claiming that the picture had exciting elements but tended to bog down dramatically, especially toward the end. A recent TV viewing confirms that they were right, and this is one of those pictures that are *not* redeemed by time. Holden's likable but somehow muted characterization is given little opportunity to shine, and director John Farrow seemed more interested in keeping the action shots percolating in lively style than in eliciting Oscar-caliber performances from Baxter, Holden, and the others, though granted the Frank Wead–Arthur Sheekman screenplay, based on the Ernest K. Gann novel, afforded scant occasion for Grade-A emoting. The four brothers—Holden, Tufts, Hayden, and Johnny Sands—start out as stunt men for a carnival, later join up with pioneer operator Howard Da Silva as mail carriers. Fatherly Da Silva tries to warn the boys that their hazardous work precludes a happy family life, but Holden falls in love with nurse Baxter and they are married. Baxter finds married life in a house full of boisterous men a trying experience, leaves Holden and then returns, and grows increasingly worried over her husband's dangerous work. She realizes, however, that his work is his life. The youngest brother, Sands, is killed; his grieving brother, Tufts, leaves fly-

With Anne Baxter

With Lloyd Corrigan, Sonny Tufts, William Bendix, Sterling Hayden, Anne Baxter, and Johnny Sands.

ing though he returns to it later, and Hayden, who secretly carries a torch for sister-in-law Baxter, is seriously injured but is nursed back to health and becomes a flight control operator, his flying days over. Eventually Holden is killed, and the picture closes rather mawkishly with the baptism of his posthumous child, with Baxter, Hayden, Tufts, and the rest smiling away. Throughout the film, an undue length of time has been given first to Holden's romantic maneuverings with Baxter, then to details of their marriage and family life, which are not presented very interestingly. Miss Baxter, who had won a supporting Oscar for her 1946 stint in *The Razor's Edge*, seemed ill-at-ease in such lightweight fare. Hayden was glum and stilted throughout (in the next few years he was to blossom into an actor of considerable range and intensity, however), and Tufts seemed to have lost much of the oafishly boyish charm that had made him a star in 1943's *So Proudly We Hail*. Bendix and Da Silva, two old pros who were never at a loss, came off best. The picture was not an auspicious post–World War II start for Holden, but at least it brought him once more before a public that had not seen him in four long years.

REVIEWS:

Time:

At its weakest, *Blaze of Noon* never quite becomes an unlikable movie. Messrs. Hayden and Holden are highly personable in their first cinemacting since the war. Paul Mantz does some good ghost stunting for all four brothers; and occasionally, without sentimentalizing, the picture really captures the obsessive dash of professional airmen. The main trouble is the story; not adequate to the emotions it tries to handle, it loses its drive, charm and eventually its shape.

John McCarten in *The New Yorker:*

There's a somewhat nostalgic air about [the film] which takes us back to the early days of flying when the number of crackups was only slightly less than the number of takeoffs . . . unless you are very young you will remember dozens of films like this, and I'm afraid there's not enough new material in [the film] to warrant your making much of an effort to see it.

Variety:

Early days of flying the air mail gets interesting treatment . . . Film has full star lineup for marquee strength, is well-played and directed . . . aerial sequences have authenticity and thrills. . . . John Farrow's actionful direction is backed with showmanly production values and a good script. Four brothers are well played by William Holden, Sonny Tufts, Sterling Hayden and Johnny Sands.

James Agee in *The Nation:*

So long as it sticks to stunt-flying and mild comedy it is pleasant enough, but the last half, during which the obsessed brothers come one by one to grief and the little woman waits it out, gets pretty monotonous.

With Johnny Sands, Anne Baxter, Sonny Tufts, and Sterling Hayden

With Edward Arnold, Mary Philips, and Joan Caulfield.

Dear Ruth

1947   Paramount

CAST:

JOAN CAULFIELD *(Ruth Wilkins)*; WILLIAM HOLDEN *(Lt. William Seacroft)*; EDWARD ARNOLD *(Judge Harry Wilkins)*; MARY PHILIPS *(Edith Wilkins)*; MONA FREEMAN *(Miriam Wilkins)*; BILLY DE WOLFE *(Albert Kummer)*; VIRGINIA WELLES *(Martha Seacroft)*; Marietta Canty *(Dora, the Maid)*; KENNY O'MORRISON *(Sgt. Chuck Vincent)*; IRVING BACON *(Delivery Man)*; ISABEL RANDOLPH *(Mrs. Teaker)*.

CREDITS:

PAUL JONES *(Producer)*; WILLIAM D. RUSSELL *(Director)*; *based on the play by* NORMAN KRASNA; ARTHUR SHEEKMAN *(Screenplay)*; HANS DREIER *and* EARL HEDRICK *(Art Directors)*; ROBERT EMMET DOLAN *(Music)*; ERNEST LASZLO *(Camera)*; ARCHIE MARSHEK *(Editor)*.

Opened at the Paramount Theater, New York, June 10, 1947. Running time, 95 minutes.

THE PICTURE:

Dear Ruth was a popular hit by Norman Krasna on Broadway in wartime 1944, its insouciance and light romantics coming at a time when the country needed some escapist laughs. Translated to the screen two years after the war, it seemed to have lost some of its timeliness and comic pertinence. But Holden's performance in it (one critic noted that he demonstrated an easy naturalness not apparent in his preservice work) helped boost his stock in 1947, and he was aided and abetted in high style by Joan Caulfield and Edward Arnold. Though the overall critical reaction tended to be on the ambivalent side, there was due credit given the zest and humor of the playing and the fast pacing of director William D. Russell. The plot, a hackneyed slew of silly misunderstandings if ever there was one, was in large measure redeemed by the slick mounting and the assets already cited. It dealt with a young Air Force lieutenant (Holden) who receives mash notes he believes are written by Joan Caulfield. However, her mischievous kid sister, Mona Freeman, has written and sent them along with Caulfield's picture. Freeman's plans are upset when Holden, on two-day leave, makes a surprise visit to their Queens home, having fallen in love with his supposed correspondent. When Caulfield learns from Freeman about the silly deception, she decides to keep it up, feeling the lieutenant will have her out of his system by the time his leave is up. But it doesn't work out that way—it never does in 1947 Hollywood—predictably, he falls more deeply in love and she finds she too is in love. Caulfield's fiancé Billy De Wolfe gets himself hysterically worked up because

With Joan Caulfield, Kenny O'Morrison, Virginia Welles, Edward Arnold, Billy De Wolfe, and Mary Philips

Holden is snitching his gal, and parents Edward Arnold and Mary Philips look on dubiously, to be relieved when Joan decides to marry her lieutenant before his leave is up.

REVIEWS:

John Thompson in New York *Mirror Movie of the Week:*

It is unlikely that 1947 will bring a more satisfying comedy than [this film]. It is humorous, heart-warming and charming. . . . The story is not especially original but it is told with such adroitness and with so many surprising and funny twists that it is a constant delight. Much of the charm is due to the playing of the principals. William Holden, only recently out of the army himself, proves to be one of the most engaging light comedians in the business. Joan Caulfield, looking prettier than ever, is equally persuasive as the girl. Mary Philips and Edward Arnold are as nice a pair of parents as anyone could want. All four conduct themselves with warmth and wit.

Mary Philips, Billy De Wolfe and Edward Arnold

T.M.P. in *The New York Times:*
There is an easy naturalness about William Holden's performance as the Army lieutenant that was not apparent in his previous acting and Joan Caulfield is a vision of loveliness (as well as a good actress) in the title role . . . the pace never drags, even though the slim story is stretched out over ninety minutes. Of course there are lulls, but then an expert blending of script-writing and directing carries the action along and there always seems to be some bit of business going on which is good for a quiet smile in any event.

Howard Barnes in the *New York Herald Tribune:*
The film has a sprinkling of engaging jests and situa-

tions. It has such principals as William Holden, Edward Arnold and Billy De Wolfe to create the pleasant impression that they are more intent on generating laughter than ornamenting close-ups. Unfortunately there is neither enough substance in the material nor gaiety in the treatment to make *Dear Ruth* the considerable delight that it was when it cut through theatrical gloom in the winter of 1944. . . . Holden does well enough as the bombardier who gets a girl by proxy and De Wolfe is excellent as the fiance who is cut out of a romantic deal. Joan Caulfield looks pretty as the lady of the title.

Billy De Wolfe, Joan Caulfield, William Holden and Virginia Welles

With Ray Milland

Variety Girl

1947   Paramount

Guest Stars:

WILLIAM HOLDEN *was one of many guest stars including* BARBARA STANWYCK, GARY COOPER, BING CROSBY, BOB HOPE, RAY MILLAND, ALAN LADD, PAULETTE GODDARD, VERONICA LAKE, DOROTHY LAMOUR, JOAN CAULFIELD, SONNY TUFTS, BURT LANCASTER, LIZABETH SCOTT, DIANA LYNN, GAIL RUSSELL, ROBERT PRESTON, STERLING HAYDEN, JOHN LUND, BARRY FITZGERALD, WILLIAM BENDIX, HOWARD DA SILVA, CASS DALEY, BILLY DE WOLFE, MACDONALD CAREY, MONA FREEMAN, ARLEEN WHELAN, PATRIC KNOWLES, JOHNNY COY, CECIL KELLAWAY, VIRGINIA FIELD, RICHARD WEBB, STANLEY CLEMENTS. *Also* MITCHELL LEISEN, CECIL B. DE MILLE, GEORGE MARSHALL, FRANK BUTLER, ROGER DANN, PEARL BAILEY, SPIKE JONES *and his City Slickers, the* MULCAYS, WANDA HENDRIX, GEORGE REEVES, SALLY RAWLINSON

CAST:

MARY HATCHER (*Catherine Brown*); OLGA SAN JUAN (*Amber La Vonne*); DE FOREST KELLEY (*Bob Kirby*); WILLIAM DEMAREST (*Barker*); FRANK FAYLEN (*Stage Manager*); FRANK FERGUSON (*J. R. O'Connell*); RUSSELL HICKS, CHARLES COLEMAN, CRANE WHITLEY, HAL K. DAWSON, EDDIE FETHERSTON (*Patrons at Steambath*); CATHERINE CRAIG (*Secretary*).

CREDITS:

DANIEL DARE (*Producer*); GEORGE MARSHALL (*Director*); EDMUND HARTMAN, FRANK TASHLIN, ROBERT WELCH, MONTE BRICE (*Screenplay*); JOSEPH J. LILLEY (*Music*); JOHNNY BURKE, JAMES VAN HEUSEN, FRANK LOESSER, ALLAN ROBERTS, DORIS FISHER (*Songs*); BILLY DANIELS, BERNARD PEARCE (*Choreography*); GEORGE TEMPLETON (*Assistant Director*); HANS DREIER, ROBERT CLATWORTHY (*Art Directors*); THORNTON HOE, WILLIAM COTTRELL (*Puppetoon Sequence*); LIONEL LINDON, STUART THOMPSON (*Editor*); GORDON JENNINGS (*Special Effects*); LEROY STONE (*Editor*).

Opened at the Paramount Theater, New York, October 15, 1947. Running time, 93 minutes.

THE PICTURE:

In this mammoth Paramount vaudeville act, full of musical numbers and brief and not-so-brief appearances on the part of every major star on the Paramount lot Holden did a song-and-dance number with Ray Milland (dapper in white tie, tails and top hat), Cass Daley, and Joan Caulfield. To his credit, he proved himself a relaxed trouper in the unfamiliar vaudeville turn, registering with pleasant aplomb and refusing to play second fiddle to his high-powered co-performers. The film was basically a tribute to the Variety Clubs of America, which was founded in 1928 by a group of theater men, its purpose being to aid underprivileged children (they started the ball rolling by adopting a foundling the first year). The almost nonexistent plot deals with Mary Hatcher (an eighteen-year-old actress who made her screen debut here), who heads out Hollywood way courtesy of the Variety Clubs and seeks a screen career. While in the film capital she visits—and gawks at—all the usual landmarks before winding up at—where else?—Paramount Studios, where she kibitzes nervously on a Cecil B. De Mille set and gets into various scrapes, unwittingly offending the studio president (Frank Ferguson). A misunderstanding has arisen, for she has been confused with her more flamboyant blonde friend, Olga San Juan, who is falsely promoted as Variety's protegé. However, Mary proves her mettle, unmasks her real identity, and winds up the toast of the Variety Club convention that forms the dénouement.

Bing Crosby and Bob Hope pop in and out more frequently than any of the other Paramount "guest stars," wowing them with the song "Harmony" (Johnny Burke and James Van Heusen") at the convention. Dorothy Lamour and Alan Ladd (the latter in an uncharacteristically expansive mood) sing "Tallahassee" (Frank Loesser) and Billy De Wolfe provides some of the comedy relief mixing his special "atomic punch" concoction for startled Frank Ferguson. Amid the general formlessness, the Frank Loesser tunes "Your Heart Calling Mine," "I Must Have Been Madly In Love," and "Impossible Things" (among other Loesser delights) provide color, as do "Romeow and Julicat" by Edward Plumb, "Tiger Rag" by the Original Dixieland Jazz Band, and "Mildred's Boogie" by Mildred and Jim Mulcay.

REVIEWS:

W.W. in the *Baltimore Sun:*

Stars are stirred into the picture like the ingredients of a pot-luck stew . . . comedy bits and musical numbers are thrown in from time to time, and there is plenty of motion and commotion . . . judging by the roars of laughter and other evidences of interest shown by the audience, Hollywood didn't guess wrong on what the public wants.

New York *Mirror Movie of the Week:*

Probably every star on the Paramount lot has been rounded up . . . there is a tenuous plot but it gets lost frequently, which is just as well . . . a flock of top names appear briefly, sometimes so briefly you barely see them. *Variety Girl* has variety for everybody.

With Ray Milland, Cass Daley, and Joan Caulfield

With Gary Gray and Loretta Young

Rachel and the Stranger

1948   RKO-Radio

CAST:

LORETTA YOUNG *(Rachel);* WILLIAM HOLDEN *(Big Davey);* ROBERT MITCHUM *(Jim);* GARY GRAY *(Davey);* TOM TULLY *(Parson Jackson);* SARA HADEN *(Mrs. Jackson);* FRANK FERGUSON *(Mr. Green);* WALTER BALDWIN *(Gallus);* REGINA WALLACE *(Mrs. Green).*

CREDITS:

JACK J. GROSS *(Executive Supervisor);* RICHARD H. BERGER *(Producer);* NORMAN FOSTER *(Director);* WALDO SALT *(Screenplay); from the story "Rachel" by* HOWARD FAST; MAURY GERSTMAN *(Camera);* LES MILLBROOK *(Editor); Songs by* ROY WEGG *and* WALDO SALT*: "Oh He Oh Hi Oh Ho," "Just Like Me," "Foolish Pride" sung by* MITCHUM; *"Tall Dark Stranger" and "Summer Song" sung by* MITCHUM *and* MISS YOUNG.

Opened at the Mayfair Theater, New York, September 18, 1948. Running time, 92 minutes.

THE PICTURE:

Loretta Young, Holden, and Robert Mitchum were the protagonists of an agreeable and unpretentious, occasionally moving and heartwarming, little domestic drama set in the unlikely Northwest Frontier country in the early 1800s. The picture was rushed out ahead of schedule that year to take advantage of the notoriety surrounding Mitchum's narcotics rap, and no one expected much of it critically, but it turned out to be a pleasant, if hardly earthshaking, plus for all concerned. True, there were complaints from some quarters that director Norman Foster kept things moving too slowly for three quarters of the film, and the basic theme was low-key, but there were far worse films shown during 1948 and many viewers tended to recall it with a glow. Widower Holden buys bondswoman Rachel (Young) for $22 to do his work and raise his son. Still in love with his dead wife, Holden mostly ignores her, and his

With Loretta Young and Robert Mitchum

With Loretta Young

young son, Gary Gray, for his part registers unconcealed disdain, so life on the frontier is a cold and cheerless proposition for Young until Holden's itinerant-hunter friend Mitchum shows up. As is the wont of human nature, Holden commences to show interest in Young in exact proportion to the growing admiration of the womanizing Mitchum, but before love gets a chance to blossom full strength, the Indians attack and the little family must defend itself forthwith. Amid the flaming arrows and loud war-whoops, Holden and Young, battling side by side, achieve the hitherto-missing depth of feeling. When danger has passed, Romeo

Mitchum, a man who knows when he has had it, takes off for greener pastures. Oh, yes, the kid warms up to her too. Miss Young, with but two changes of costume throughout, eschewed her usual iron-butterfly glamour, and gave one of her more sincere performances. Holden was stalwart and sensible, Mitchum wry and roguish. During the proceedings there were even some interludes of song (see credits) that somehow did not seem inappropriate; in fact, they blended in rather nicely. Director Foster managed to achieve forgiveness for the relatively slow pacing of his earlier sequences with that aforementioned Indian attack, as rousing and

With Tom Tully, Sara Haden, and Gary Gray

82

With Gary Gray

action-filled as any male viewer could wish. What with the women rooting for Rachel, the film managed to have it both ways.

REVIEWS:

Time:

[The film] is content to examine a small domestic situation of no conceivable importance to citizenship classes, and to suggest the hard, lonesome beauty of the frontier and the way life was lived there. In other words, it is a better piece of history than most. There is pleasant work by Miss Young and Mr. Mitchum, and a skillful, comic, notably engaging performance by William Holden . . . on its own terms, *Rachel* is an engaging and unpretentious show.

Brog in *Variety:*

[The picture] plods an agreeable, if unexciting, entertainment path in narrating story of pioneer days and love in the wilderness . . . mood of the picture is pleasant but is so even that interest isn't too strong . . . flam-

With Robert Mitchum and Gary Gray

With Gary Gray, Robert Mitchum,
and Loretta Young

ing arrows and war whoops pinpoint pioneer danger but, unfortunately, there isn't enough of it in preceding footage.

Jack Thompson in the *New York Sunday Mirror Magazine:*
Our brave and hardy pioneers have usually been depicted on the screen as either very noble heroes or very despicable villains and never as human beings at all. It is therefore a pleasure to see them as normal people [in this film] . . . unfortunately director Norman Foster has directed the first part of the film at too leisurely a pace, but by the time the Indians arrive the action rips along. The principals are all attractive and pleasant, and while no Academy Awards are indicated, it all adds up to a good evening's entertainment.

With Gary Gray and Loretta Young

With Edmund Gwenn and Jeanne Crain

Apartment for Peggy

1948   Twentieth Century-Fox

CAST:

JEANNE CRAIN *(Peggy)*; WILLIAM HOLDEN *(Jason)*; EDMUND GWENN *(Prof. Henry Barnes)*; GENE LOCKHART *(Prof. Edward Bell)*; GRIFF BARNETT *(Dr. Conway)*; RANDY STUART *(Dorothy)*; MARION MARSHALL *(Ruth)*; PATI BEHRS *(Jeanne)*; HENRI LETONDAL *(Prof. Roland Pavin)*; HOUSELEY STEVENSON *(Prof. T. J. Bick)*; HELEN FORD *(Della)*; ALMIRA SESSIONS *(Mrs. Landon)*; CHARLES LANE *(Prof. Collins)*; RAY WALKER *(Carson)*; CRYSTAL REEVES *(Librarian)*; RONALD BURNS *(Delivery Boy)*; GENE NELSON *(Jerry)*; BOB PATTON *(Student)*; BETTY ANN LYNN *(Wife)*; THERESE LYON, ANN STAUNTON *(Nurses)*; HAL K. DAWSON, FRANK SCANNELL, ROBERT B. WILLIAMS *(Salesman)*; PAUL FRISON *(Boy)*.

CREDITS:

WILLIAM PERLBERG *(Producer)*; GEORGE SEATON *(Director)*; written by GEORGE SEATON; from a story by FAITH BALDWIN; CLEMENS FINLEY *(Associate)*; DAVID RASKIN *(Music)*; LIONEL NEWMAN *(Musical Direction)*; HERBERT SPENCER, MAURICE DE PACKH *(Orchestral Arrangements)*; HARRY JACKSON, A.S.C. *(Director of Photography)*; LYLE WHEELER, RICHARD IRVINE *(Art Direction)*; THOMAS LITTLE, WALTER M. SCOTT *(Set Decorations)*; ROBERT SIMPSON *(Editor)*; CHARLES LE MAIRE *(Wardrobe)*; KAY NELSON *(Costume Design)*; BEN NYE *(Make-up Artist)*; FRED SERSEN *(Special Photographic Effects)*; E. CLAYTON WARD, ROGER HEMAN *(Sound)*; Color by Technicolor; Technicolor Director, NATALIE KALMUS.

Opened at the Roxy Theater, New York, October 15, 1948. Running time, 96 minutes.

*With Jeanne Crain and
Edmund Gwenn*

THE PICTURE:

One of Holden's more felicitous assignments since returning from the service was *Apartment for Peggy*, which he did on loanout to 20th Century-Fox. In this he was teamed with Jeanne Crain, at the time one of 20th's bright young lights, and Edmund Gwenn, the talented British character actor who had just won a supporting Oscar for his role of Kris Kringle in the highly successful *Miracle on 34th Street.* George Seaton, who had directed *Miracle*, succeeded in injecting much of the same human appeal into this story of a young GI student and his wife who find themselves up against postwar living conditions. The critics were almost unanimous in their praise of this film, commenting on

With Charles Lane

its intelligence, sensitive direction, true-to-life situations, and extraordinary insight into the rootlessness of many returned GI's and their efforts to achieve a balanced orientation. Faithful likewise was the film's depiction of the lives of young couples endeavoring to build a more sane and livable world after the tremendous social and economic upheavals brought about by World War II. The story is simple: Holden and Crain are living in a trailer while he struggles through college on the GI bill. They look for more comfortable quarters, and Miss Crain in her search encounters an elderly college professor (Gwenn) who has come to feel that life has passed him by and contemplates suicide. Gwenn portrays with his usual winning expertise an aging man of ideals, compassion and sensibility whose life is dedicated to the concept of usefulness and who finds that life has lost its savor if he cannot feel wanted and needed. Miss Crain persuades Gwenn to let them rent the attic of his house, which they proceed to turn into comfortable and homey living quarters. As Gwenn warms his hands at the fires of the young couple's hopes, dreams, and valiantly resilient approach to life in an era that is unusually complicated and difficult for all young people, he finds that his flagging will to live is gradually restored, and he develops a new zeal and positivism in pursuing his own future aims, determining as he does to make what few years he has left as fruitful as possible. Holden ably captures the determination and occasional bafflements of a well-meaning, decent young vet battling for a place in the postwar scheme of things. His reviews at the time were quite good—his best since resuming his career. Much of the emotional power and warm charm of the film come from Seaton's feel for the small details that make a film

With Jeanne Crain

and its characters come alive. On this level the work is ably realized and fully presented. Seaton avoided the mawkish and cloying, and gave his audience a feeling of genuine participation and catharsis. He also worked in some sly yet pointed comments on the unfeeling greed of hustling American commerce, the sly chicaneries and opportunisms that disillusioned many returned GIs. The trailer life, launderettes, dog-walking, tension over a chemistry exam, attempts to create a harbor of domestic felicity amidst changing external fortunes, encounter with used-car salesmen and their moneygrubbing, search for parttime work—all are depicted realistically. The distinguished Mr. Gwenn was never in finer fettle, and his scenes with the young people were genuinely affecting. Miss Crain, too, was excellent. The picture gave Holden a much-needed boost at a slack point in his career and enhanced his burgeoning cinematic image.

REVIEWS:

Cue:

Intelligently written and directed without resort to camera tricks; it is played honestly and happily, without the coyness and cuteness that too often prevail in comedies that deal in the small joys and worries of the younger generation. The actors are human beings; what they have to say has meaning, wisdom and compassion; and the manner of their living bears solid resemblance to the minor dramas that fall in all our lives.

. . . Jeanne Crain and William Holden make a thoroughly believable and ingratiating young couple. Edmund Gwenn is an excellent choice as the professor who helps, and is helped by, the student GI and his bride.

Bosley Crowther in *The New York Times:*

A little picture of seeming unimportance which has remarkable persuasive power . . . a tender and genuine comprehension of a real slice of modern life . . . refreshingly honest and respectful in its relation of youth to age. The boy and the girl are credible youngsters, good-natured, confident but disturbed, and the old boy, whom Mr. Gwenn plays grandly, is a person of compassion . . . a first-rate experience for observers with comprehending minds.

Jack Thompson in the *New York Mirror of the Week:*

An extremely pleasant and amiable comedy dealing with the problems of ex-GIs. George Seaton, who wrote and directed last year's successful *Miracle on 34th Street,* in which Gwenn won an Academy Award, is responsible for the current offering. This one is of the same genre as its predecessor, although Seaton strains at times to get the picture so heartwarming it is almost heartburning. Gwenn does his usual beautiful job, aided immensely by Miss Crain and Holden, two of the most able and attractive young actors in films. This is fine entertainment for the whole family.

With Nina Foch (left)

The Dark Past

1948   Columbia

CAST:

WILLIAM HOLDEN *(Al Walker)*; NINA FOCH *(Betty)*; LEE J. COBB *(Dr. Andrew Collins)*; ADELE JERGENS *(Laura Stevens)*; STEPHEN DUNNE *(Owen Talbot)*; LOIS MAXWELL *(Ruth Collins)*; BERRY KROEGER *(Mike)*; STEVEN GERAY *(Professor Fred Linder)*; WILTON GRAFF *(Frank Stevens)*; ROBERT OSTERLOH *(Pete)*; KATHRYN CARD *(Nora)*; BOBBY HYATT *(Bobby)*; ELLEN CORBY *(Agnes)*; CHARLES CANE *(Sheriff)*; ROBERT B. WILLLIAMS *(Williams)*.

CREDITS:

BUDDY ADLER *(Producer)*; RUDOLPH MATE *(Director)*; MALVIN WALD *and* OSCAR SAUL *(Adaptation)*; PHILIP MACDONALD, MICHAEL BLANKFORT *and* ALBERT DUFFY *(Screenplay); based upon the play* Blind Alley *by* JAMES WARWICK; JOSEPH WALKER *(Camera)*; VIOLA LAWRENCE *(Editor)*.

Opened at the Ambassador Theater, New York, December 22, 1948. Running time, 75 minutes.

THE PICTURE:

After the relatively gentle felicities of *Apartment for Peggy*, Holden gave yet another demonstration of his versatility with *The Dark Past*, and under Rudolph Matè's direction he offered a compelling study of an escaped convict haunted by kinks in his mental and emotional makeup that dated from his early life. The reviews for his acting in this ranged from "extraordinarily fine" to "excellent" to "believable", and the film—and Holden's performance—still holds up rather well. A remake of a 1939 Columbia film called *Blind Alley* with Chester Morris in the Holden role and Ralph Bellamy in the part played by Lee J. Cobb in the 1948 version, the story relates the escape of cold-blooded killer Holden from prison with his moll (Nina Foch) and his gang joining him at the country home of psychiatrist Cobb, where they break in. They proceed to hold the doctor and his family as hostages until a confederate can arrange a getaway. Cobb senses that Holden is in serious mental trouble, and in his pipe-smoking, quietly clinical way goes about probing the

With Lee J. Cobb

criminal's mind despite initial resistance. In time Cobb lays bare the distortions in Holden's past that had turned him into a criminal. The duel between the two men is fascinating to watch—one a man accustomed to using force and brawn to obtain his will, the other a man of brain and sensibility who seeks to heal. Holden, it seems, has some nightmarish dreams which terrify him as much as do the law agencies he knows to be in pursuit. As Cobb leads him ever nearer to the truth about himself—it turns out to be that standard Oedipus complex that proved his undoing—Holden discovers that the ultimate self-revelation dissipates his murderous urges; he then proves an easy capture for the police. There was some publicity given at the time to the necessity for psychiatric understanding, and treatment, of the warped criminal mind, and for furtherance of the recognition that criminals are human beings, not animals, with their own share of emotional problems and psychic complexities. A coddle-versus-castigate debate raged in some sections of the press after the film was released. Though the action drags in spots, suspense is built up admirably toward the conclusion. Perhaps

With Lee J. Cobb

Holden's most complex performance until *Sunset Boulevard, The Dark Past* did much to focus attention on his solidly burgeoning acting abilities.

REVIEWS:

Time:

A swift and sometimes brutal melodrama, [the film] makes a frank plea for sympathetic understanding, rather than harsh punishment, of young criminals. Smooth performances by Holden and Cobb put the point across without undue sentimentality...but the picture loses sight of the fact that the intimate details of a psychoanalysis are apt to be more interesting to the patient and the doctor than to a kibitzer.

John McCarten in *The New Yorker:*

Although somewhat diffuse in method [the film] does have its tense moments, and Lee J. Cobb, as the psychiatrist, and William Holden, as the convict, are excellent.

Jack Thompson in the New York *Sunday Mirror Magazine:*

The idea that adult crime would be drastically reduced if juvenile delinquents were treated by psychiatry has been made into an absorbing thriller.... Holden gives an extraordinarily fine performance as the trigger-happy lad. His disintegration from cocky gang leader into terrified psychopath is admirably done. Cobb is exactly right as the psychiatrist and Nina Foch is appealing as Holden's loyal sweetheart. Rudolph Matè, whose directional debut this is, does a generally good

With Nina Foch

job, though occasionally he has allowed the action to drag, which is unfortunate in a film of this type.

Variety:

Under Rudolph Matè's skillful direction, the cast builds a firm aura of suspense in the grim period when the thugs hold the upper hand. Always self-assured, the pipe-smoking Cobb racks up a neat portrayal of the medico. Holden is believable as the high-strung con on the lam. Nina Foch handles her role well as Holden's moll.

With Lee J. Cobb

With Glenn Ford and Jerome Courtland

The Man from Colorado

1949   Columbia

CAST:

GLENN FORD *(Colonel Owen Devereaux);* WILLIAM HOLDEN *(Captain Del Stewart);* ELLEN DREW *(Caroline Emmett);* RAY COLLINS *(Big Ed Carter);* EDGAR BUCHANAN *(Doc Merriam);* JEROME COURTLAND *(Johnny Howard);* JAMES MILLICAN *(Sgt. Jericho Howard);* JIM BANNON *(Nagel);* WILLIAM "BILL" PHILLIPS *(York);* DENVER PYLE *(Easy Jarrett);* JAMES BUSH *(Dickson);* MIKEL CONRAD *(Morris);* DAVID CLARK *(Mutton Mc-Guire);* IAN MACDONALD *(Jack Rawson);* CLARENCE CHASE *(Charlie Trumbull);* STANLEY ANDREWS *(Roger MacDonald);* MYRON HEALEY *(Powers);* CRAIG REYNOLDS *(Perry);* DAVID YORK *(Rebel Major).*

CREDITS:

JULES SCHERMER *(Producer);* HENRY LEVIN *(Director);* BORDEN CHASE *(Original Story);* ROBERT D. ANDREWS *and* BEN MADDOW *(Screenplay);* WILLIAM SNYDER *(Camera);* CHARLES NELSON *(Editor);* GEORGE DUNING *(Score); Color by Technicolor.*

Opened at the Capitol Theater, New York, January 20, 1949. Running time, 99 minutes.

THE PICTURE:

Holden found himself again involved with psychiatric problems in *The Man From Colorado,* but this time it was the other guy's hangup, not his. And in a nineteenth-century Western, no less. Some critics pointed out that director Henry Levin had his work cut out for him mixing Western action with mental malaise, but Levin did manage to work in a fair share of excitement, and the oater elements were not unduly neglected in the midst of the psychiatric probing. Holden had little to do but be stalwart, sincere, and likable in this, with Glenn Ford, his old buddy from *Texas,* getting the juicier assignment as a sadistic ex–Civil War colonel who gets so trigger-happy that he kills for the love of it—even after the formal shooting is over. After he gets out of the Union Army, this savory character gets himself appointed a federal judge in Colorado. Instead of living a normal judicial existence, he sets out to apply the law in the same way he did his gun, with disastrous results for everyone, including himself. Holden is Ford's former adjutant who follows him to Colorado and tries to help the man he knows to have a weird psychological twist by setting up as his marshal. Though Ford proceeds to do such destructive things as wiping out recalcitrants even after they hoist white flags, and passing death sentences on anyone he pleases whether he deserves it or not, Holden tries to ameliorate his evil-doing. However, the enforcing of Ford's strict rules leads to a mass revolt. Ultimately, fed up with Ford's ungovernable bloodlust, Holden quits as marshal and joins a group of ex-soldiers forced to become outlaws because Ford has taken away their gold-mining concessions. Ellen Drew is along for the ride as Ford's wife who eventually leaves him for Holden after she too has had her fill of his twisted impulses. Of course it all ends in a violent confrontation between Ford and his enemies, with Ford dying a fiery death when a burning building collapses on him and his antagonist during a fistfight. There was criticism of Ford's performance as the mentally ill judge—some felt he overplayed. Holden for his part couldn't help but get good notices—his was the role of the solid-stalwart-sensible throughout.

REVIEWS:

Cue:

A reasonably interesting, pictorially exciting drama in

With Glenn Ford

which the chief suspense develops out of waiting to see how long it will take before the tyrannical territorial judge gets his come-uppance . . . the outdoor scenes are well photographed in Technicolor; the posse chases, holdups and murders are properly exciting; and the romantic interludes are restrained, as befits a Western in which the heroes carefully distribute their affections between their horses and their ladies . . . Glenn Ford is glum, grim and morosely effective as the psychopathic judge; William Holden is a friendly and likeable marshal.

With Edgar Buchanan, Ellen Drew, and Glenn Ford

With cast members

Time:

The movie becomes an unusual western by seeming to ask: "Is there a psychiatrist in the house?" *The Man From Colorado* has no more humor than a lawyer's shingle, but it has suspense and some exciting shots of fist fights and burning houses. All in all, it's a better than average horse opera.

Jose in *Variety:*

While the action values of [the film] have been dissipated to some extent by the introduction of psychiatric motives, there's enough color and excitement to insure healthy returns. . . . Henry Levin had to overcome some difficult problems inasmuch as he had to blend mental medicine with gunplay, and frequently had to subordinate one for the other. Under these circumstances, it was virtually impossible to sustain a mood.

With Jerome Courtland

With Mona Freeman

Streets of Laredo

1949   Paramount

CAST:

WILLIAM HOLDEN *(Jim Dawkins);* WILLIAM BENDIX *(Wahoo Jones);* MAC DONALD CAREY *(Lorn Reming);* MONA FREEMAN *(Ronnie Carter);* STANLEY RIDGES *(Major Bailey);* ALFONSO BEDOYA *(Charley Calico);* RAY TEAL *(Cantrel);* CLEM BEVANS *(Pop Lint);* JAMES BELL *(Ike);* DICK FOOTE *(Pipes);* JOE DOMINGUEZ *(Francisco);* GRANDON RHODES *(Phil Jessup);* PERRY IVINS *(Major Towson).*

CREDITS:

ROBERT FELLOWS *(Producer);* LESLIE FENTON *(Director);* CHARLES MARQUIS WARREN *(Screenplay); based on a story by* LOUIS STEVENS *and* ELIZABETH HILL; RAY RENNAHAN *(Camera);* ARCHIE MARSHEK *(Editor);* VICTOR YOUNG *(Music); Song by* JAY LIVINGSTON *and* RAY EVANS. *Color by Technicolor.*

Opened at the Paramount Theater, New York, May 11, 1949. Running time, 92 minutes.

THE PICTURE:

Streets of Laredo was in many of its plot ingredients a rehash of Paramount's earlier *Texas Rangers* (1936) and *Rangers of Fortune* (1940)—dressed-up, recast, and refurbished for 1949 tastes, of course. The reviews were somewhat mixed, though all credited the picture's vitality and pace, and commended the handsome Technicolor photography. Holden garnered his share of good personal reviews, but the always dynamic William Bendix and MacDonald Carey, quite swaggering and glamorous in his outlaw role, gave him some tough competition. Mona Freeman, the kid-sister vixen of *Dear Ruth*, showed herself a grown-up young lady in this, and all four were supported by a slew of fine character actors headed by the always reliable Stanley Ridges. Leslie Fenton kept the direction brisk and well-paced, and Ray Rennahan's Technicolor camera caught all the vivid hues of the Arizona–New Mexico location background. The story begins with outlaws Holden, Bendix, and Carey robbing banks and stagecoaches at

a reckless clip. They encounter and rescue a young girl (who later grows up to be Miss Freeman) who is menaced by a villainous tax collector (Alfonso Bedoya). Some years later they encounter the girl again, and a triangle of sorts ensues, with Holden mooning over Miss Freeman who in turn moons over the more dashing and colorful Carey. During one of their melées, the three bandits are separated, and Holden and Bendix team up with the Texas Rangers, headed by sturdy Stanley Ridges, as a blind to track down and rejoin their missing confederate Carey. As is usual in such plots, they get to take their side-of-the-law duties seriously and develop the "Ranger spirit"; then pangs of conscience arise. Miss Freeman has meanwhile nursed Carey after he sustains a bullet wound. Later, in a showdown between Holden and Carey, who is an expert gunman, Miss Freeman, who has come to realize Holden's true worth, saves him by killing Carey. The arbitrary editing of the ninety-two-minute film keeps the plot strands somewhat disconnected at times, but the action never flags, and 1949 audiences found the picture an attention-holder. It holds up well after nearly a quarter century.

REVIEWS:

Lawrence J. Quirk in *Movies in Boston:*

It's all been done before, of course—after all, how many Western variations *can* one come up with—but Bill Holden is stalwart and eminently sensible, as always; Mona Freeman is prettily sincere in a passionate

With Mona Freeman

sort of way that is slightly inappropriate to such a milieu, and MacDonald Carey is as silky and snaky a villain as one could wish. And director Leslie Fenton has invested that tense finale with the proper excitement any Western worthy of the designation is inevitably due.

Cue:

Handsomely photographed in Technicolor against some of the most impressive scenery in Arizona and New Mexico, "Streets" is played hard and tough by a good cast, and is in most respects a fair example of the current vogue for large-scale, slam-bang Westerns.

With Mona Freeman and MacDonald Carey

With MacDonald Carey and William Bendix

Brog in *Variety:*

For the genuine Western fans, [the film] treats many of its situations a bit too flippantly, and there are a number of erratic cuts in its footage that make for jumpy story development. Otherwise, though, it goes about its business of telling a rather standard Western tale with the proper pace . . . three male toppers please . . . direction by Leslie Fenton gets plenty of sweep and movement into the chase sequences.

Jack Thompson in the New York *Mirror's Movie of the Week:*

It has every possible ingredient to delight the fans—a personable cast, fast action, deep-dyed villains, courageous heroes, an engaging theme song and a pretty and spirited heroine . . . all of the principals acquit themselves handsomely and Leslie Fenton's adroit direction keeps the plot whisking along.

With Stanley Ridges and William Bendix

97

With Lucille Ball

Miss Grant Takes Richmond

1949   Columbia

CAST:

LUCILLE BALL *(Ellen Grant)*; WILLIAM HOLDEN *(Dick Richmond)*; JANIS CARTER *(Peggy Donato)*; JAMES GLEASON *(J. Hobart Gleason)*; GLORIA HENRY *(Helen White)*; FRANK MC HUGH *(Kilcoyne)*; GEORGE CLEVELAND *(Judge Ben Grant)*; STEPHEN DUNNE *(Ralph Winton)*; ARTHUR SPACE *(Willacombe)*; WILL WRIGHT *(Roscoe Johnson)*; JIMMY LLOYD *(Homer White)*; LOREN TINDALL *(Charles Meyers)*; OLA LORRAINE *(Jennie Meyers)*; CLAIRE MEADE *(Aunt Mae)*; ROY ROBERTS *(Foreman)*; CHARLES LANE *(Woodruff)*; HARRY HARVEY *(Councilman Reed)*; HARRY CHESHIRE *(Leo Hopkins)*; NITA MATHEWS *(Ruth)*.

CREDITS:

S. SYLVAN SIMON *(Producer)*; LLOYD BACON *(Director)*; NAT PERRIN, DEVERY FREEMAN, FRANK TASHMAN *(Screenplay)*; based on a story by DEVERY FREEMAN; CHARLES LAWTON *(Camera)*; JEROME THOMS *(Editor)*; HEINZ ROEMHELD *(Music)*; MORRIS STOLOFF *(Musical Director)*.

Opened at Loew's Lexington Theater, New York, September 20, 1949. Running time, 88 minutes.

THE PICTURE:

In an interesting, and well-timed, departure from Western fare, Holden showed himself an excellent light comedian in *Miss Grant Takes Richmond*, and this against that formidable exponent of the genre, Miss Lucille Ball, who for her part was never in finer fettle. The fact that Holden did not permit her, or expert scene-stealers Frank McHugh and James Gleason, to outshine him, gives strong indication of the formidable acting range he had developed by age thirty-one. The film itself was well-received, with kudoes thrown out for Lloyd Bacon's clever, quickly paced comedy direction, the crackling, witty screenplay by Nat Perrin, Devery Freeman, and Frank Tashman (who proved with this that three cooks, could, on occasion, *improve* a comic broth), and the fine trouping of the leads and character players. The public agreed with the critics that here was indeed an amusing, literate farce, and the picture did well crosscountry. Some critics pointed out that a comedy on the housing problem, one of the most serious national concerns of 1949, was just what was needed to shorten long faces, and perhaps it was, at the time. Similar in some respects to *Born Yesterday*, which

*With James Gleason and
Lucille Ball*

was to be one of Holden's film hits the following year, the movie had to do with dumb-cluck secretary Lucille Ball, who is hired by a bookie gang headed by Holden and designed to serve as an innocent front for their real-estate office, a dummy for their real operation. But Miss Ball has been underestimated, both in ability and zeal, by her employers, and she starts sympathizing fervently with the homeless. Result: Holden finds himself involved in the promotion of a low-cost housing project. At first negative in his reaction, Holden then decides to milk the project for $50,000 to pay off a bet owed to a syndicate. While Ball furthers her housing

*With Lucille Ball, James Gleason,
and Frank McHugh*

With Frank McHugh and James Gleason

aims with crusading fervor, Holden and Co. manipulate the books brazenly and siphon off the cash. With the investor's money gone, Ball, still unaware of her boss's perfidy, takes the rap for the project's failure. But Holden runs true to 1949 movie-form, and turns out to be a righty guy after all. He gets back the lost $50,000 by selling out his bookie joint to syndicate head Janis Carter, who has been carrying a torch for Holden throughout the proceedings. After assorted complications are ironed out, Holden and Miss Ball decide to face the future as man and wife. Many amusing situations are woven into the plot, all directed crisply by Bacon: Holden acting as chairman of a weighty conference on housing with solid citizens while handling bets on the side; Miss Ball, toward the fade-out, breaking into Miss Carter's home pretending she's a gun moll who means to have her guy back or else. Frank McHugh is in great form as a whiz with the figures, and James Gleason is a harried bookie of the first water. Miss Carter, as the other woman, is sex

William Holden (center)

personified. The editing is as tight as Miss Carter's gowns. All in all, it's a slick, well-turned-out product with built-in audience appeal—and above all, a refreshing, needed change-of-pace for Holden.

REVIEWS:

Herm in *Variety:*

This neat comedy will keep the turnstiles clicking at a merry rate. Placing a group of bookies in charge of a local housing project, [the film] builds a wacky structure of yocks on a solid gag foundation. It's a frothy item spun out of a lightweight yarn and skillfully sewn together under Lloyd Bacon's deft direction . . . screenplay crackles with bright dialog in a broad farce set up for the comedic talents of Lucille Ball and, in a subordinate way, for James Gleason and Frank McHugh. William Holden, as the romantic lead and bookie chieftain, also displays a nice flair for the flip line and the fast double-take, rounding out a quartet of performances that carry the pic at a pace that never lags.

Lawrence J. Quirk in *Movies in Boston:*

One of the more delightful comedies of the season, with William Holden proving in spades that he is an actor of considerable range and versatility. He stands up to that excellent comedienne Lucille Ball at every turn, refusing to settle for passive straight-man status, and he even gives veteran farceurs Gleason and Mc-Hugh a run for their money.

Jack Thompson in New York *Mirror Movie of the Week:*

The housing problem, which is anything but comic to most people, forms the background. . . . [Miss Ball's] efforts to actually operate the construction company and her losing battles with cranes, bulldozers, mud and blueprints are fine comedy. It gives one pause to think of ladies actually running large corporations as they are supposed to in the future. It also reveals that Miss Ball is a very stalwart girl to go through so much and look so well afterward. Lloyd Bacon has directed the film at a rocket-like pace in keeping with the spirit of the story.

With James Gleason, Lucille Ball and Frank McHugh

Dear Wife

1950   Paramount

CAST:

WILLIAM HOLDEN *(Bill Seacroft)*; JOAN CAULFIELD *(Ruth Seacroft)*; BILLY DE WOLFE *(Albert Kummer)*; MONA FREEMAN *(Miriam Wilkins)*; EDWARD ARNOLD *(Judge Wilkins)*; ARLEEN WHELAN *(Tommy Murphy)*; MARY PHILIPS *(Mrs. Wilkins)*; HARRY VAN ZELL *(Jeff Cooper)*; RAYMOND ROE *(Ziggy)*; ELISABETH FRASER *(Kate Collins)*; BILL MURPHY *(Dan Collins)* MARY FIELD *(Mrs. Bixby)*; IRVING BACON *(Mike Man)*; GORDON JONES *(Taxicab Driver)*; MARIETTA CANTY *(Dora)*; DON BEDDOE *(Metcalfe)*; STANLEY STAYLE *(An Early Riser)* *portrayed by director* RICHARD HAYDN.

CREDITS:

RICHARD MAIBAUM *(Producer)*; RICHARD HAYDN *(Director)*; ARTHUR SHEEKMAN *and* N. RICHARD NASH *(Screenplay)*; *written as a sequel to* NORMAN KRASNA'S Dear Ruth; STUART THOMPSON *(Photography)*; ARCHIE MARSHEK *(Editor)*; HANS DREIER *and* EARL HEDRICK *(Art Directors)*.

Opened at the Paramount Theater, New York, February 1, 1950. Running time, 87 minutes.

THE PICTURE:

It has always been an unwritten law of the movies that if a film works, give it a sequel or rehash of some kind. This is what happened with the pleasant 1947 comedy *Dear Ruth*. It didn't measure up to the original, not that *that* was flawless. This time the feyly amusing Richard Haydn took over as director and even worked in a small part for himself. The same principals—Holden, Caulfield, Arnold, and Philips—were on hand. The Arthur Sheekman—N. Richard Nash screenplay was on the slim side, as to both plot and situational inventiveness. It seems that three years later Holden and Caulfield are young marrieds, encountering the standard in-law trouble. Father-in-law Judge Arnold and Holden don't get on too well. When our boy informs the judge that he doesn't think much of grapefruit for breakfast (it's the judge's favorite dish), the temperature really goes into deep-freeze. Irritations major and minor ensue, but the payoff comes when Mona Freeman, the mischievous kid sister of the earlier romp now grown into a social-conscious, politics-crazy type, slyly maneuvers Holden into running for state senator against his father-in-law. Then hell really breaks loose on the domestic front, and when a radio commentator comes to the house for a breakfast interview no one is speaking. Political worker Arleen Whelan introduces triangular romantic mischief with Holden and Caulfield, the housing shortage keeps everyone jammed in together, and Billy De Wolfe, who had to surrender Caulfield to Holden in the earlier film, hangs around hoping for marital trouble and contributing *his* share of mischief on occasion. Complications continue to bedevil the protagonists, most of them trivial and foolishly motivated, but finally the strained Holden–Caulfield marriage is placed on a firmer footing and peace reigns at the crowded Seacroft–Wilkins menage. Mona Freeman had a bigger part in this film than she had had in the first picture, and by 1951 found herself the principal in yet another rehash of the theme, *Dear Brat*.

REVIEWS:

Time:

The movie sequel is an old Hollywood custom designed to repeat a success by imitating it. More often, as with this pale wraith of 1947's *Dear Ruth*, it succeeds only in running a good story into the ground—with the same principals playing for farce in the same suburban setting. [The film] sadly lacks a script to measure up to the original. It is played largely on the comic level of

With Joan Caulfield

With Joan Caulfield, Edward Arnold, Marietta Canty, Mary Philips, and Mona Freeman

With Arleen Whelan and Joan Caulfield

With Joan Caulfield

such crude gags as the eye that blackens right after the punch. One bright spot: radio announcer Harry Van Zell trying desperately to get a cheery broadcast out of a family breakfast table where no one is speaking. Holden and Joan Caulfield are likeable enough.

Cue:

The further adventures of *Dear Ruth*, playwright Norman Krasna's heroine who had so dizzily comical a career on stage and screen, are here continued in a similar spirit of dizzy, carefree levity . . . a generally amusing family comedy, with squabbles, tears and

laughter mixed in about equal proportions through a frothy plot wherein husband Holden runs for Senator against his judicial father-in-law.

Brog in *Variety:*

. . . comes to the screen as an adequate sequel. The family humor is continued in an amusing vein, the same cast principals repeat their *Ruth* characters and altogether it adds up to a promising boxoffice entry. William Holden and Joan Caulfield as the man and wife couple of the title, further their *Dear Ruth* romance.

With Billy De Wolfe, Gordon Jones, Edward Arnold, and Joan Caulfield

Father Is
a Bachelor

1950   Columbia

CAST:

WILLIAM HOLDEN (*Johnny Rutledge*); COLEEN GRAY (*Prudence Millett*); MARY JANE SAUNDERS (*May Chalotte*); CHARLES WINNINGER (*Professor Mordecai Ford*); STUART ERWIN (*Pudge Barnham*); CLINTON SUNDBERG (*Plato Cassin*); GARY GRAY (*Jan Chalotte*); SIG RUMAN (*Jericho Schlosser*); BILLY GRAY (*Feb Chalotte*); LLOYD CORRIGAN (*Judge Millett*); FREDERIC TOZERE (*Jeffrey Gilland Sr.*); PEGGY CONVERSE (*Genevieve Cassin*); ARTHUR SPACE (*Lucius Staley*); WARREN FARLOW (*March*); WAYNE FARLOW (*April*).

CREDITS:

S. SYLVAN SIMON (*Producer*); NORMAN FOSTER *and* ABBY BERLIN (*Directors*); ALLEN LESLIE *and* JAMES EDWARD GRANT (*Screenplay*); *from a story by* JAMES EDWARD GRANT; BARNETT GUFFEY (*Camera*); ARTHUR MORTON (*Musical Score*); JEROME THOMAS (*Editor*).

Opened at the Palace Theater, New York, February 22, 1950. Running time, 83 minutes.

THE PICTURE:

The hoary cliché that it is always darkest just before the dawn certainly applied to Holden with *Father Is a*

With Sig Ruman and Gary Gray

Bachelor, a turkey into which Columbia for no reason that anyone could discern, shoved him for results that boded no good for anyone concerned. Directed haphazardly by Norman Foster and Abby Berlin (they got in each other's way stylewise), the film had the additional disadvantage of a cliché-ridden, meandering, foolishly sentimental script by Allen Leslie and James

Edward Grant, from a story by the often-able Grant that he must have wished later he had left in his trunk. At any rate, this movie, all eighty-three minutes of it, must represent in retrospect Holden's creative dark-night-of-the-soul, coming as it did six months before the happier morning of his next, *Sunset Boulevard.* Labeled by the critics "old-fashioned," "insipid," and "uninspired," the story, or whatever of it could be deciphered from the hodgepodge of song and sentiment, dealt with Holden, a tramp and ne'er-do-well, who prefers fishing to work. Charles Winninger, an excellent character actor who deserved a better fate, was also on hand as owner of a medicine show that is put out of business, whereupon Holden concentrates strictly on the fish. Lo and behold, there appear at this point a family of five simply adorable moppet orphans, with the coy names (as if you didn't know) of Jan (January), Feb (February), March, April, etc. These sugar-plums proceed to revamp the tramp, again as if you didn't know, reactivating his ambition, resurrecting his manly self-respect, getting him to work like a Trojan— all for a true rejuvenation of Holden's allegedly lost soul (Thoreau might not have agreed) and a happy ending which features the standard (in 1950 almost obligatory) fadeout embrace with Coleen Gray, a village beaut who has been standing by hoping Holden will hear those old wedding bells. Holden is called upon (for no good reason) to warble some old tunes,

With Arthur Space

there is mouth-organ tootling, a lot of cutesy-cute kid stuff of the kind that was wearing thin in the heyday of Jackie Cooper (or even Jackie Coogan)—and well, you've got the general idea. So did the critics, and the verdict was: thumbs down.

REVIEWS:

Brog in *Variety:*

Almost a complete waste of money and talent. For the bucolic date, it will just get by, and family audiences will find it strictly minor entertainment.... Old-fashioned and insipid ... story brings in some uninspired complications strictly from the paperbacked novels of yesteryear before it resolves into a happy ending with Holden in a clinch with Coleen Gray, Village belle.

Otis L. Guernsey, Jr., in the *New York Herald Tribune:*

The easy competence of William Holden's acting makes a fairly palatable comedy of sentiment ... the script relies on all the usual plot devices in motion pictures on this theme, but the execution is unpretentious, even disarming. With Holden keeping a tight rein on his own performance and thereby setting the pace for almost every scene, the film is restrained enough to develop more pleasant sequences than might be expected from this sort of heartstring concerto ... [the film]

With Gary Gray

proves nothing except that William Holden is a top-notch actor who deserves the best of material. It does, however, spin a genial yarn.

H.H.T. in *The New York Times:*

Saccharine ... paper-thin ... at least one spectator at the Palace yesterday couldn't take it—a tot of about 4, wearing a cowboy suit, who aimed a toy pistol at the screen and popped off the cast one by one.

With Gary Gray, Billy Gray, Mary Jane Saunders, Warren Farlow, and Wayne Farlow

With Gloria Swanson and Erich Von Stroheim

Sunset Boulevard

1950   Paramount

CAST:

WILLIAM HOLDEN *(Joe Gillis)*; GLORIA SWANSON *(Norma Desmond)*; ERICH VON STROHEIM *(Max Von Mayerling)*; NANCY OLSON *(Betty Schaefer)*; FRED CLARK *(Sheldrake)*; LLOYD GOUGH *(Marino)*; JACK WEBB *(Artie Green)*; FRANKLYN FARNUM *(Undertaker)*; LARRY BLAKE *(First Finance Man)*; CHARLES DAYTON *(Second Finance Man)*; CECIL B. DE MILLE, HEDDA HOPPER, BUSTER KEATON, ANNA Q. NILSSON, H. B. WARNER, ROY EVANS, JAY LIVINGSTON as themselves.

CREDITS:

CHARLES BRACKETT *(Producer)*; BILLY WILDER *(Director)*; CHARLES BRACKETT, BILLY WILDER *and* D. M. MARSHMAN, JR. *(Screenplay); Based on the story "A Can of Beans" by* CHARLES BRACKETT *and* BILLY WILDER. JOHN F. SEITZ *(Photography)*; HANS DREIER *and* JOHN MEEHAN *(Art Direction)*; FRANZ WAXMAN *(Music)*; SAM COMER *and* RAY MOYER *(Sets)*; DOANE HARRISON *and* ARTHUR SCHMIDT *(Editors)*.

Opened at Radio City Music Hall, August 10, 1950. Running time 110 minutes.

THE PICTURE:

Then came the picture which Holden himself has always maintained did more to accelerate his career and bring him serious critical respect than any ten he had done before. In this he revealed himself, at thirty-two, as an actor of considerable depth and wide range, replete with an unique quality of personality and an intrinsic creative strength that could hold its own with any in 1950 Hollywood. *Sunset Boulevard* has been dissected and analyzed by some of the best critical minds in film writing, and twenty-three years after its original release it fulfills the late James Agee's prediction that it would linger long in memory and exert a classic and widespread influence on film standards. The film, for one thing, posed several aspects that were on the revolutionary side for a 1950 movie: it dared to suggest that a sordid, utilitarian sexual involvement between a woman of 50 and a man roughly half her age was not as uncommon as supposed, and it presented Hollywood's glittering silent era in direct and surprising juxtaposition to a Hollywood present (as of 1950) that somehow seemed drab, trivial, and pedestrian by comparison. Other films had harked back to the movies'

With Gloria Swanson

role. Even her somewhat arrant posturings and rococo overplaying seemed suited to the mood and content of her characterization, and Erich von Stroheim as her butler and former director (as well as husband), who tries to protect her from the crass infringements of the irreverent present and who helps foster her pathetically grandiose illusions of enduring filmic greatness, admirably fleshes out the decadent, spiritually musty ambience sought by producer-writer Brackett and director-writer Wilder. Holden as a down-and-out screenwriter, Joe Gillis, drives his about-to-be-impounded sports car into a private roadway while on the lam from creditors. He encounters Swanson and von Stroheim when he hides his car in the garage of her mansion, stays to do a screenplay for Swanson's projected return to the screen as *Salome*, finds himself half-fascinated and half-repelled by her grotesqueries, and is gradually drawn into her spider web. Soon she is buying him clothes, shortly she is in love with him, and because he is, for all his surface bravado, an essentially dependent, weak, and unadmirable path-of-least-resistancer, he guiltily and self-hatingly accommodates her insatiable needs. When he tries to break away, after initiating a tentative romance with studio employee Nancy Olson, he dies at Swanson's hands, and his bullet-riddled body is removed by police from her swimming pool. The now completely demented Swanson is lured downstairs by the police while her saddened butler, once more a "director," pretends to guide her through a *Salome* scene—giving the original occasion for the oft-repeated camp line "I'm ready for my closeup now, Mr. De-

past, of course, but not with this depth of penetration or tragic grandeur of concept. As the faded silent luminary who lives in memories of a more robust era in Hollywood's—and her—existence, Gloria Swanson, who of course in actual fact had lived through the baroque twenties as one of Hollywood's top silent stars, was as convincing as anyone could hope to be in the

With Gloria Swanson

Mille." The movie is replete with superbly inventive scenes: Swanson doing a wryly apt imitation of Chaplin, or shaking a fist at her shadow up on the screen and shouting her defiance of the unheeding present; her visit to Cecil DeMille on a movie set where DeMille (who shows himself a surprisingly effective actor) tactfully and gently fobs off her comeback ambitions; her colorfully enacted suicide try on the night Holden leaves her alone in the mansion to return temporarily to that newer Hollywood world where he feels more at home. Originally *Sunset Boulevard* had a prologue and epilogue that took place in a morgue where Holden's body lay after the murder. This was later excised from the footage when it inspired mixed reactions and puzzled laughter at a preview. Holden is magnificent in the picture, projecting all the inner complexities of a Hollywood also-ran disappointed in his ambitions and looking for the easy way, finally disillusioned and rank with self-disgust. Holden recalled on a recent talk show the excitement and wonder he felt on the *Sunset Boulevard* set as he listened to Swanson reminisce about the past, with silent players like Buster Keaton, H. B. Warner, and Anna Q. Nilsson—the famed "waxwork" bridge players of one of the film's most nostalgically evocative scenes joining in. For this picture Holden won his first nomination for an Academy Award, but lost to José Ferrer's *Cyrano de Bergerac*.

With Gloria Swanson

REVIEWS:

James Agee in *Sight and Sound:*
[The film] is Hollywood craftsmanship at its smartest and at just about its best, and it is hard to find better craftsmanship than that, at this time, in any art or country. It is also, in terms of movie tradition, a very courageous picture. A sexual affair between a rich woman of fifty and a kept man half her age is not exactly a usual version of boy meets girl . . . nor, as a rule, is a movie hero so weak and so morally imperfect that he can less properly be called a "Hero" than an authentic, unlucky and unadmirable human being. "Unhappy endings" are not so rare, by now, but it is rare to find one as skillful, spectacular and appropriate as this one. Besides all that, *Sunset Boulevard* is much the most ambitious movie about Hollywood ever done, and is the best of several good ones into the bargain. . . . Miss Swanson, required to play a hundred percent gro-

With Gloria Swanson

With Gloria Swanson

With Nancy Olson

tesque, plays it not just to the hilt but right up to the armpit, by which I mean magnificently. . . . Mr. Holden and his girl and their friend, not to mention Fred Clark acting a producer, are microscopically right in casting, direction and performance.

Otis L. Guernsey, Jr., in the *New York Herald Tribune:*
Charles Brackett and Billy Wilder have slashed open Hollywood in a brilliantly moody melodrama . . . a weird, fascinating motion picture about an art form which, new as it is, is already haunted by ghosts . . . Brackett and Wilder have built a series of acute dramatic observations on the business they love. Some of them are witty, some ruefully accurate and some heartbreaking. This is no mere show business story; it examines the slag heap rather than the front window, and it finds there a drama more powerful than most of the imaginary sound stage theatricals. Miss Swanson was an excellent choice for the role of the wildly eccentric silent star wearing her frayed reputation as though it were brand new. . . . Holden's casual, natural performance is an authentic background against which Miss Swanson can project herself. . . . *Sunset Boulevard* [says] that pictures are made by people, and people get hurt. Under the tutelage of the Messrs. Brackett and Wilder, it says it with conviction and magnificent style.

William Holden

T.M.P. in *The New York Times:*
It is such a clever compound of truth and legend—and is so richly redolent of the past, yet so contemporaneous —that it seemingly speaks with great authority. *Sunset Boulevard* is that rare blend of pungent writing, expert acting, masterly direction and unobtrusively artistic photography which quickly casts a spell over an audience and holds it enthralled to a shattering climax . . . playing the part of Joe Gillis, the script writer, William Holden is doing the finest acting of his career. His range and control of emotions never falters and he engenders a full measure of compassion for a character who is somewhat less than admirable.

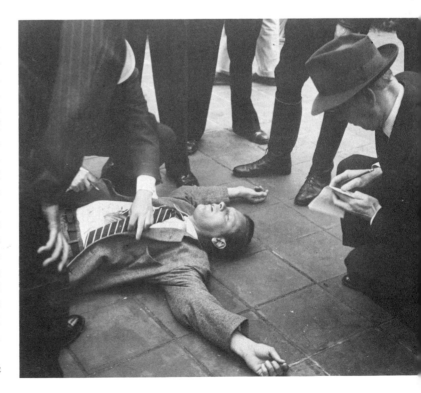

With Nancy Olson

Union Station

1950   Paramount

CAST:

WILLIAM HOLDEN *(Police Lt. William Calhoun)*; NANCY OLSON *(Joyce Willecombe)*; BARRY FITZGERALD *(Inspector Donnelly)*; LYLE BETTGER *(Joe Beacon)*; JAN STERLING *(Marge Wrighter)*; ALLENE ROBERTS *(Lorna Murchison)*; HERBERT HEYES *(Henry Murchison)*; DON DUNNING *(Gus Hudder)*; FRED GRAFF *(Vince Marley)*; JAMES SEAY *(Detective Shattuck)*; PARLEY E. BAER *(Detective Gottschalk)*; RALPH SANFORD *(Detective Fay)*; RICHARD KARLAN *(Detective Stein)*; BIGELOW SAYRE *(Detective Ross)*; CHARLES DAYTON *(Howard Kettner)*; JEAN RUTH *(Pretty Girl)*; PAUL LEES *(Young Man Mosher)*; HARRY HAYDEN *(Conductor Skelly)*.

CREDITS:

JULES SCHERMER *(Producer)*; RUDOLPH MATE *(Director)*; SYDNEY BOEHM *(Screenplay); based on a story by* THOMAS WALSH; DANIEL FAPP *(Camera)*; ELLSWORTH HOAGLAND *(Editor)*; IRVIN TALBOT *(Score)*.

Opened at the Paramount Theater, New York, October 4, 1950. Running time, 81 minutes.

THE PICTURE:

Holden was reunited with his *Sunset Boulevard* girlfriend Nancy Olson in this film, which was a reasonably exciting melodrama about a kidnapping, with a railway terminal used as a payoff location. Holden is chief of the railway police and Olson a passenger who on arrival at Union Station, reports to his outfit on two suspicious characters who have been on her train. It develops that Olson is the secretary to a wealthy man (Herbert Heyes) whose blind daughter (Allene Roberts) has been kidnapped by Lyle Bettger and his confederate. The terminal is designated by the Bettger gang as the payoff area for the ransom, which the blind girl's father is to deliver. There is much scurrying in and out of phone booths, payoff red-herrings, and spotting of kidnappers, as Holden and Co. gradually zero-in on the miscreants, one of whom eventually dies under the hooves of stockyard cattle while being pursued by the cops. Bettger himself expires under the Holden gunfire after an exciting underground chase that is the most suspenseful thing in the film. Meanwhile Holden and Olson develop a romance, and Barry

With Nancy Olson

Fitzgerald is on hand as a top cop who oversees the apprehension of the criminals. Jan Sterling is along for the ride as Bettger's moll. The Holden–Olson chemistry was on striking display in this (they were to do several more films together), and Holden was quietly assured and at times strikingly forceful as the cop determined to get his man. Miss Roberts had some fine moments registering terror of Bettger as he kept the terrified blind woman captive in the underground. Some critics thought *Union Station* a comedown for Holden, following as it did on the heels of that milestone *Sunset Boulevard* (which had been released only two months before). As one of his associates pointed out, however, "Great parts in great films don't grow on every tree." Holden himself, though recognizing that the film was standard fare, did not consider it detri-

mental to his progress. Neither did it represent an advance for him. Director Rudolph Matè kept things moving at a fast clip. Fitzgerald, in a rather radical casting departure, was in fine form, and all in all, the public responded positively.

REVIEWS:

Variety:

The Thomas Walsh story holds together in logical fashion. (The scripters) build a good feeling of suspense and keep the pace moving properly.... William Holden, while youthful in appearance to head up the railway policing department of a metropolitan terminal, is in good form and will be liked ... [the film] catches the feel of a large terminal and its constantly shifting scenes of people arriving and departing ... the

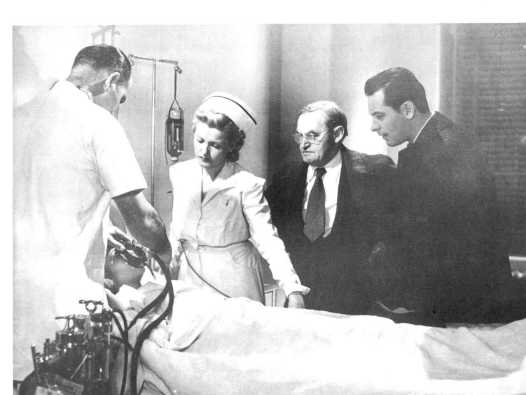

With Barry Fitzgerald

William Holden

With Nancy Olson and Barry Fitzgerald

elements of chase and danger, against an offbeat locale, hold the attention. Romance angle in having Holden and Miss Olson strike a finale clinch is ordinary but okay theater.

The New York Times:

Despite its occasional excitements, the goings-on in *Union Station* only add up to the muscular derring-do likely to turn up in any standard cops-and-robbers adventure . . . it unfolds in fits and starts. After quickly opening in expert fashion as a kidnapping is revealed, it proceeds along familiar routes to a denouement which is also according to a traditional formula . . . although he seems a mite young to head the police force of the undesignated city's terminal, William Holden is a serious, alert dick, who can spot a con man or a masher, if not a kidnapper, before you can say Grand Central.

Howard Barnes in the *New York Herald Tribune:*

So aggressive in its violence is *Union Station* that it frequently prompts one to laughter rather than shock, even in its most lurid moments. . . . Holden fortunately underplays [his role], letting the prodigal complications of the continuity lead him into a highly organized but haphazard act of heroism and the successful wooing of a sharp-eyed girl. . . . *Union Station* is striking if highly unpersuasive.

With Barry Fitzgerald

With Broderick Crawford, Howard St. John, and Judy Holliday

Born Yesterday

1950   Columbia

CAST:

BRODERICK CRAWFORD *(Harry Brock)*; JUDY HOLLIDAY *(Billie Dawn)*; WILLIAM HOLDEN *(Paul Verrall)*; HOWARD ST. JOHN *(Jim Devery)*; FRANK OTTO *(Eddie)*; LARRY OLIVER *(Norval Hedges)*; BARBARA BROWN *(Mrs. Hedges)*; GRANDON RHODES *(Sanborn)*; CLAIRE CARLETON *(Helen)*.

CREDITS:

S. SYLVAN SIMON *(Producer)*; GEORGE CUKOR *(Director)*; ALBERT MANNHEIMER *(Screenplay)*; *from the stage play by* GARSON KANIN; JOSEPH WALKER *(Camera)*; CHARLES NELSON *(Editor)*; FREDERICK HOLLANDER *(Music Score)*; MORRIS STOLOFF *(Musical Director)*; JEAN LOUIS *(Gowns)*.

Opened at the Victoria Theater, New York, December 26, 1950. Running time, 103 minutes.

With Judy Holliday

day, who made a brilliant stage success in it, but in true Hollywood fashion, when it came time to cast the movie everybody *but* Judy got tested for the role. Then, after three patient years of trying for the movie part, Judy landed it, to the rousing cheers of her many supporters—and her performance, just as fine on screen as on stage, gave reviewers of the period ample grounds for wondering how any other actress could have dared aspire to the role of the comically ignorant blonde chorine who becomes a companion-mistress of junk tycoon Broderick Crawford (Paul Douglas played the role on the stage). He uses her as an unwitting catspaw in his suspect business dealings, getting her to sign papers that bring her possession of important junkyard concessions coveted by Crawford. The junk king, however, is ashamed of her illiteracy and lack of polish. He decides to recruit the services of a scholarly and literate young journalist, William Holden, to improve Judy's mind. Holden, who is secretly out to expose Crawford's nefarious Washington maneuverings, succeeds in his task only too well. Before he is done he has not only educated his naturally bright pupil in social and intellectual essentials but has also imbued her with democratic views that effectively pull the rug out from Crawford's undemocratic practices. Holden incidentally wins his girl's heart and hand from Crawford. Her performance in this superbly droll and vulgarly larkish part won Holliday the Oscar for 1950 over Bette Davis (*All About Eve*) and Gloria Swanson, Holden's *Sunset Boulevard* co-star. Holden and Crawford are overshadowed by Holliday throughout, though Holden garnered some good notices for his telling projection of scholarly authority and earnest good will in a role that had been built up for the screen.

REVIEWS:

Life:

Judy Holliday is back in her by-now-classic role of Billie Dawn, the junk dealer's mistress unexpectedly educated into virtue. The movie is not much more than a photographed version of the play which ran 1,642 performances on Broadway. The male leads are played, more or less competently, by Broderick Crawford and William Holden. But the whole picture is Judy's, and in the intervals between guffaws you have time to reflect that you are seeing the top comic performance by an actress in American movies this year.

Hollis Alpert in *Saturday Review:*

In spite of Miss Holliday's magical presence—her voice runs the gamut from a shrill squeak to a noisy whine—the movie hardly dims the play version. The setting of the hotel suite in Washington is, as one would expect,

THE PICTURE:

Born Yesterday opened as a play on Broadway in 1946, and turned out to be one of Garson Kanin's more felicitous literary efforts, running for 1,642 performances. It also did wonders for the career of Judy Holli-

With Broderick Crawford

larger and more lavish in the picture; the camera can show Judy trotting around to monuments and public buildings; there are good performances from Broderick Crawford and William Holden as the writer. But the play had no dull moments, never sagged. The movie falters, curiously, now and then . . . the translation from play to movie was made too literally.

Jack Thompson in the *New York Sunday Mirror Magazine:*

One of the most brilliant and hilarious performances to flash across the screen in a long time is Judy Holliday's wonderful job [in this film] . . . Holden is first rate as usual as the newspaperman, a part more important in the film than in the play.

*With Judy Holliday and
Broderick Crawford*

Variety:

Miss Holliday delights . . . William Holden is quietly effective as the newspaperman hired to coach her in social graces so she will better fit in with her junkman's ambitious plans . . . George Cukor's direction, always with emphasis on the chorine character, belts many laughs as he sends the players through their paces. In spots, however, timing permits audience laughter to step on punch lines so that some of the play's wit and satire are drowned out.

With Judy Holliday

Force of Arms

1951   Warners

CAST:

WILLIAM HOLDEN *(Peterson)*; NANCY OLSON *(Lt. Eleanor McKay)*; FRANK LOVEJOY *(Major Blackford)*; GENE EVANS *(Sgt. McFee)*; DICK WESSON *(Sgt. Klein)*; PAUL PICERNI *(Sheridan)*; KATHERINE WARREN *(Major Waldron)* ROSS FORD *(Hooker)*; SLATS TAYLOR *(Yost)*; RON HAGERTHY *(Minto)*; MARIO SILETTI *(Signor Maduvalli)*; ARGENTINA BRUNETTI *(Signcra Maduvalli)*; AMELIA COVA *(Lea Maduvalli)*; DONALD GORDON *(Webber)*; BOB ROARK *(Frank)*; ANNA DEMETRIO *(Mama Mia)*.

CREDITS:

ANTHONY VEILLER *(Producer)*; MICHAEL CURTIZ *(Director)*; ORIN JANNINGS *(Screenplay) from a story by* RICHARD TREGASKIS; TED MC CORD *(Camera)*; MAX STEINER *(Music)*; OWEN MARKS *(Editor)*.

Opened at the Warner Theater, New York, August 13, 1951. Running time, 98 minutes.

THE PICTURE:

Holden appeared to great advantage in 1951 in *Force of Arms* (originally titled *A Girl For Joe)*. It contains some excellently staged (by Michael Curtiz) battle scenes (some footage of the actual World War II Italian campaign was interpolated briefly); a fine, forceful, sincere performance by Holden; able support from Nancy Olson and Frank Lovejoy; and first-class production values all around. A poignant story of a romance played out against the horrors of World War II combat-zone conditions, it has also the benefit of a literate script by Orin Jannings from that warwise writer Richard Tregaskis's original story. Max Steiner does his usual exceptional job in fitting mood music to the action, as well as the more private emotions of the players. The story has Holden a sergeant in the American Army on the San Pietro front. The outfit is pulled out of active duty for a rest, and during this period Holden meets WAC Lieutenant Olson. They get off to a hostile start, but then man-woman chemistry asserts itself predictably. Back in action, Holden deliberately holds back during a crucial engagement which sees the lives of his commanding officer, Lovejoy, and other buddies sacrificed. He then develops the feeling that he has shirked his duty because of his anxiety to return to Olson. Later they marry, but he passes up a chance at limited service to return to combat dangers because, as he tells her, he must keep faith with his conscience and sense of duty. In a subsequent engagement he is wounded, left behind and presumed dead. The moving climax finds Olson, who refuses to believe her husband is dead, tracing him along the battle line all the way to Rome, where she finds him among liberated prisoners-of-war being billeted for treatment. Olson and Holden, in their third film together, played their more intimate scenes with the naturalistic conviction and telling mutual chemistry that in the early fifties had resulted in their becoming a rather frequent romantic teaming on screen.

REVIEWS:

James S. Barstow, Jr., in the *New York Herald Tribune:*
A stark, uncompromising picture of men at war . . . the screenplay depicts with a maturity surprising in a Hollywood film both the savagery of soldiers under fire and their animal enjoyment of a five-day pass. . . . In its romantic aspects . . . [the film] is only partially successful in combining a conventional love story with the more vivid impact of Tregaskis's outline. But on the

With Nancy Olson

With Paul Picerni (right)

William Holden (left)

whole honesty outweighs contrivance in an arresting study of the moral and physical structure after the shooting starts. . . . Holden does an excellent job with the uneven character of the sergeant . . . Nancy Olson is equally good as the lady in question.

The New York Times:

The drama, which treats of two young people, bone-tired and sick of the war in which they are pawns, is honest romance and cynicism made adult, moving and palatable by an intelligent cast, director, writers and producer . . . particularly praiseworthy is William Holden's characterization of Peterson, at once hard, brittle and sentient. Nancy Olson is equally sensitive . . . a forceful amalgam of ruggedness and romance.

Variety:

A tender, dramatic love story played off against a World War II background . . . its entertainment values have popular appeal, being expertly fashioned for both femme and masculine reaction . . . the story line is filled out with many gripping scenes. The romance rings true and the battle action sequences are dangerously alive under the forthright staging of Curtiz. . . . Miss Olson and Holden, not new to romantic teaming are most effective in the natural reactions to the circumstances in which they are plunged. Frank Lovejoy makes his role of the friendly major a standout . . . battle footage is among some of the most realistic yet staged for a picture and has the added authenticity of using some brief clips from the actual Italian campaign.

With Frank Lovejoy (top right)

121

With Nancy Olson

Submarine Command

1952   Paramount

CAST:

WILLIAM HOLDEN *(Commander White)*; NANCY OLSON *(Carol)*; WILLIAM BENDIX *(C.P.O. Boyer)*; DON TAYLOR *(Lt. Cmdr. Peter Morris)*; ARTHUR FRANZ *(Lt. Carlson)*; DARRYL HICKMAN *(Ensign Wheelwright)*; PEGGY WEBBER *(Mrs. Alice Rice)*; MORONI OLSEN *(Rear Admiral Joshua Rice)*; JACK GREGSON *(Commander Rice)*; JACK KELLY *(Lt. Barton)*; DON DUNNING *(Quartermaster Perkins)*; JERRY PRIS *(Sgt. Gentry)*; CHARLES MEREDITH *(Admiral Tobias)*; PHILIP VAN ZANDT *(Gavin)*.

CREDITS:

JOSEPH SISTROM *(Producer)*; JOHN FARROW *(Director)*; JONATHAN LATIMER *(Screenplay) from a story by* LATIMER; *made with the Cooperation of the U.S. Department of Defense and the U.S. Submarine Service; locations shot partly at bases in San Diego and Mare Island.*

Opened at the Globe Theater, New York, January 18, 1952. Running time, 87 minutes.

THE PICTURE:

Having chased kidnappers and fought valiantly in World War II (along with having perpetrated a lot of other standard movie heroics) it was, perhaps, inevitable that Holden should find himself commanding a submarine—and command it he did in this. Umpteen other male stars had gotten mixed up with submarines over the years, including Jack Holt *(Submarine,* 1928) and even Charles Laughton *(Devil and the Deep,* 1932), and Holden probably sensed by 1952 that his fate was inevitable when it came to affecting heroics in such a milieu. The fact that he followed closely upon John Wayne's submarine-commander stint the year before in *Operation Pacific* (even some of the plot setups were the same) must not have sent Holden to his task particularly exhilarated, but he did his standard stuff, as always, managing to make some of the goings-on look reasonably compelling. It was the old chestnut about the submarine executive officer forced to submerge under enemy attack to save his ship and crew

With Don Taylor

can't sleep nights, though assured by fellow officers that he had made the correct decision, all things considered. He has fits of melancholia, quarrels with pals, tiffs with his wife, played with an expression of forebearing patience by the now-ubiquitous Nancy Olson, who in previous pictures had helped Holden find kidnappers and weather World War II army vicissitudes after attempting his last-minute rescue from tigress Swanson in *Sunset Boulevard*—all of which cinematic experience demonstrated that Miss O. was well-equipped for her latest task—as indeed she was. By the fadeout, Holden has proved his heroism in a spectacular sea action off Korea, Olson manages to come up with a pregnancy to clinch a marital reconciliation (we *knew* she was up to the challenge), and all is well that ends well, even if damply, what with all the clichés gumming things up. There is much exciting action, however, and an authentic feel and look were supplied with the more-than-competent assistance of the U.S. Submarine Service at West Coast bases such as Mare Island and San Diego. Don Taylor is winning as Holden's fellow-submariner and William Bendix is—well, William Bendix—as another seadog. John Farrow, who knew his sea stuff (his *Two Years Before The Mast* had done Alan Ladd no harm in 1946) did right well by all hands. Though admittedly derivative, and far from the best picture of 1952, it was a worthy example of its rather overworked milieu.

despite the necessity of leaving his wounded captain topside, to inevitably drown. After this unfortunate circumstance, Holden does much conscience-churning and soul-searching, telling himself he should have surfaced to rescue his superior despite the risks. Though the plot comes across as hackneyed and artificial, the fact was that such real-life melodramas actually occurred in the Pacific during World War II. In any event Holden

With William Bendix and Don Taylor

REVIEWS:

Cue:

Except for a rather soapily carpentered finish, [the film] is a lively and gripping, quite realistic drama of the underseas service, filled with enough naval action and seagoing authenticity to give the picture the excitement it requires. The scenes afloat are excellent and the shore sequences convincing enough. The cast [is] excellent.

Joe Pihodna in the *New York Herald Tribune:*

The film which concerns the crew of the *Tiger Shark* and their highly dramatic problems is quite probably technically correct in revealing the operation of a submarine. When the emotional problems of the officers and men are discussed, the contrast with the efficient shipboard scenes is remarkable. On land *Submarine*

With William Bendix

With William Bendix and Don Taylor

Command loses a lot of power.... John Farrow has directed the film with an eye to making most of the photogenic possibilities of the *Tiger Shark.* Indeed the romance stuck on the views of the submarine like a superstructure seems to be more of a dressing than a necessity. William Holden, William Bendix and Don Taylor carry themselves with dignity and charm as Navy men. Nancy Olson is a pretty and practical Navy wife.

Bosley Crowther in *The New York Times:*

The screenplay by Jonathan Latimer is a compact and levelheaded job, the direction of John Farrow is naturalistic and the performers are uniformly good. William Holden is human and compelling as the distracted officer and Nancy Olson is pretty and respectable as his uncomprehending wife ... the ways of submariners and the atmosphere of Navy life, both afloat and ashore, are represented with remarkable plausibility and power.

With Johnny Stewart

Boots Malone

1952   Columbia

CAST:

WILLIAM HOLDEN *(Boots Malone)*; JOHNNY STEWART *(The Kid)*; STANLEY CLEMENTS *(Stash Clements)*; BASIL RUYSDAEL *(Preacher Cole)*; CARL BENTON REID *(John Williams)*; RALPH DUMKE *(Beckett)*; ED BEGLEY *(Howard Whitehead)*; HUGH SANDERS *(Matson)*; HENRY MORGAN *(Quarter House Henry)*; ANN LEE *(Mrs. Gibson)*; ANTHONY CARUSO *(Fee)*; BILLY PEARSON *(Eddie Koch)*; JOHN W. FRYE *(Foxy Farrell)*; HARRY HINES *(Goofy Gordon)*; TONI GERRY *(Penny West)*; HURLEY BREEN *(Red)*; WHIT BISSELL *(Lou Dyer)*; EARL UNKRAUT *(Cabbage Head)*; HARRY SHANNON *(Colonel Summers)*; JOHN CALL *(Touting Clocker)*.

CREDITS:

MILTON HOLMES *(Producer)*; WILLIAM DIETERLE *(Director)*; MILTON HOLMES *(Writer)*; CHARLES LAWTON JR. *(Camera)*; ELMER BERNSTEIN *(Music)*; AL CLARK *(Editor)*; *a presentation of the* SIDNEY BUCHMAN *Enterprises unit.*

Opened at the Paramount Theater, New York, March 12, 1952. Running time, 102 minutes.

THE PICTURE:

Having survived the rigors of submarine derring-do at Paramount, Holden then found himself back at Columbia in a racetrack story written by Milton Holmes and directed by William Dieterle who, like his star, had certainly drawn more prestigious assignments in the past. Not that the film was all that bad, though on the longish side at 102 minutes. But it was slight stuff at this point in the Holden career, though he turned in his customary sincere job. The story, redolent of many another in this genre, dealt with a jockey's agent, Holden, who is down on his luck. He meets up with Johnny Stewart, a rich teenager whose career-crazy mother neglects him. The boy is horse-mad and race-mad, and the opportunistic Holden, sensing money in these enthusiasms, decides to kid him along while the dough holds out, pretending meanwhile to teach the revved-up fifteen-year-old how to be a winning jockey. The plot thickens when the mother locates the boy and tries to interfere with his blossoming career; other complications rear their ugly heads when Holden is forced to tell the boy he must deliberately lose the big race or be murdered by a syndicate that is betting on a rival. Of course, as in all good little human-interest yarns, the crooks are bested, the boy's faith in his mentor is salvaged, and all ends on a sentimental note, the sincere affection and camaraderie between boy and man having developed during their association. Much of the photography was done at actual race tracks and horse havens—and it looks it. Nothing like an authentic feel, Holmes and associates probably reasoned, and they

With Stanley Clements, Basil Ruysdael, and Johnny Stewart

were right. The more seedy, sordid side of racing—its touts, its hangers-on, its phonies and also-rans—are depicted graphically. Holden gives out with some honest human sentiment and solid character delineation as the

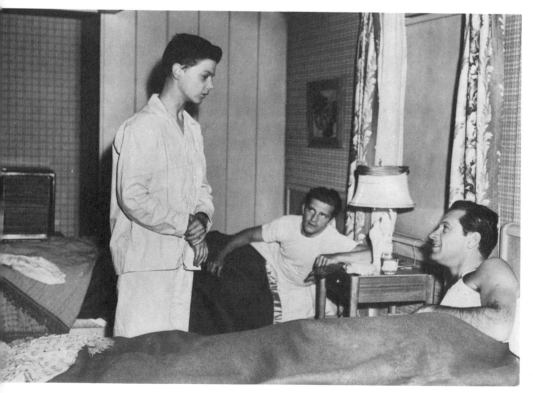

With Johnny Stewart and Stanley Clements

126

With Stanley Clements and Johnny Stewart

With Johnny Stewart

With Johnny Stewart

cynical opportunist redeemed by genuine affection for a sincere kid. The picture did nothing to further Holden's career—in fairness, however, it did nothing to hinder it either.

REVIEWS:

The New Yorker:

No man who has devoted as much time, thought and cash to horses as I have is a trustworthy guide to the merits of any picture dealing with contests between the beasts, but it seems to me that even people who don't know a mare from a gelding will find the racing lore in *Boots Malone* entertaining here and there. While the plot is pretty standard stuff, the doings around the track have an authentic look; as a matter of fact, most of the photography was done at real horse plants. Some of the animals prancing about are very pleasant to watch, and those of you who use a bet-the-jockey system may be interested to know that [the film] includes a lot about the training of the boys. . . . William Holden, Johnny Stewart, Stanley Clements and Basil Ruysdael all do an admirable job.

Brog in *Variety:*

About average boxoffice results shape up for [the film], a well-done drama effectively presenting the attachment between a man and a boy against a racing stable background. Appeal is particularly good for the family trade. . . . Milton Holmes has told the story with good

emotional moments and sentiment without being maudlin. This handling also is reflected in the direction by William Dieterle. . . . Story is run off against an authentic racetrack background, drawing a good picture of the less prosperous side of racing and the hangers-on. . . . Holden and Stewart get excellent support from the handpicked cast playing the assorted racing types. . . . Holmes and Dieterle have put the film together creditably.

With Basil Ruysdael and Stanley Clements

The Turning Point

1952   Paramount

CAST:

WILLIAM HOLDEN (Jerry McKibbon); EDMOND O'BRIEN (John Conroy); ALEXIS SMITH (Amanda Waycross); TOM TULLY (Matt Conroy); ED BEGLEY (Eichelberger); DON DAYTON (Ackerman); ADELE LONGMIRE (Carmelina); RAY TEAL (Clint); TED DE CORSIA (Harrigan); DON PORTER (Joe Silbray); HOWARD FREEMAN (Fogee); NEVILLE BRAND (Red).

CREDITS:

IRVING ASHER (Producer); WILLIAM DIETERLE (Director); WARREN DUFF (Screenplay); based on a story by HORACE MC COY; LIONEL LINDON (Camera); HAL PEREIRA and JOSEPH MC MILLAN JOHNSON (Art Directors) GORDON JENNINGS (Special Photographic Effects); FARCIOT EDOUART (Process Photography); SAM COMER and GRACE GREGORY (Set Decoration); IRVIN TALBOT (Music Direction); EDITH HEAD (Costumes); GEORGE TOMASINI (Editor); WALLY WESTMORE (Makeup Supervisor); JOHN COPE (Sound Recording).

Opened at the Globe Theater, New York, November 15, 1952. Running time, 85 minutes.

THE PICTURE:

The Turning Point saw Holden back on his usual yoyo Columbia-to-Paramount-to-Columbia swing—this time it was Paramount's turn—and while the new picture was not exactly apropos in its titling, it was shortly to be followed by some true "turning point" fare for Holden—one of which was to win him an Oscar. The picture in question, however, was a standard crime melodrama, no better and no worse than hundreds that had preceded it. Holden again found himself working with director William Dieterle, who must have found race tracks and crime stuff a distinct comedown after directing plush historical dramas. Be that as it may, the pace and action were kept percolating in this confection about a state crime investigation. Chief investigator Edmond O'Brien wants his old school pal, newspaper reporter Holden, to help him "get" a tough syndicate headed by wily Ed Begley. Alexis Smith is O'Brien's assistant, she is also supposed to be his girlfriend—until she gets a look at crusading-journalist-with-an-eye-for-the-ladies Holden. Then, as you knew it would, that old ugly triangle-specter rears its head. Reviewers commented at the time that the film was possibly inspired

Edmond O'Brien and Alexis Smith

by the Kefauver investigations, but since these were yesterday's news as of 1952, the picture seems to have been somewhat late in exploiting such headlines. The plot thickens when Smith and Holden discover that O'Brien's father, cop Tom Tully, is in league with the syndicate, which later rubs him out. When a prime witness spills the beans on the inner machinations of the mob, the jig is up for them—but unfortunatley also for Holden, who dies at the hands of a hired killer after a cat-and-mouse chase in a fight stadium, with Miss Smith on hand to bid Holden a tearful adieu, after which, presumably, she gets reinherited by O'Brien, who arrives

in time for the death scene. Holden delivered in his usual style, Smith was her beautiful self (and who could ask for more?), and O'Brien was grim and forceful as always. A bevy of good supporting players helped things along.

REVIEWS:

Variety:

[The film] apparently draws its inspiration from last year's Kefauver investigation . . . with William Holden, Edmond O'Brien and Alexis Smith as marquee lures, comfortable returns are indicated in most situations. Unfortunately the Horace McCoy story as screenplayed by Warren Duff is now somewhat dated since both

Edmond O'Brien (right)

With Alexis Smith

Senator Kefauver and his crime committee have stepped from the public eye. But despite its lack of topicality, the script contains enough melodrama to satisfy the action fans . . . occasionally the movement of the script tends to lag in a rash of superfluous dialogue. This is especially apparent at the midway point. However, the action accelerates thereafter and the closing reels are highlighted by a successful hunt for an all-important femme witness . . . performances of the cast help considerably in making the yarn credible. Holden is calm and self-assured as the fearless scribe who comes close to knowing all the answers. O'Brien pursues his chores with grim determination. Besides providing pulchritude, Miss Smith nicely fills the demands of her role . . . director William Dieterle displays a sure hand in the action sequences.

Joe Pihodna in the *New York Herald Tribune:*

[The film] directed by William Dieterle, moves along fast but without too much conviction . . . a good-guys-and-bad-guys melodrama which shades the handicaps by some fierce and unpremeditated violence . . . this reviewer hopes that movies based on the existing Senate Crime Investigating Committee appearances have about had it.

H.M.T. in *The New York Times:*

A sober but uninspired drama of anti-crime crusading

With Edmond O'Brien

With Adele Longmire

...with William Holden, Alexis Smith and Edmond O'Brien as the game principals of an almost completely reminiscent undertaking. For while the crisp playing of the actors and the alert, if unimaginative, directing by William Dieterle often vibrate a formula structure, [the film] gives its sizzling text a lukewarm once-over.... Mr. O'Brien and Mr. Holden grapple admirably with some starchy, overwritten dialogue. Pretty Miss Smith is confined to answering the telephone and trotting at the heels of both.

With police

With distaff admirers

Stalag 17

1953   Paramount

CAST:

WILLIAM HOLDEN *(Sefton)*; DON TAYLOR *(Lt. Dunbar)*; OTTO PREMINGER *(Oberst Von Scherbach)*; ROBERT STRAUSS *(Stosh)*; HARVEY LEMBECK *(Harry)*; RICHARD ERDMAN *(Hoppy)*; PETER GRAVES *(Price)*; NEVILLE BRAND *(Duke)*; SIG RUMAN *(Schulz)*; MICHAEL MOORE *(Manfredi)*; PETER BALDWIN *(Johnson)*; ROBINSON STONE *(Joey)*; ROBERT SHAWLEY *(Blondie)*; WILLIAM PIERSON *(Marko)*; GIL STRATTON JR. *(Cookie)*; JAY LAWRENCE *(Begradian)*; ERWIN KAISER *(Geneva Man)*; EDMUND TRCZINSKI *(Triz)*; HAROLD D. MARESCH *(German Lieutenant)*; JERRY SINGER *(The Crutch)*; ROSS BAGDASARIAN *(Prisoner of War)*; SVETLANA MC LEE *(Russian Woman Prisoner)*; LYDA VASHKULAT, AUDREY STRAUSS *(Other Russian Women Prisoners)*.

CREDITS:

BILLY WILDER *(Producer and Director)*; BILLY WILDER *and* EDWIN BLUM *(Screenplay); based on the play by* DONALD BEVAN *and* EDMUND TRCZINSKI; WILLIAM SCHORR *(Associate Producer)*; DOANE HARRISON *(Editorial Advisor)*; FRANZ WAXMAN *(Music)*; ERNEST LASZLO *(Director of Photography)*; HAL PEREIRA *and* FRANZ BACHELIN *(Art Direction)*; GEORGE TOMASINI *(Editor)*; GORDON JENNINGS *(Special Photographic Effects)*; SAM COMER *and* RAY MAYER *(Set Decoration)*; WALLY WESTMORE *(Makeup)*; HAROLD LEWIS *and* GENE GARVIN *(Sound)*.

Opened at the Astor Theater, New York, July 1, 1953. Running time, 119 minutes.

THE PICTURE:

Holden won his first and (to date) only Academy Award for his vital and blistering rendition of the cocky, self-serving individualist Sefton in *Stalag 17*, a rousing, biting, astringent depiction of the raw, tense conditions among American servicemen in a prisoner-of-war camp in World War II Germany. All the cruel ironies and prickling happenstances, the jousting and scheming and upmanship games, the temporary loyalties and rampaging feuds, the accumulated tensions of young and vital men confined in conditions that were barely endurable, are set forth admirably by producer-director Billy Wilder, who also collaborated on the screenplay from the Broadway hit by Donald Bevan and

Edmund Trczinski. This was Holden's and Wilder's first film together since *Sunset Boulevard*. Wilder seems to have been Holden's first real "good luck" director, since Holden received an Oscar nomination for the first film with Wilder and the Oscar itself for the second. Holden gave his most versatile and full-bodied performance to date as the cynical, shifty Seton, an opportunist in spades who juggles any and all situations to further his own comfort and well-being and who is intent on just one goal: the survival of Sefton, in style if possible, in comfort at the minimum. After two soldiers die while attempting a well-planned escape, the other inmates of the prison barracks realize that there is an informer in their midst. Suspicion falls on the widely disliked and distrusted Holden, a surly, sarcastic, swaggering character who rides too high, safe, and secure for the men's taste. When Don Taylor, a newcomer, is later exposed as the guy who blew up a German ammunition train, the fellows decide that Holden has ratted yet again, and they beat him up brutally. Holden happens to be innocent, however, and the rest of the story is taken up with his ultimately successful attempts to uncover the real informer, after which he makes a clever escape from the compound. Otto Preminger, on sabbatical from directing, is glitteringly saturnine as the camp commander. Sig Ruman delivers in his customary burlesque style as a barracks guard. Gil

With Don Taylor

With the guys (Richard Erdman, second from left; Neville Brand, third from left)

Stratton, Jr., gets in a telling portrayal as Holden's craven stooge, and Neville Brand, Harvey Lembeck, and others convey tellingly the tensions of men at bay. But it is Holden's many-faceted, tensely authoritative performance that carries the picture; it is the center-piece on which all else hangs. There are fine individual vignettes and small incidents, all of which helped make the play a long-run hit: the guys doing a mass imitation of Hitler; the clowning at Christmastime around a pathetically haphazard tree; the invasion of a nearby camp where Russian women prisoners are lodged. Some of the play's gamy humor and masculine ribaldry has been deleted from the film version, but enough of it remains to promote the effect of a gutsy, rowdy show indeed.

REVIEWS:

Bosley Crowther in *The New York Times:*
The movie which Billy Wilder has made from the stage play *Stalag 17* is one of which any film-maker and any nation's film production might be proud . . . [the film] blinks none of the ugly realities or the wicked ironies

With Otto Preminger

Otto Preminger gets nasty

of being a prisoner of war—at least, under circumstances set up by the Nazis in World War II, and graphically and sensibly reported by sober fellows who were there. . . . Mr. Wilder has very cleverly and aptly coated the pill of this ugly and sobering revelation with some very funny business from his men . . . he has got in this picture, which seems on the surface to be a lusty and raucous reminiscence of a bitter and painful phase of war, a sharply perceptive indication of the ironies contained in modern men.

Life:

As acted by William Holden, *Stalag 17*'s hero-heel emerges as the most memorable character to come out of Hollywood this year. As directed by Billy Wilder and adapted from a 1951 Broadway play of the same name, the movie emerges as the finest comedy drama out of Hollywood this year. Raucous and tense, heartless and sentimental, always fast-paced, it has already been assigned by critics to places on their lists of the year's best ten movies.

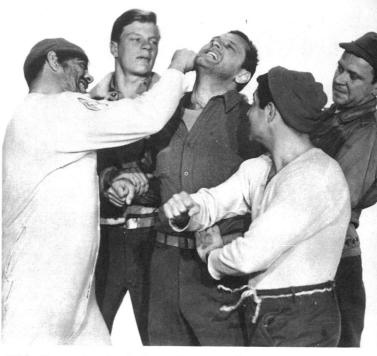

With Harvey Lembeck, Peter Graves, Robert Strauss, and Richard Erdman

With Neville Brand (center), Richard Erdman, and Peter Graves

136

With Robert Strauss and Harvey Lembeck

The New Yorker:

This description of life in a German prison camp during the last war offers some slick melodrama and Billy Wilder has seen to it that there are few lulls in the action . . . we have a fairly incisive depiction, by William Holden, of a crafty manipulator who manages, despite his confinement, to put into effect all kinds of schemes designed to make life easy for himself . . . all in all, though, the people we meet in this German jail are too oppressive to have with us for any length of time, and I doubt whether Mr. Wilder's dramatic stratagems quite overcome that major handicap.

Brog in *Variety:*

A lusty comedy-melodrama, loaded with bold, masculine humor and as much of the original's uninhibited earthiness as good taste and the Production Code will permit. Its raucous flavor will set well with male viewers and even the distaffers should find it acceptable entertainment most of the time. William Holden's name heads the good cast. . . . Holden is very good in his cynical character.

With Neville Brand, Don Taylor, Harvey Lembeck, Peter Graves, Robert Strauss, Richard Erdman, and others

With Maggie McNamara and Gregory Ratoff

The Moon Is Blue

1953   United Artists

CAST:

WILLIAM HOLDEN *(Donald Gresham)*; DAVID NIVEN *(David Slater)*; MAGGIE MC NAMARA *(Patty O'Neill)*; TOM TULLY *(Mr. O'Neill)*; DAWN ADDAMS *(Cynthia Slater)*; FORTUNIO BONANOVA *(TV Singer)*; GREGORY RATOFF *(Taxi Driver)*.

CREDITS:

OTTO PREMINGER *and* F. HUGH HERBERT *(Producers)*; OTTO PREMINGER *(Director); from the play by* F. HUGH HERBERT; ERNEST LASZLO *(Camera)*; HERSCHEL BURKE GILBERT *(Music)*; OTTO LUDWIG *(Editor)*.

Opened at the Victoria and Sutton Theaters, New York, July 8, 1953. Running time, 99 minutes.

THE PICTURE:

The Moon Is Blue set off a controversy in 1953 that seems silly and trivial in the extreme twenty years later. The then rampant and all-pervasive Motion Picture Production Code raised all kinds of hell with it on moral grounds and denied the film a Code seal (a necessity for most films to win if they wished ample dis-tributional outlets) though it passed the censor boards in New York and Pennsylvania. Bosley Crowther, irritated in the face of such nitpicking and puritanism, did not hesitate to point out, along with other right-thinking critics, that the Code folk were merely handing the picture a prime publicity gimmick that would have all kinds of people running to the theater to find out exactly of what the allegedly sinful angle of the "hot potato" movie consisted. If they expected something really wild, they were doomed to disappointment, for the picture has to do with a clever young girl who neatly fends off would-be wolves by asking them disarming questions ("Would you try to seduce me?" "Do you have a mistress?") along with making equally disarming statements ("I would rather be preoccupied than occupied"). *The Moon Is Blue* is actually a pretty moral little tale in which the determined virgin wins her point and states it at tedious length: she is out for an honorable man in an honorable relationship, meaning marriage. Does the whole brouhaha sound incredibly old-fashioned and prim? In permissive 1973 it certainly does, but in 1953 it amounted to an explosive *affaire-*

de-scandale, with producer-director Otto Preminger, always a ready man with a controversy of this kind, jousting at the bluenoses with avid glee (two years later he went into the same kind of tournament for his *Man with the Golden Arm*). In the process he garnered a million dollars' worth of publicity for his film. *The Moon Is Blue* was a version of the 1951 stage hit that starred Barbara Bel Geddes, Barry Nelson, and Donald Cook in the roles later played by Maggie McNamara, Holden, and David Niven. Holden seemed listless and preoccupied in his performance, which well he might, for if the truth be known, the actual plot, such as it was, along with the dialogue, was on the tedious side. Holden picks up McNamara, who forthwith informs him that while he can neck and even attempt seduction if he wants to, his designs on her virginity will prove fruitless, as virgin she will remain come hell and high guys of all kinds and persuasions. Until marriage, of course—she has no plans for single status. The jousting goes on interminably, with aging roué David Niven showing up to try to go Holden one better in the getting-Maggie's-garter maneuverings. Then there is Niven's daughter, Dawn Addams, who has a grudge against Holden because it seems he was too gentlemanly and nonaggressive for her taste on their last date. To repeat, Holden finally gets the girl—but on her terms. By 1973 standards the concoction is so coy, silly, dated, and antiseptically innocuous that revivals of it might occasion more than a little unsolicited levity. Perhaps that is why the film is seldom or ever seen. As for 1973-style women's view of it, these Pill-takers would probably

With Dawn Addams

With David Niven

139

With Maggie McNamara

regard the proceedings as a monstrous bore and a museum piece of the first water—which, let's face it, it is.

REVIEWS:

Bosley Crowther in *The New York Times:*

For all this candid conversation, and this playing around with the thought of a possible seduction (which is not entirely new to the screen) Mr. Herbert is actually telling a highly moral tale. In it a decent little lady completely upsets the pawing wolves by asking disarming questions. She gets her man fairly in the end. Now this may not be the most inventive or amusing little romance ever filmed. As a matter of fact, its limited movement and its talking make it tedious at times. And its slightly labored performance by William Holden, David Niven and Maggie McNamara, does not endow it too strongly with essential vivacity or charm. But moral it is, beyond question, beneath its pretentious

With Maggie McNamara and David Niven

With Maggie McNamara

talk. And that's why it seems so foolish—again, to this corner at least—that this film should have been permitted to become a cause celebre . . . the custodians of the industry's Production Code should have realized that the better part of wisdom and intelligence would have been to approve it for the screen.

Arthur Knight in *Saturday Review*:

A film, like water, can rise no higher than its source, and Herbert, for all his commercial talents, is no Schnitzler. But the question here at issue is neither one of great art nor even of particularly good taste. It is rather a question of whether American movies are continually to be hamstrung by rules that confine picture themes, picture morals and picture language to what is deemed fit for children—or for childlike mentalities. *The Moon Is Blue* is what the trade refers to as "a good, commercial picture." It is amusing, has neat comedy performances by William Holden and David Niven, and introduces an enchanting young actress, Maggie McNamara.

Variety:

The entertaining adult comedy of this film version of the legit play would enjoy healthy grosses in most dates even without the exploitation lift a controversy over its lack of a Production Code seal may provide. As key city fare the romantic farce seems a natural and, as the less cosmopolitan centers are just as hep to what makes the world go 'round, its release chances generally are good. . . . Preminger's guidance gives it pace within the confines of a few sets and much dialogue by using extremely mobile camera angles and the natural stage movement of the players. The cast work is standout with William Holden and David Niven breaking about even for male honors and newcomer Maggie McNamara presenting an interesting talent as the femme lead. . . . Niven's middleaged playboy is mighty fancy laugh acting and Holden takes no back seat in the comedic battle over a dame.

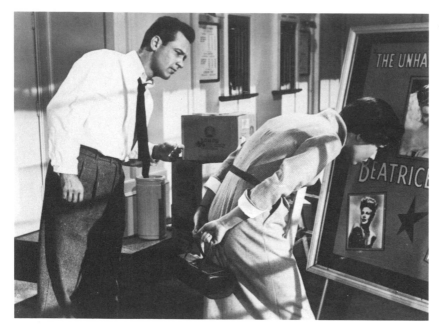

Forever Female

1954   Paramount

CAST:

GINGER ROGERS *(Beatrice Page);* WILLIAM HOLDEN *(Stanley Krown);* PAUL DOUGLAS *(E. Harry Phillips);* JAMES GLEASON *(Eddie Woods);* JESSE WHITE *(Willie Wolfe);* MARJORIE RAMBEAU *(Herself);* GEORGE REEVES *(George Courtland);* KING DONOVAN *(Playwright);* VIC PERRIN *(Scenic Designer);* RUSSELL GAIGE *(Theatrical Producer);* MARION ROSS *(Patty);* RICHARD SHANNON *(Stage Manager);* KATHRYN GRANDSTAFF, RAND HARPER *(Young Hopefuls);* HENRY DAR BOGGIA *(Felix);* VICTOR ROMITO *(Maitre d');* HYACINTHE RAILLA *(Waiter);* and PAT CROWLEY *as Sally Carver.*

CREDITS:

PAT DUGGAN *(Producer);* IRVING RAPPER *(Director);* JULIUS J. *and* PHILIP G. EPSTEIN *(Writers); suggested by the play* Rosalind *by* JAMES M. BARRIE; HARRY STRADLING *(Director of Photography);* HAL PEREIRA *and* JOSEPH MAC MILLAN JOHNSON *(Art Direction);* GORDON JENNINGS *(Special Photographic Effects);* FARCIOT EDOUART *(Process Photography);* SAM COMER *and* ROSS DOWD *(Set Decoration);* DOANE HARRISON *(Editorial Advisor);* EDITH HEAD *(Costumes);* ARCHIE MARSHEK *(Editor);* JOHN COONAN *(Assistant Director);* WALLY WESTMORE *(Makeup);* HARRY LINDGREN *and* JOHN COPE *(Sound);* VICTOR YOUNG *(Music).*

Opened at the Victoria Theater, New York, January 13, 1954. Running time, 93 minutes.

THE PICTURE:

If Sir James M. Barrie had only known that his relatively sedate play, *Rosalind,* would wind up a bitchy, fast-paced, hard-nosed Broadway showbiz affair, he might have turned turtle in his last resting place—and then maybe he wouldn't have, for his could be a whimsical, ironic intelligence on occasion. In any event, director Irving Rapper presented a typical man-woman and woman-woman free-for-all with nice romantic overtones, and Julius and Philip Epstein gave Sir James's original a groovy going-over for generally fair results. The film is rarely revived, and probably doesn't deserve more than a fair share of attention anyway, being distinctly on the lightweight side. Ginger Rogers was no Bette Davis as an aging stage star still trying to play it young. Holden is a supermarket clerk who writes a play. It's about a teenage girl (nineteen, it says here) and her domineering mother. Holden, who thinks he has written something immortal, encounters Rogers and her ex-husband, Paul Douglas, a stage producer. Douglas decides to stage the play IF the nineteen-year-old character is moved up to age twenty-nine so that Miss Rogers can take it over and shine for her fans. Then there's ambitious young Pat Crowley who wants to be Eve to Rogers' Margo, it would appear, for she sees the teenage role as star-potential for *her*. Despite her efforts, the play is readjusted to fit Rogers' requirements, and naturally it flops in tryout. Meanwhile Rogers has fallen in love with Holden and so has Crowley. Predictably enough, Douglas gets into the act to engineer matters so that Holden gets Crowley (and vice-versa), and Douglas gets Rogers for a marital reprise. There was some criticism of Miss Rogers' hyper-mannered and affected performance as the Margo Channing–type star determined to turn back the clock. Possibly she felt it called for bravura playing in spades. Holden, in the enviable position of being chased by two women at once, gave out with more than his usual aplomb under the ego-inflating circumstances. Miss Crowley, a pert little thing, shone briefly—but *then* what became of her?

With Pat Crowley

With Pat Crowley and Paul Douglas

With Pat Crowley

With Jesse White and Ginger Rogers

REVIEWS:

Variety:

A slickly-devised Broadway-show-biz romantic comedy, cast with familiar names, that should have easy going at the boxoffice in its key dates. It bears down a bit hard on the show world flavor for the more general entertainment taste, and the plot structure is on the lightweight side, but the comedy values are excellent, presentation polished and playing amusing; so it adds up to acceptable screenfare. There's special appeal to the trade hangers-on . . . writing team cloaks the plot in nifty dialogue that zips along with tradey quips, and Irving Rapper's direction makes the most of this in handling the situations and players for chuckles. Holden and Douglas give the offering solid acting support . . . Miss Rogers bears down on the stage queen character but hits her peak in the sequence where she acknowledges her age.

With Paul Douglas and
Ginger Rogers

145

With Eleanor Parker and Richard Anderson

Escape from Fort Bravo

1954   Metro-Goldwyn-Mayer

CAST:

WILLIAM HOLDEN *(Captain Roper)*; ELEANOR PARKER *(Carla Forrester)*; JOHN FORSYTHE *(Captain John Marsh)*; WILLIAM DEMAREST *(Campbell)*; WILLIAM CAMPBELL *(Cabot Young)*; JOHN LUPTON *(Bailey)*; RICHARD ANDERSON *(Lieutenant Beecher)*; POLLY BERGEN *(Alice Owens)*; CARL BENTON REID *(Colonel Owens)*.

CREDITS:

NICHOLAS NAYFACK *(Producer)*; JOHN STURGES *(Director)*; FRANK FENTON *(Screenplay)*; PHILIP ROCK *and* MICHAEL PATE *(Story)*; JEFF ALEXANDER *(Music)*; *Photographed in Ansco Color*; ROBERT SURTEES *(Photography)*; ALVARD EISEMAN *(Color Consultant)*; CEDRIC GIBBONS *and* MALCOLM BROWN *(Art Directors)* EDWIN B. WILLIS *and* RALPH HURST *(Set Decoration)*; WARREN NEWCOMBE *(Special Effects)*; HELEN ROSE *(Women's Costumes)*; SYDNEY GUILAROFF *(Hair Styles)*; WILLIAM TUTTLE *(Makeup)*.

Opened at the Mayfair Theater, New York, January 22, 1954. Running time, 98 minutes.

THE PICTURE:

With *Escape From Fort Bravo*, Holden returned to his first Western setting since *Streets of Laredo* and made his first movie at MGM. Eleanor Parker and John Forsythe co-starred, and director John Sturges kept the proceedings moving smoothly. Though nothing terribly original materialized, the writing and acting proved of sufficient quality to maintain interest. In this, Holden is a Union captain in charge of Confederate prisoners at a stockade in Arizona; the year, 1863. Holden is disliked by his fellow officers, to say nothing of the Confederates, because of his harsh treatment of escapees, whom he always recaptures. When he drags a sensitive young prisoner, John Lupton, back to the fort with a rope around his neck, ostensibly to set an example for

other would-be escapees, the men turn their backs on him and his commanding officer, Carl Benton Reid, remonstrates. Holden, however, is a man of integrity beneath his rigid code, and he reminds his superior that discipline is essential and that after all, he isn't responsible for the world he finds himself living in. To the fort comes Eleanor Parker, ostensibly for the marriage of her friend, the commandant's daughter, to a young officer. In reality she is a Confederate agent who proceeds to engineer the escape of Forsythe, the officer who leads the prisoners, and some of his men. She cultivates Holden, comes to know him for the man he really is (a thoughtful, sensitive fellow who grows plants behind his billet) and soon finds herself in love with him. But

duty comes first, and she leaves with the escapees under cover of night in the cart of a tradesman who is a Confederate ally. A disillusioned Holden sets out in pursuit. When he catches up with them, he engages in a fistfight with Forsythe, who is also in love with Miss Parker, and treats the lady with cool scorn. The party set out to return to the fort, but are waylaid by Indians and pinned down behind a small ridge. Lupton captures one of the horses that have strayed and disappears; he

is branded a cowardly deserter. The Indians rain arrows on the small band, and Forsythe and others are wounded. Forsythe begs Holden to take Parker and make a run for it. He reveals to Holden that the woman, though adamant in her fidelity to her cause, was and is truly in love with him. Holden decides to try to save the group by pretending to the Indians that he is the sole survivor of their brutal "arrow-artillery" barrage. After leaving a loaded pistol with Parker, he exposes himself to them and opens fire. He is wounded, but at that moment a rescue detachment from the fort arrives, led by Lupton, who proves no cowardly deserter after all. Forsythe dies, but the others return to the fort. All these plot elements had, of course, been done to death in many a prior oater, but Sturges, as before noted, kept it all quick-paced, slick, and professional. The film proved popular with 1954 audiences.

REVIEWS:

Brog in *Variety:*

A well-made drama of the early west, cavalry versus Indians school, a cut above the usual run of outdoor feature in its star names, plot development and fresh scenic backgrounds. Ticket-buyers who don't demand action just for action's sake will find it a rewarding drama. The film carries a constantly mounting tension as it builds carefully to the exciting climax, which is actionful enough for anyone. The air of expectancy is well established in the excellent Frank Fenton script and by the response of stars William Holden, Eleanor Parker and John Forsythe to John Sturges' meticulous direction. The trouping is top-grade and gives validity to the drama.

The *New York Times:*

A basically standard triangle that perks up for some random, tingling Indian skirmishes but remains radiantly dwarfed nearly all the way by the towering grandeur of the Ansco color backgrounds . . . but the most exasperating paradox of this off-keel "class" horse opera is the undercurrent of arch badinage flavoring the dialogue, from the lengthy lovelorn sequences of Mr. Holden and Miss Parker to the bloodiest moments. The cast consequently seems confused throughout, although Mr. Holden's dour, cryptic performance comes off best.

The *New York Herald Tribune:*

There is hardly time to notice the personalities in the midst of so much action, yet William Holden manages to register from time to time in a firm performance of a brusque young officer forging ahead with the business of war . . . these essentials of rough work in a rough country are vigorously presented by director Sturges.

William Holden (left) with Richard Anderson (right)

With June Allyson

Executive Suite

1954   Metro-Goldwyn-Mayer

CAST:

WILLIAM HOLDEN *(McDonald Walling)*; FREDRIC MARCH *(Loren Phineas Shaw)*; BARBARA STANWYCK *(Julia O. Tredway)*; JUNE ALLYSON *(Mary Walling)*; WALTER PIDGEON *(Frederick Alderson)*; SHELLEY WINTERS *(Eva Bardeman)*; PAUL DOUGLAS *(Josiah Dudley)*; LOUIS CALHERN *(George Nyle Caswell)*; DEAN JAGGER *(Jesse Q. Grimm)*; NINA FOCH *(Erica Martin)*; TIM CONSIDINE *(Mike Walling)*; WILLAM PHIPPS *(Bill Ludden)*; LUCILE KNOCH *(Mrs. George Nyle Caswell)*; EDGAR STEHLI *(Julius Steibel)*; MARY ADAMS *(Sara Grimm)*; VIRGINIA BRISSAC *(Edith Alperson)*; HARRY SHANNON *(Ed Benedeck)*.

CREDITS:

JOHN HOUSEMAN *(Producer)*; ROBERT WISE *(Director)*; ERNEST LEHMAN *(Screenplay)*; *adapted from the novel by* CAMERON HAWLEY; JUD KINBERG *(Associate Pro-* *ducer)*; GEORGE FOLSEY *(Photographer)*; CEDRIC GIBBONS *and* EDWARD CARFAGNO *(Art Directors)*; DOUGLAS SHEARER *(Recording Supervisor)*; RALPH E. WINTERS *(Editor)*; EDWIN B. WILLIS *and* EMIL KURI *(Set Decorators)*; HELEN ROSE *(Gowns)*; SYDNEY GUILAROFF *(Hairstyles)*; WILLIAM TUTTLE *(Makeup)*; GEORGE RHEIN *(Assistant Director)*.

Opened at Radio City Music Hall, New York, May 6, 1954. Running time, 115 minutes.

THE PICTURE:

Holden co-starred with Fredric March for the first time in *Executive Suite*, a compelling story of the assorted machinations of vice-presidential would-be successors to the dynamic head of a prosperous furniture company who has just dropped dead. Holden plays the idealistic and honest young designer who wants to see standards

With Barbara Stanwyck

With Fredric March and Walter Pidgeon

and quality enhanced in the company product. March portrays the ruthless, self-seeking company controller whose materialistic outlook promises to up profits while diluting the product quality. These two are joined in their struggle for the top spot by other aspirants, one a man incapable of firm decisions, another a production man who essentially wants to retire, and the third a married man who has been dallying with an office mistress. March, who stops at nothing to achieve power, attempts to apply some refined-blackmail pressure on the latter. The spirit of Cameron Hawley's exciting bestseller was retained, and indeed improved, with much of the novel's underbrush cleared away by screenwriter Ernest Lehman and director Robert Wise so as to adhere to the basic story line uncluttered by side excursions. Also on hand are such distaff assets as Nina Foch, as a secretary devoted to her boss who is crushed by his

With Shelley Winters

With Walter Pidgeon

death, Barbara Stanwyck as the dead man's mistress, and June Allyson in another variation of the steadfast, faithful wife. Eventually matters reach a boil at the meeting to elect the new president, and of course intrepid young Holden wins the day after an impressive speech during which he wins the deciding vote of jaded, disillusioned board member Stanwyck. Holden and March played well against each other (they were to team up again in a picture made shortly thereafter). The climactic scene is well-handled and suspenseful, with Holden the essence of intrepid purpose and March accepting his eventual defeat with sickly-sour politeness. The critics gave March—deservedly—most of the acting honors (March made the most of the meatiest role in the picture). Holden, however, held his own very well in the more sympathetic role. Everyone concerned gave competent accounts of themselves, including fine character stars Walter Pidgeon and Louis Cal-

With Louis Calhern, Paul Douglas, Fredric March, and Nina Foch

hern, and Barbara Stanwyck, who found herself in her first picture with Holden since *Golden Boy* fifteen years before. In a recent letter to the author, Mr. March spoke graciously of Holden. He wrote, "As to Bill Holden, he's one of the finest men I've ever known—an excellent actor and a joy to work with, kind and generous to his fellow actors. I have never seen him give anything but an outstanding performance."

REVIEWS:

The *New York Herald Tribune:*

The film demonstrates in many personal frictions how the best-qualified man finally gets the job, and why this should be so. Under Robert Wise's direction, it is as politely guarded as a junior executive's opinion—the beating heart under the dark blue lapel rarely shows through. The interplay of the characters is cleverly presented, though, and the rarefied atmosphere of upper echelon politics is carefully established. At home with his bright young wife (June Allyson) and baseball-

minded son (Tim Considine) or clashing with his fellow-executives, it is (Holden's) assignment to be both likeable and strong-minded, and he carries it out efficiently . . . by far the most acute performance in the movie is that of Fredric March.

Bosley Crowther in *The New York Times:*

It is a not pretty but very lucid portrait of a rodent that Mr. March draws. On the other hand Mr. Holden's blueprint of a smartly-tailored young executive is in the agreeable tradition of the success-magazine ideal. He runs a nice home with June Allyson. He plays baseball with his kid. He is respectful toward his elders. He is diligent in trying to perfect a new veneer. The only trouble with all these people as directed by Robert Wise is that they are strictly two-dimensional. They are what you might call prototypes. Neither Mr. Wise nor the actors ever make humans out of them. They give no substantial illusion of significance, emotion or warmth.

With Paul Douglas, Fredric March, Dean Jagger, and Walter Pidgeon

With Humphrey Bogart, Walter Hampden, and Nella Walker

Sabrina

1954   Paramount

CAST:

HUMPHREY BOGART *(Linus Larrabee);* AUDREY HEPBURN *(Sabrina Fairchild);* WILLIAM HOLDEN *(David Larrabee);* WALTER HAMPDEN *(Oliver Larrabee);* JOHN WILLIAMS *(Thomas Fairchild);* MARTHA HYER *(Elizabeth Tyson);* JOAN VOHS *(Gretchen Van Horn);* MARCEL HILLAIRE *(The Professor);* NELLA WALKER *(Maude Larrabee);* MARCEL DALIO *(Baron);* FRANCIS X. BUSHMAN *(Mr. Tyson);* ELLEN CORBY *(Miss McCardle).*

CREDITS:

BILLY WILDER *(Producer and Director);* BILLY WILDER, SAMUEL TAYLOR *and* ERNEST LEHMAN *(Screenplay); based on the play* Sabrina Fair *by* SAMUEL TAYLOR; CHARLES LANG JR. *(Director of Photography);* FREDERICK HOLLANDER *(Music);* HAL PEREIRA *and* WALTER TYLER *(Art Directors);* SAM COMER *and* RAY MOYER *(Set Decorations);* EDITH HEAD *(Costumes);* WALLY WESTMORE *(Makeup);* ARTHUR SCHMIDT *(Editor);* C. C. COLEMAN, JR. *(Assistant Director);* HAROLD LEWIS *and* JOHN COPE *(Sound);* JOHN P. FULTON *and* FARCIOT EDOUART *(Special Effects).*

Opened at the Criterion Theater, New York, September 22, 1954. Running time, 113 minutes.

THE PICTURE:

Fresh from tilting with furniture-company malefactors in *Executive Suite* at MGM, Holden returned to Paramount to play the pace-changing role of the spoiled younger brother of a wealthy Long Island family in *Sabrina.* In this film he found himself outclassed by an ironically wry Humphrey Bogart and a scintillatingly chic Audrey Hepburn. With his hair unaccountably lightened to ash blond for the part, Holden at age thirty-six had difficulty sustaining credibility as a dapper society playboy of a particularly juvenile cast, and his co-stars garnered the best reviews and the most attention. Billy Wilder produced and directed; he gave the lightly-amusing and deliciously-subtle proceedings a tone and style that would have done credit to the late lamented Lubitsch himself. Based on the Broadway play *Sabrina Fair*, which had starred Margaret Sullavan, and boasting a pungent, witty screenplay by Wilder, Taylor, and Ernest Lehman, the picture turned out to be one of the biggest hits of 1954. The fact that it starred no less than three recent Oscar winners (Miss Hepburn and Holden for 1953, Bogart for 1951) certainly didn't hurt the box office or the film's prestige values. Miss Hepburn was never more delightful, fey, and charming than as Sabrina, the chauffeur's daughter who hopelessly loves the wastrel son of the house, Holden, who lives only for fast cars and champagne and a good time. When Sabrina attempts suicide after languishing over the unattainable Holden, who can't see his wispy chauffeur's daughter for dust, her father, John Williams, packs her off to Paris to learn cooking. When she returns she is a chic, beautifully groomed young international sophisticate. At last the womanizing Holden sits up and takes notice. But his socialite parents, Walter Hampden and Nella Walker, have other plans for Holden; to marry him off to well-connected Martha Hyer. It then falls to the stuffy, forbiddingly efficient older son and head of the Larrabee enterprises, Humphrey Bogart, to distract Miss Hepburn with a simulated courtship. However, Bogart finds he has

With Audrey Hepburn and Humphrey Bogart

fallen in love with the lady himself, and in the end they go off to Europe together. The proceedings are handled throughout with soufflé expertise and the requisite light touch. Situations, dialogue, and acting are topnotch, Miss Hepburn and Bogart especially delivering with crisp professionalism. The role of Sabrina was tailor-made for Miss Hepburn. Though Bogart reportedly did not care for his part, he revealed here that his years as a drawing-room lead on Broadway had stood him in good stead and lent a needed versatility to his film

With Audrey Hepburn

With Audrey Hepburn

image; his was a delightful performance. Holden is overshadowed throughout; his role is ill-defined, essentially a foil for the others. Though billed third under Bogart and Hepburn, he nonetheless shared in this comedy's warm reception.

With Ellen Corby and Humphrey Bogart

REVIEWS:

Time:

When Hollywood's abracadabblers find a new formula for turning celluloid into gold, they overwork it every time. For *Sabrina*, based on Samuel Taylor's Broadway hit, Paramount's magicians used the same elements that worked so well in *Roman Holiday:* actress Audrey Hepburn, Director Billy Wilder, a switch on the old Cinderella story. Gold, in a word, is guaranteed at the boxoffice, and this is never less than a glittering entertainment, but somehow a certain measure of lead has found its way into the formula. Actress Hepburn's appeal, it becomes clearer with every appearance, is largely to the imagination; the less acting she does, the more people can imagine her doing, and wisely she does very little in *Sabrina*. That little she does skillfully. By contrast, actor Holden seems almost too true to a banal type to be good. Bogart, however, being as much a symbol as the Hepburn is—and a cunning scene stealer besides—holds his own with ease, and sometimes even sets little Audrey down, toreador pants and all, as a Vogue model who has risen above her station.

Alex Barris in *Casting About:*

Perhaps the happiest thing about this generally happy movie is the bright dialogue that Samuel Taylor, Ernest Lehman and Wilder have sprinkled throughout... Miss Hepburn is a natural for these Cinderella roles, and Holden and Bogart can handle themselves skillfully in light comedy.

Variety:

A slick blend of heart and chuckles makes *Sabrina* a sock romantic comedy that should catch on... a class, adult comedy that will be liked by the masses.... Bogart is socko as the tycoon with no time for gals until he tries to get Miss Hepburn's mind off Holden. The latter sells his comedy strongly, wrapping up a character somewhat offbeat for him. Miss Hepburn again demonstrates a winning talent for being Miss Cinderella and will have audiences rooting for her all the way.

The Christian Science Monitor:

Miss Hepburn is principally required to be bewitching, a requirement she fulfills with no trouble at all. Mr. Bogart makes an avuncular wooer of the big tycoon. Mr. Holden to some extent redeems, with a relaxed comedy style, one of the silliest parts he has been called upon to play.

With Grace Kelly and Bing Crosby

The Country Girl

CAST:

1954   Paramount

BING CROSBY *(Frank Elgin)*; GRACE KELLY *(Georgie Elgin)*; WILLIAM HOLDEN *(Bernie Dodd)*; ANTHONY ROSS *(Phil Cook)*; GENE REYNOLDS *(Larry)*; JACQUELINE FONTAINE *(Singer-Actress)*; EDDIE RYDER *(Ed)*; ROBERT KENT *(Paul Unger)*; JOHN W. REYNOLDS *(Henry Johnson)*; IDA MOORE *(First Woman)*; FRANK SCANELL *(Bartender)*; RUTH RICKABY *(Second Woman)*; HAL K. DAWSON, HOWARD JOSLIN, RICHARD KEENE, JACK KENNEY *(Actors)*; CHARLES TANNEN *(Photographer)*; LES CLARK *(Another Actor)*; ALLAN DOUGLAS *(Man)*; DON DUNNING *(Expressman)*; MAX WAGNER *(Second Expressman)*; BOB ALDEN *(Bellboy)*; CHESTER JONES *(Ralph)*; JOHN FLORIO *(Photographer)*; JACK ROBERTS *(Man)*.

CREDITS:

WILLIAM PERLBERG *(Producer)*; GEORGE SEATON *(Director and Screenwriter)*; *from the play by* CLIFFORD ODETS; JOHN F. WARREN *(Director of Photography)*; HAL PEREIRA *and* ROLAND ANDERSON *(Art Direction)*; JOHN P. FULTON *(Special Photographic Effects)*; SAM COMER *and* GRACE GREGORY *(Set Decoration)*; FRANCISCO DAY *(Assistant Director)*; ELLSWORTH HOAGLAND *(Editor)*; ARTHUR JACOBSON *(Assistant to the Producer)*; EDITH HEAD *(Costumes)*; WALLY WESTMORE *(Makeup Supervision)*; GENE MERRITT *and* JOHN COPE *(Sound Recording)*; ROBERT ALTON *(Musical Sequence Staging)*; VICTOR YOUNG *(Music)*; *Songs by* IRA GERSHWIN *and* HAROLD ARLEN.

Opened at the Criterion Theater, New York, December 15, 1954. Running time, 104 minutes.

THE PICTURE:

Holden also drew third billing after Bing Crosby and Grace Kelly in *The Country Girl*, the Paramount movie version of the striking Clifford Odets play that had starred Uta Hagen on Broadway. This film, however, proved as much a dramatic plus for him as had his other third-billing 1954 picture, *Sabrina*—in fact more so, for this time around he had a strong, well-conceived role and delivered in fine, forceful, manly style. Nor was he on this occasion overshadowed by his two co-stars, as he had been in *Sabrina*. Director George Seaton, who had helped boost Holden's postwar career

157

With Grace Kelly

with *Apartment for Peggy*, saw to it that Holden profited from his well-staged sequences as much as did Kelly (who won an Oscar for her portrayal) and Crosby. The literate and adult screenplay dealt with a director of Broadway shows, Holden, who seeks to help a faded stage star, Crosby, recover his lost eminence in a new role. Crosby is timid and unsure of his ability to stage a major comeback, and when Holden encounters Crosby's dour, embittered, and forbidding spouse, Miss Kelly, he develops the impression that she is responsible for the dive in her husband's morale and career fortunes. A contest of wills develop between Holden and his star's wife. He attempts to banish her from her husband's vicinity, but it develops that she is the strong one of their marriage. Crosby, it seems, had become depressed after their small son had been killed by a car while his father let go of his hand to pose for a picture. For the following decade he is consumed by guilt while his neglected career slides downhill. Miss Kelly, it develops, had patiently stood by him, humored his moods, tolerated his drinking—and as Holden comes to know her, and at last comprehends her long-suffering heroism, he finds he has fallen in love. Between them, wife and director put the star on his feet, and he is a Broad-

With Bing Crosby and Grace Kelly

With Bing Crosby

way hit. Holden offers his love to Miss Kelly, but she decides that now that Crosby is his own man again, there is a chance for their marriage; she returns to her now self-confident husband. Holden and Miss Kelly played their scenes together extremely well, delineating with consummate delicacy and wise restraint Holden's gradual evolvement from contemptuous dislike to admiring respect and finally to deep love. Miss Kelly, in a role that represented a radical departure from her prior glamour roles, amply deserved her Oscar, submerging her personality in a sound and well-thought-out characterization. Nor was Crosby found lacking, his sound depiction of the escapist-minded Frank Elgin, who finally recovers his independence and self-respect, being one of his finest screen portrayals. The picture, in summation, was first-rate in all departments, including direction, photography, and writing, and certainly ranks as one of Holden's more creditable vehicles.

REVIEWS:

Look:

A stark film, with the deceptively cheerful title of *The Country Girl*, hurls the dramatic thunderbolt of the year ... this is an important movie event because the

With Grace Kelly

With Anthony Ross

stars, in surprising roles, have the courage to give uncompromising performances. [The actors] play this human tragedy with a compassion and psychological insight reaching the best traditions of dramatic skill.

Crosby is the most likely candidate for the year's best dramatic performance by an actor. He's that good. Which is not to suggest that the fine supporting performances by Grace Kelly as his loyal wife, and by William Holden as the director who helps him make a comeback, do not help enormously. They do. Actually it is the trio that make *The Country Girl* the prize-winner it is bound to be. The Crosby-Kelly-Holden team comes just about as close to theatrical perfection as we are likely to see onscreen in our time.... Odets' dialogue is literate and realistic, the backgrounds are authentic, the direction swift, natural and dynamic, and the performances superbly conceived.

John Beaufort in *The Christian Science Monitor:*
As Bernie Dodd, William Holden gives the solid, tremendously vital kind of performance that has made him one of Hollywood's most valuable actors. In *The Country Girl* he employs an astute actor's skills to tell the truth about a somewhat familiar theater type—a bristling egocentric whose talent influences people but whose arrogance doesn't win friends. Bernie's only home is his work.

With Bing Crosby

With Grace Kelly

The Bridges at Toko-Ri

1955   Paramount

CAST:

WILLIAM HOLDEN *(Lt. Harry Brubaker, USNR)*; FREDRIC MARCH *(Rear Adm. George Tarrant)*; GRACE KELLY *(Nancy Brubaker)*; MICKEY ROONEY *(Mike Forney)*; ROBERT STRAUSS *(Beer Barrel)*; CHARLES MC GRAW *(Cdr. Wayne Lee)*; KEIKO AWAJI *(Kimiko)*; EARL HOLLIMAN *(Nestor Gamidge)*; RICHARD SHANNON *(Lt. Olds)*; WILLIS B. BOUCHEY *(Capt. Evans)*; NADENE ASHDOWN *(Kathy Brubaker)*; CHERYL LYNN CALLOWAY *(Susie)*; JAMES JANKINS *(Assistant C.I.C. Officer)*; MARSHALL V. BEEBE *(Pilot)*; CHARLES TANNEN *(M.P. Major)*; TERU SHIMADA *(Japanese Father)*.

CREDITS:

WILLIAM PERLBERG *(Producer)*; MARK ROBSON *(Director)*; *a* PERLBERG–SEATON Production; VALENTINE DAVIES *(Screenplay)*; adapted from the novel by JAMES A. MICHENER; LOYAL GRIGGS *(Photographer)*; CHARLES G. CLARKE *(Aerial Photography)*; WALLACE KELLEY *and* THOMAS TUTWEILER *(Second Unit Photography)*; HAL PEREIRA *and* HENRY BUMSTEAD *(Art Directors)*; LYN MURRAY *(Music)*; ALMA MACRORIE *(Editor)*; EDITH HEAD *(Costumes)*; WALLY WESTMORE *(Makeup)*; HUGO GRENZBACH *and* GENE GARVIN *(Sound)*; COMMANDER M. U. BEEBE, USN *(Technical Advisor)*; Color by Technicolor.

Opened at Radio City Music Hall, New York, January 20, 1955. Running time, 102 minutes.

THE PICTURE:

Holden and March were reunited in *The Bridges at Toko-Ri*, one of those overblown, flag-waving, superchauvinistic war epics that were already becoming *déja vu* relics by 1955. Holden is an aircraft-carrier-based pilot, March is the admiral who has to send pilots out to dangerous missions in Korea and grieves when the death toll soars, and Grace Kelly is the lovely, worried wife of Holden who watches and waits, and visits him in Tokyo. There is no little philosophizing about war and fate, but the action hogs the scene. Charles G. Clarke's aerial photography is spectacular, there are second-unit photography exploits that advance cinema art in this genre, and Mark Robson's direction

161

of the story, taken from a James A. Michener novel, is about as competent as the subject permits. But there was some critical regret expressed over the waste of Robson's talents, *and* March's, *and* Holden's, to say nothing of Grace Kelly, who at the time was up for an Academy Award for *The Country Girl* (which she subsequently won). At any rate, Holden gets in some intimate scenes with Miss Kelly. March gets to make an affecting speech about men who fly off a treacherously tossing deck, perform difficult missions in strange terrain, then return to find (from the air) a tiny speck of deck in a wide, angry sea. March as the admiral is dignified and solid; he lends the picture no little substance. Holden has the lion's share of footage and makes the most of it, clambering in and out of planes, romancing his wife Miss Kelly, conducting weighty discussions with March, kidding with his buddies, and giving the enemy hell from the air. While genuine opportunities for fine acting are simply not afforded Holden, given the nature of his part, he does get in a lot of physical action, which no doubt kept his physique, if not his art, limber. The bridges of the title are key spots in North Korea, and it is up to Holden and his pals to annihilate them in order to forestall enemy movements. The boys do their work well, but at the cost of their lives, including Holden's. He does *not* finale (as is usual in such films) for a clinch with Miss Kelly. A clever production, a plethora of energy

With Grace Kelly

in all departments, lavish settings, the aforementioned prodigious photography, a sterling performance by March, an action-matinee-idol-style competent one by Holden, an affecting if perfunctory one by Miss Kelly— the 102-minute film had all these. Today, though, it seems, on viewing, dated and superpatriotic and somehow glossy, due partly to the current national disillusionment with war as a policy instrument.

REVIEWS:

Saturday Review:

Although well and professionally cast, the film has no

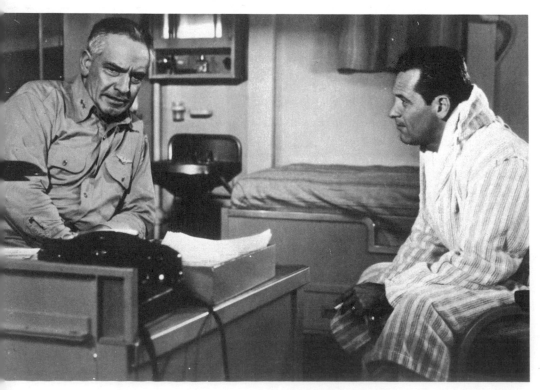

With Fredric March

With Mickey Rooney and Earl Holliman

of carrier flying are shown so beautifully that it is enormously satisfying to hear the admiral's period to the piece, as he says with wonder and sorrow, "Where do we find such men?"

Cue:

A taut, thrilling, top-flight documentary drama of men, war, ships and planes. For all the film's explosively exciting naval and aerial action—brilliantly photographed in color—the film is a study of men's minds as well as their military actions.

William K. Zinsser in the New York Herald Tribune:

Holden is his usual competent self throughout, and Miss Kelly—well, everybody knows how nice it is to have *her* around.

The New Yorker:

[The Film] undertakes to show why a peace-loving thirty-five-year-old lawyer from Denver is willing to risk his life piloting a jet plane over Korea. Directed by Mark Robson, it includes some spectacular footage of jet planes . . . and some high-altitude photography that is quite exciting, but the picture is not all of a piece, and when it interrupts its aerial maneuvers to explore the motivations of its chief character, it sometimes becomes rather pedestrian . . . in the role of the jet pilot, William Holden does all right as a solid American warrior.

single performance markedly above the level of high motion-picture competence. The difference is in the development, which has been purged of untruth. There are heroics in this film, but they are in what men do, not in what they say. . . . The fascination and danger

With Earl Holliman and Mickey Rooney

163

With Jennifer Jones

Love Is a Many-Splendored Thing

1955   20th Century-Fox

CAST:

WILLIAM HOLDEN *(Mark Elliott)*; HAN SUYIN *(Jennifer Jones)*; TORIN THATCHER *(Mr. Palmer-Jones)*; ISOBEL ELSOM *(Adeline Palmer-Jones)* MURRAY MATHESON *(Dr. Tom)*; ANN RICHARDS *(Virginia Gregg)*; RICHARD LOO *(Robert Hung)*; SOO YONG *(Nora Hung)*; PHILIP AHN *(Third Uncle)*; JORJA CURTRIGHT *(Suzanne)*; DONNA MARTEL *(Suchen)*; CANDACE LEE *(Oh-No)*; KOM TONG *(Dr. Sen)*; JAMES HENG *(Fifth Brother)*; HERBERT HAYES *(Father Lon)*; ANGELA LOO *(Mei Loo)*; MARIE TSIEN *(Rosie Wu)*; ELEANOR MOORE *(English Secretary)*; BARBARA JEAN WONG, HAZEL SHON *(Nurses)*; KEI CHUNG *(Intern)*.

CREDITS:

BUDDY ADLER *(Producer)*; HENRY KING *(Director)*; JOHN PATRICK *(Screenplay); from the* HAN SUYIN *novel,* A Many-Splendored Thing; LEON SHAMROY *(Photography)*; ALFRED NEWMAN *(Music)*; Song *"Love is a Many-Splendored Thing"* by SAMMY FAIN and PAUL FRANCIS WEBSTER. *Color by Deluxe; CinemaScope.*

Opened at the Roxy Theater, New York, August 18, 1955. Running time, 102 minutes.

THE PICTURE:

Love Is a Many-Splendored Thing is a quotation from the poet Francis Thompson's work, *The Kingdom of God*—and one wonders what the late distinguished religious bard would have thought of the 1955 movie whose title reflects his words, although applied in quite a different context, due to the question whether Thompson would have felt any affinity with woo-pitching Hollywood style. *Love* was considerably touted at the time of its original release, but to my mind it has not held up well after eighteen years. The romance of Jennifer Jones, quite good as the Eurasian doctor in Hong Kong,

With Jennifer Jones

and William Holden, his usual manly and assured self as the married American war correspondent, had elements of the tired and the banal in it then, and has even more so now. But the women just loved it back there in the still-romantic fifties, and the handkerchiefs got damp in theaters all over the United States—or anyway those that TV hadn't emptied. Certainly this interracial romance is presented in a more creditable manner than the cheap, falsely sentimental, and mendacious treatment of a similar theme in Holden's 1960 *World of Suzie Wong*. Suzie was, of course, a prostitute while the Jones character is a doctor, but there is a pungent taste of soap to the proceedings as viewed in 1973. One can't help wondering just how much the Sammy Fain–Paul Francis Webster tune, which was phenomenally popular (same title as the film) and which blared endlessly from jukeboxes during 1955, contributed to the film's popularity. One is also inclined to blame the then-hyperactive 20th Century-Fox publicity bandwagon for much of the hue and cry. Director Henry King, who lathered on the soap effectively in the 1925 *Stella Dallas* (and who got a more effective performance out of Jennifer Jones in *Song of Bernadette* than in *Love*), guided this elegant and well-mounted tearjerker for maximum effect, and there was no denying the lavish production values provided by Buddy Adler. The John Patrick screenplay from the Han Suyin novel tended to slowness and an excess of talk, which King's directorial pacing only occasionally relieves. I for one have never thought that Jones and Holden as a pair of impassioned lovers ever threatened to eclipse the legend of Garbo and Gilbert. The plot, such as it is: Eurasian medico Jones meets correspond-

With Jennifer Jones

165

With Jennifer Jones

With Jennifer Jones

166

ent Holden in Hong Kong. They fall deeply in love and for a time things are idyllic. Then Jones encounters standard prejudices against Eurasians at the hospital where she works. Holden's married status is another heartache. The petty-minded dowagers of the snide British colony do their best to belittle the affair. Holden's wife won't give him a divorce. Compromised and jobless at the film's conclusion, Jones persists in loving loyally and completely while Holden goes off on a Korean War assignment. When word comes that he has been killed, she goes to the verdant hill that she associates with his spirit and their love, and there communes as best she can while the Fain–Webster tune bellows deafeningly from the soundtrack. There's lots of gooey Deluxe color, too. To repeat, an awful lot of people have admired this film since 1955, but I have always been able to think of at least twenty love pictures I liked better. There was always something too exotically pat about this one, at least for my taste, and too many of the novel's subthemes were sacrificed to the love stuff, or were presented fleetingly and superficially.

REVIEWS:

Hollywood Reporter:

In this beautiful and sensitive motion picture . . . Buddy Adler has concentrated the highly skilled efforts of many technicians on the telling of a very simple bittersweet love story about a lovely Eurasian doctor . . . one of the best women's pictures made in some years. . . . Jennifer Jones paints a picture that few men will be able to resist. . . . Henry King, who piloted her to greatness in *The Song of Bernadette*, makes every small thing eloquent. . . . Bill Holden quietly throws all his vitality as an actor into the task.

Daily Variety:

A beautiful, absorbing motion picture. Women particularly will be attracted by it. . . . Men will find themselves just as engrossed in the poignant story. . . . *Love* should be a boxoffice winner . . . Buddy Adler's production scores on all counts. . . . Henry King's direction captures all the tenderness and moving qualities. . . . Miss Jones is excellent as Han Suyin, her performance rating favorably with anything else she has done in the past. She captures the audience to the point of complete absorption. . . . Holden turns in another excellent performance, carrying sympathy all the way.

Fred Hift in *Weekly Variety:*

Love, as portrayed and dramatized in this fine and sensitive Buddy Adler production based on the Han Suyin bestseller, is indeed a many-splendored thing and, unless audiences have lost their romantic inclinations, it ought to make for a plenty strong boxoffice. Miss Jones' accomplishment in a very difficult part is quite remarkable and contributes greatly to the film's success. Her love scenes with Holden sizzle without ever being cheap or awkward. In her the spirit of the book is caught completely.

With Jennifer Jones and director Henry King

With Kim Novak

Picnic

1956   Columbia

CAST:

WILLIAM HOLDEN *(Hal Carter)*; ROSALIND RUSSELL *(Rosemary Sydney)*; KIM NOVAK *(Madge Owens)*; BETTY FIELD *(Flo Owens)*; SUSAN STRASBERG *(Millie Owens)*; CLIFF ROBERTSON *(Alan Benson)*; ARTHUR O'CONNELL *(Howard Bevans)*; VERNA FELTON *(Mrs. Helen Potts)*; RETA SHAW *(Linda Sue Breckenridge)*; NICK ADAMS *(Bomber)*; RAYMOND BAILEY *(Mr. Benson)*; ELIZABETH W. WILSON *(Christine Schoenwalder)*; PHYLLIS NEWMAN *(Juanita Badger)*; DON C. HARVEY *(First Policeman)*; STEVE BENTON *(Second Policeman)*.

CREDITS:

FRED KOHLMAR *(Producer)*; JOSHUA LOGAN *(Director)*; DANIEL TARADASH *(Screenplay); Based on the play "Picnic" by* WILLIAM INGE; *Produced on the stage by* the Theatre Guild, Inc. and JOSHUA LOGAN; JAMES WONG HOWE *(Camera)*; JEAN LOUIS *(Gowns)*; GEORGE DUNING *(Music)*; MORRIS STOLOFF *(Musical Conductor)*; WILLIAM FLANNERY *(Art Director)*; JO MIELZINER *(Production Designer)*; CHARLES NELSON *and* WILLIAM A. LYONS *(Film Editors)*; ROBERT PRIESTLEY *(Set Decorator)*; CARTER DE HAVEN JR. *(Assistant Director)* CLAY CAMPBELL *(Makeup)*; HELEN HUNT *(Hair Styles)*; JOHN LIVADARY *(Recording Supervisor)*; GEORGE COOPER *(Sound)*; ARTHUR MORTON *(Orchestrations)*; FRED KARGER *(Music Advisor)*; RAY DARY *(Second Unit Photography); Color by Technicolor; Technicolor Color Consultant,* HENRI JOFFA; *CinemaScope.*

Opened at Radio City Music Hall, New York, February 16, 1956. Running time, 115 minutes.

THE PICTURE:

Holden next starred in the film version of William Inge's sensitive, concentrated depiction of smalltown Kansas life, *Picnic*, which had been a successful 1953 Broadway play with Ralph Meeker and Janice Rule in the roles essayed in the film by Holden and Kim Novak. Joshua Logan directed both versions. As the charming but shiftless drifter who sends the Salinson, Kansas, women's blood-pressure soaring when he makes a sudden appearance in their town, Holden gave a thoughtful, sincere and at times powerful performance but there were two things wrong with it: At thirty-seven he was simply too old for the role and looked it (a number of people thought Meeker should have repeated his role, but box-office considerations required a Hollywood "name"), and moreover, he was forced to delineate the complexities, internal and external, of a character quite opposite to his own and with which he was not subconsciously in sympathetic identificatory rapport. As noted elsewhere, Holden was to some extent limited to playing various extensions of his own personality, and the rootlessness, the dreamy escapism, and the

unrealistic outlook of Hal Carter were fundamentally alien to Holden's temperament and mystique as a man. The play itself had been a simple and intimately observed slice-of-life piece, of the kind that Inge made his own, and when blown up with color and Cinema-Scope into a host of extraneous scenes thought cinematic, it tended to lose some of its poignant humanity. Even in 1956 there was a certain stilted self-consciousness to the picture, a strong hint of reality forced and twisted somewhat out of shape. As seen on TV recently, its dated aspects are apparent. They indicate how far we have come from manners and mores accepted unquestioningly in the fifties. Today much of Inge's work tends to seem quaint, grainily sentimentalized, humanistically forced, and posturing. These flaws are all the more noticeable in the film version, in which everything is magnified in peaches-and-cream photography. The picnic that gives the film (as the play) its title comes on as an overblown Busby Berkeley-style, Brobdingnagian-Hollywood idea of how the simple folk of a Kansas town would amuse themselves on holiday. The plot has the drifter coming to town to look up an old

With Susan Strasberg

169

With Cliff Robertson

schoolmate, Alan (Cliff Robertson), who is the town rich-man's son and from whom he hopes to obtain work. Robertson is patronizingly kind at first—until Holden starts making time successfully with his light o' love Madge (Kim Novak), a restless, vaguely discontented woman of great beauty who feels men are attracted only to her surface attributes. Her less attractive sister (Susan Strasberg) also falls for Holden as does every other woman around, especially after he disports himself half-naked, dances suggestively at the picnic with Novak, and brags about incidents in his past. At the picnic matters reach a climax when repressed, unmarried schoolteacher Roz Russell loses her self-control while drunk and practically accosts Holden on the dance floor, tearing his shirt. When he rebuffs her she turns on him with lacerating scorn; later she begs shy bachelor Arthur O'Connell to marry her. Some critics thought Russell overplayed; *I* thought her vivid and arresting in a bravura way that spiked up the proceedings. Betty Field is on hand as the worried mother who fears for Novak's happiness if she passes up Robertson, and Verna Felton is the kindly neighbor who initially employs him. After Holden and Novak use Robertson's car for spooning, he accuses Holden of stealing it and gets him run out of town. Holden begs Novak, now emotionally awakened, to come with him. Though Field

With Rosalind Russell, Arthur O'Connell, and Susan Strasberg

170

With Susan Strasberg, Arthur O'Connell, and Cliff Robertson

begs her to stay, fearful that in like-mother-like-daughter style she will repeat her own unhappy marriage, the woman follows the fleeing drifter, obviously preferring to be unhappy with a flawed man she loves than to be happy with a solid citizen she does not. Among the players, Miss Novak was physically attractive but emotionally wooden; Miss Strasberg vice-versa; Miss Field warm and wise and womanly; Miss Felton gently compassionate; Miss Russell tangy and vital; Mr. Robertson passable in a role Paul Newman, incidentally, had played on Broadway; and Mr. O'Connell (repeating his stage role) delightfully down-to-earth as the hapless guy Russell finally ropes into matrimony.

REVIEWS:
The New Yorker:

William Inge's modest play, adapted to the vastness of CinemaScope under the direction of Joshua Logan, has become a sort of Middle Western Roman holiday. Mr. Logan's notion of an outing in the corn country includes a choir of at least a hundred voices, a camera so alert that it can pick up the significance of the reflection of a Japanese lantern in a pool (futility, wistfulness, the general transience of life, as I get it) and a sound track let loose in the most formidable music I've heard in my time at the movies. All this surging background stuff is applied to nothing more than the story of a kind

With Cliff Robertson, Don C. Harvey, Raymond Bailey, and Steve Benton

171

With Kim Novak

of literate tramp who hops off a freight train in a Kansas town and sets every female heart to yearning. I presume that the young fellow is a variant on Pan, but in the person of William Holden he's a very gloomy type. His influence on the community is profound, however. Within a half hour of debouching from his rattler, he has the women, young and old, figuring out their emotional life like a mob of accountants and coming up with the notion that they've all been short-changed at the store called love.

With Kim Novak

William K. Zinsser in the *New York Herald Tribune*:
Logan and Mielziner shape their drama with hundreds of images and vignettes, meticulously chosen to capture not only the fun but the stifling social climate of small-town life. It is ironic that all these passions erupt at the picnic which represents tradition and organized wholesomeness. The actors are excellent. Holden is handsome, weak, irresponsible and, somehow, appealing in his enthusiasm.

John Beaufort in *The Christian Science Monitor*:
Mr. Holden paints a portrait in depth of the confused, lonely, sometimes comically absurd hero of the story. The actor sees beneath Hal's awkwardness and callow bragging to the young man's uncertainty and harrowing desperation. By the time Hal has blundered in and out of the vulnerable backyard world of Flo Owens and her Salinson, Kansas neighbors, Mr. Holden has given a major screen performance.

Variety:
The boards-to-screen transplanters correctly refrained from making any basic changes with Inge's characters and the circumstances in which they're involved. William Holden is the drifter, sometimes ribald, partly sympathetic and colorful and giving a forceful interpretation all the way.

With Kim Novak

With Betty Field, Cliff Robertson, Verna Felton, Kim Novak, Rosalind Russell, Arthur O'Connell, and Susan Strasberg

With Deborah Kerr

The Proud and the Profane

1956   Paramount

CAST:

WILLIAM HOLDEN *(Lt. Col. Colin Black)*; DEBORAH KERR *(Lee Ashley)*; THELMA RITTER *(Kate Connors)*; DEWEY MARTIN *(Eddie Wodcik)*; WILLIAM REDFIELD *(Chaplain-Lt. (J.G.) Holmes)*; ROSS BAGDASARIAN *(Louis;)* ADAM WILLIAMS *(Eustace Press)*; MARION ROSS *(Joan, Red Cross Worker)*; THEODORE NEWTON *(Bob Kilpatrick)*; RICHARD SHANNON *(Major)*; PETER HANSEN *(Lt. (J.G.) Hutchins)*; WARD WOOD *(Sgt. Peckinpaugh)*; GERALDINE HULL *(Helen, Red Cross Worker)*; ANN MORRISS *(Pat, Red Cross Worker)*; DON ROBERTS *(Lt. Fowler)*; DON HAUSE *(Marine)*; BOB KENASTON *(Soldier)*; TAYLOR MEASOM *(Marine-Serviceman)*; JACK RICHARDSON *(Sailor)*; FREEMAN MORSE *(Paul)*; GEORGE BRENLIN *(3rd Casualty)*; ROBERT MORSE *(2nd Casualty)*; RAY STRICKLYN *(1st Casualty)*; ANTHONY MORAN *(Case)*.

CREDITS:

WILLIAM PERLBERG *(Producer)*; GEORGE SEATON *(Director and Screenwriter)*; *based on a novel by* LUCY HERNDON CROCKETT; JOHN F. WARREN *(Camera)* HAL PEREIRA *and* EARL HEDRICK *(Art Direction)*; JOHN P. FULTON *(Special Photographic Effects)*; VICTOR YOUNG *(Music)*; FARCIOT EDOUART *(Process Photography)*; SAM COMER *and* FRANK R. MC KELVY *(Set Decorations)*; ALMA MACRORIE *(Editor)*; RIC HARDMAN *(Assistant to the Producer)*; EDITH HEAD *(Costumes)*; WALLY WESTMORE *(Makeup)*; FRANK BAUR *(Asst. Director)*; HUGO GRENZBACH *and* GENE GARVIN *(Sound)*. LT. JOHN W. ANTONELLI, USMC; MARGARET HAGAN, LOUISE A. WOOD, MARY LOUISE DOWLING *of the American National Red Cross (Technical Advisors)*; VistaVision.

Opened at the Astor Theater, New York, June 13, 1956. Running time, 111 minutes.

THE PICTURE:

The publicists assigned to this film made much of sensitive, ladylike Deborah Kerr's meeting—and achieving sensational chemistry with—manly, forceful William Holden, but advance buildups for the film, its stars, and its general content proved in the fullness of time to be both proud and profane. Shot on location

With Deborah Kerr

in the Virgin Islands, the picture certainly had a good starting premise: Kerr loves Holden, Kerr loses Holden, Kerr gets him back—but as spelled out in the screenplay of George Seaton, who also directed, and as acted by the principals and an able supporting cast, it just didn't convince or move. Anyway, it seems that Miss Kerr is a war widow who comes to New Caledonia during World War II to locate the grave of her dead lieutenant husband, who died at Guadalcanal, and to learn, if possible, of his last days. While on the staff of the Red Cross unit headed by wry yet motherly Thelma Ritter, she meets, and runs afoul of, tough Marine officer Holden. He scorns sentiment, lives only for his outfit, and thinks Red Cross doughnut-dispensers don't belong in the realistic world of combat danger. In line with the opposites-attract principle, Holden pursues Kerr, who is at first repelled by his crass directness and lack of sensibility but finally goes along with him in the hope he will tell her about her deceased mate. The cue now is love—and plenty of it—and Miss Kerr shortly finds herself pregnant by the brash officer. It seems, however, that he is married, and upon discovering this Kerr attempts to end it all. Holden frustrates her suicide attempt, but she loses the unborn child. The colonel then returns to combat, the plot con-

With Deborah Kerr

veniently jettisons the obstructive wife by killing her off (she was an alcoholic, it seems), and when the wounded Holden returns in comatose state on a cot murmuring "forgive me," Kerr's womanly heart melts once more. Dewey Martin is on hand as a leatherneck with a crush on Miss Kerr; he later dies in combat. William Redfield is a chaplain, and he is given some really icky dialogue, poor guy. Adam Williams is the attendant in the Marine cemetery whose gentle words trigger in Kerr the realization that her approach to her late husband had been essentially a shallow and selfish one. Thelma Ritter was her usual self as the lovable Red Cross supervisor; she is given a few good lines to deliver, which she exploits as much as she can. But critics roasted the picture as poorly motivated and unconvincing, what with its spurious plot developments, turgid romance, and distracting subplots, all of which countered to deadly effect that overly ballyhooed "Kerr-Holden chemistry."

REVIEWS:

John Beaufort in *The Christian Science Monitor:*
Lieutenant Colonel Colin Black, a part Indian, is played with a bristling moustache and a fierce impacted aggression by William Holden. . . . Miss Kerr is ladylike without being insipid, forthright yet extremely feminine. . . .

The Proud and the Profane is skillfully enough acted, under Mr. Seaton's direction, to acquire a monetary validity. But its emotions are shallow, its motivations cliché-ridden, and its plot developments include such a fortuitous dodge as having the colonel's alcholic wife expire conveniently before the picture ends . . . it seems doubtful that [the film] will do much to enhance the reputation of the team which produced *The Country Girl.* But the damage, if any, will doubtless be no more than temporary.

Gene in *Variety:*

Holden and Miss Kerr have name weight which, together with the bally buildup, ought to assure good openings. But the story doesn't stand up, taking spurious turns and inviting neither audience participation nor sympathy for any of its characters. Entry is a shaky one for the long haul . . . the script comes off as if authored by a soap opera practitioner trying for a follow-up to *From Here To Eternity.* Seaton's a good man with the pen as attested by previous credits but this time out he seems to have lost some balance. . . . Holden, Miss Kerr [and other cast members] can't overcome the unconvincing script.

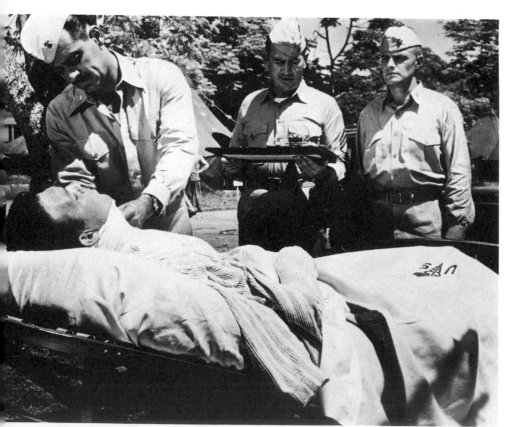

William Holden

Toward the Unknown

1956   Warners

CAST:

WILLIAM HOLDEN *(Maj. Lincoln Bond);* LLOYD NOLAN *(Brig. Gen. Banner);* VIRGINIA LEITH *(Connie Mitchell);* CHARLES MC GRAW *(Col. Mickey McKee);* MURRAY HAMILTON *(Maj. Bromo Lee);* PAUL FIX *(Lt. Gen. Brian Shelby);* JAMES GARNER *(Maj. Joe Craven);* L. Q. JONES *(Lt. Sweeney);* KAREN STEELE *(Polly Craven);* MALCOLM ATTERBURY *(Hank);* BARTLETT ROBINSON *(Senator Black);* RALPH MOODY *(H. G. Gilbert);* MAURA MURPHY *(Mrs. Sara McKee);* CAROL KELLY *(Debby).*

CREDITS:

A Toluca Production; MERVYN LE ROY *(Producer and Director);* BEIRNE LAY, JR. *(Writer and Associate Producer);* HAL ROSSON *(Photographer);* PAUL BARON *(Music);* WILLIAM ZIEGLER *(Editor);* RUSS SAUNDERS *(2nd Unit Director);* HAROLD E. WELLMAN *(2nd Unit Photographer);* LEO E. KUTER *(Special Effects); Photographed in WarnerColor.*

Opened at the Paramount Theater, New York, September 27, 1956. Running time, 114 minutes.

THE PICTURE:

Holden went "independent" for the first time with *Toward the Unknown,* which was made for Warners by his Toluca Productions. The day of the actor-producer was getting into high, James Stewart having led the parade, and Alan Ladd, Burt Lancaster, John Wayne, Gary Cooper, and other stars were assuming creative control of their productions and garnering percentage deals. The days of star contracts with studios, what with the TV threat and stars' distaste for heavy tax bites, was about over, and with a number of box-office films and an Oscar in his background, Holden was ready to hold his own with the best. Photographed in handsome WarnerColor and written by Beirne Lay, Jr., who doubled as associate producer, this film about jet pilots and hazardous tests of untried craft was a far cry from the earlier *Blaze of Noon,* which had dealt with primitive airmail transport in the 1920s. Directed tautly by Mervyn LeRoy, who also produced, and with the complete cooperation of the U.S. Air Force to bolster its authenticity, the drama, set against the background of the Air Force flight test center, was well photo-

With Virginia Leith, Karen Steele, and James Garner

Lloyd Nolan and Virginia Leith

graphed by Hal Rosson, with Paul Baron's music an underplayed-yet-expressive element in stressing the testing heroics. Holden plays Major Lincoln Bond, who would rather test planes than do anything else in life; he has on his record, however, a history of having cracked under brainwashing in Korea, and his commanding general, Lloyd Nolan, at first refuses to allow him to test complex new jets, feeling he is not reliable and will break at crucial moments. Loyally backing Holden in his attempts to prove he has recovered his nerve is Virginia Leith, the general's secretary and steady date, who was once involved with Holden and had been hurt by his withdrawal from her since his misfortunes overtook him. He tries to explain to her that he needs time to recover, but she protests that her love for him had remained constant throughout and that he should have let her help. Nolan, who is also in love with Miss Leith, senses a renewal of her interest in Holden, and his distrust of Holden's air performances, which he has reluctantly allowed him to resume, is complicated by his jealousy. But Holden proves himself an able test pilot, exposing "Wing Wrinkles" as authentic structural defects despite the manufacturer's protests, and when he rescues Nolan from a tight spot during a test flight, the general begins to regard him more favorably. When an important new jet is to get a final test, Nolan wants to fly it, though he is not in the best of health and is overage. The two men quarrel when Holden tries to tell him the truth, warning him that his

pride and stubbornness are jeopardizing the entire operation. Holden later tests the jet himself, barely escaping with his life. Nolan finally faces the fact that he isn't the man he used to be, and accepts a transfer. Miss Leith chooses to stay with Holden, who has now redeemed her faith in him and his faith in himself. The picture is well-acted and splendidly executed in all departments, with such sterling character players as Paul Fix and Charles McGraw lending the principals solid support. James Garner has a small part as a pilot who dies in a test, leaving behind a wife who bears up courageously when his pal Holden gives her the news. "Man will not only endure—he will prevail" is the motto of Nolan, who all but steals the picture from the nominal star, so sure and cool and poised and utterly authoritative is he in his role. Miss Leith is adequate in her part, the color is striking, the jet-testing scenes look authentic. Of course 1956-style testings can't help looking somewhat dated in 1973, but the action is keen, the acting has bite—and we have all seen worse examples of the genre.

REVIEWS:

John Beaufort in *The Christian Science Monitor:*

As Bond, Mr. Holden gives another of his solid portrayals of a man tensely at grips with a personal problem. Mr. Nolan is first-rate as the general. The other players behave for the most part in a fashion which reflects nothing but credit on Air Force pilots and their wives. The screen play includes the admissible editorializing which helps secure official Air Force cooperation for films like *Toward the Unknown* ... the picture naturally achieves its highest and most breathtaking drama in the aerial sequences.

A. H. Weiler in *The New York Times:*

Producer-director Mervyn LeRoy has taken advantage of the special attributes of the terrain, the men and their highly specialized and risky tasks ... [it] makes for authentic pictorial excitement. The personal saga of Maj. Lincoln Bond whom Mr. Holden portrays with tight-lipped sincerity, is a less absorbing matter, however. As the flier for a test pilot's berth while laboring under the stigma of having broken under Korean Communist brainwashing, he encounters situations that are not entirely inspired ... the principals, to put it briefly, are never as fascinating as the aircraft pointed at the future.

Joe Pihodna in the *New York Herald Tribune:*

William Holden [plays] with admirable restraint ... [the film] is undoubtedly effective as a recruiting de-

With Virginia Leith

vice. Those uniforms and shiny new air machines certainly have a strong appeal ... take-offs, landings, parachute jumps and special acrobatics by Thunderbirds take up enough of the ... running time to relieve the monotony of the command tactics and love-making.

With Lloyd Nolan

The Bridge on the River Kwai

1957   Columbia

CAST:

WILLIAM HOLDEN *(Shears)*; ALEC GUINNESS *(Colonel Nicholson)*; JACK HAWKINS *(Major Warden)*; SESSUE HAYAKAWA *(Colonel Saito)*; JAMES DONALD *(Major Clipton)*; GEOFFREY HORNE *(Lieutenant Joyce)*; ANDRE MORELL *(Colonel Green)*; PETER WILLIAMS *(Captain Reeves)*; JOHN BOXER *(Major Hughes)*; PERCY HERBERT *(Grogan)*; HAROLD GOODWIN *(Baker)*; ANN SEARS *(Nurse)*; HENRY OKAWA *(Captain Kanematsu)*; K. KATSUMOTO *(Lieutenant Miura)*; M. R. B. CHAKRABANDHU *(Yai)*; *Siamese Girls:* VILAIWAN SEEBOONREAUNG, NGAMTA SUPHAPHONGS, JAVANART PUNYNCHOTI, KANNIKAR WOWKLEE.

CREDITS:

SAM SPIEGEL *(Producer)*; DAVID LEAN *(Director)*; PIERRE BOULE *(Screenplay. from his own novel)*; JACK HILDYARD *(Photography)*; MALCOLM ARNOLD *(Music)*; PETER TAYLOR *(Editor)*; *Color by Technicolor; Photographed in Ceylon.*

Opened at the Palace Theater, New York, on a two-a-day run, December 18, 1957. Running time, 161 minutes.

THE PICTURE:

Rolewise, Holden played a distinct second fiddle to Alec Guinness in *The Bridge On the River Kwai* (Guinness won the 1957 Academy Award for his performance as the martinet British officer), but there were compensating elements for Holden: The film has netted him, via a wisely charted percentage deal, a generous annuity that promises to go on forever. At the time of its initial release the film had cost $2 million; by 1960 it had grossed $30 million in worldwide rentals. A rousing adventure film with a World War II period background, and shot on location against the fascinating terrain of the island of Ceylon, the picture features vivid characters who seem to be drawn from life. The point driven home by Pierre Boule in his novel on which the movie is based, "war is madness" is set forth in stark and clear terms during the steadily intensifying action and the controlled, subtly rhythmic mood established by the masterly hand of director David Lean. Guinness is truly superb as the British colonel who is an impossible prig and rigid martinet, but nonetheless a brave and dedicated soldier who lives strictly by the book. His regiment has been captured by the Japanese, and his men are later ordered to build a

With Jack Hawkins and Geoffrey Horne

With Alec Guinness

bridge over the canyon of the River Kwai. Guinness refuses to order his officers to do manual labor, and the Japanese commander, Sessue Hayakawa, who is also a consummate and rigid egotist, find that they are unable to budge Guinness from his stand by torture or any other means. His ace with the Japs is that his officers alone have the engineering skill to construct the bridge. When construction does begin, Guinness insists on per-fection in every detail. The fact that the completed structure will serve enemy purposes is a truth that Guinness ignores; all that matters to him is that he demonstrate what British manpower can accomplish even under desperate and handicapped circumstances. Holden plays an American sailor masquerading as a commander who escapes from the Jap prison camp commanded by Hayakawa. After undergoing many

William Holden

hardships, Holden reaches a base hospital and declares himself a coward, applying for a medical discharge. Opportunistic shirking and self-preservation are his only interests. But he is then partly cajoled, partly browbeaten into joining a raiding party that is to push through the thick jungle to blow up the bridge, which Allied air patrols have spotted. The bridge does get destroyed, with a now-demented Guinness, carried away by the "glories" of the bridge, dying in its defense, and at the last, accidentally falling on the detonator that destroys his men's masterwork. Holden etches a compelling portrait of a shirker who is forced against his will into becoming a hero of sorts. Jack Hawkins too is splendid as a typical English martinet. But the picture is Guinness's and he is magnificent throughout.

REVIEWS:

C. A. Lejeune in the *London Observer:*

There is a great deal to admire in [the film]. Pierre Boule's novel about the conflict between different sorts of high fanaticism had iron in its blood, and whenever David Lean's direction is able to catch that irony the effect is prodigious. . . . Mr. Holden, to be quite frank, is rather in the way of the main development, and Jack Hawkins, as Major Warden, can't quite wrench life out of an army type over-simplified. Alec

With Jack Hawkins and Geoffrey Horne

182

With Jack Hawkins

Guinness hits off Colonel Nicholson brilliantly, as a Commanding Officer of supreme fearlessness with no emotional concessions.

Alton Cook in the *New York World Telegram:*

[The film] may rank as the most rousing adventure film inspired by the last World War . . . its characters run to a strange variety but they remain valid, seeming to spring out of the background of the picture. Their casual rise to exploits of foolhardy valor makes the deeds seem credible. . . . Holden is understandable as the shirker who could be goaded into heroism only when there was no recourse. A ramrod of British military strength and devotion is played by Jack Hawkins. Good as these performances are, they are overshadowed by the gem of a paradox offered by Guinness, with his perverted ideas of loyalty and duty so long as regulations were observed . . . along with his director, David Lean, and his scenarists (Sam Spiegel) found humor, roaring robust laughter and the agony and hardship of war. His eye for spectacle and scenic majesty never was relaxed.

184

William Holden

Arthur Knight in the *Saturday Review:*

Unlike so many of the multimillion-dollar super-spectacles which seem to equate sheer bulk with entertainment value, *Kwai* starts out with something important to say, something to prove. "War is madness" is M. Boule's central theme—a madness that afflicts conquered and conquerors alike. And all the time, all the money, sweat and inspiration expended on this production have gone into the elaboration of this theme into an affecting, dramatic, suspenseful motion picture. . . . David Lean's direction, while never obscuring this philosophic base, gives the film an aura of high adventure by pacing it in the tempo of an action picture. Each incident, imaginatively staged and tersely edited, leads swiftly to the nerve-wracking finale, the blowing up of the bridge. . . . The playing, especially of Guinness and Hayakawa as proud, obsessed, opposing martinets, is overwhelmingly effective; they make their forbidding characters understandably human.

Kap in *Variety:*

A gripping drama, expertly put together and handled with skill in all departments . . . there are notable performances from the key characters but the film is unquestionably Guinness's. He etches an unforgettable portrait of the typical British army officer, strict, didactic and serene in his adherence to the book. . . . Holden turns in another of his solid characterizations, easy, credible and always likeable in a role that is the pivot point of the story.

With Ann Sears

The Key

1958   Columbia

CAST:

WILLIAM HOLDEN *(David Ross)*; SOPHIA LOREN *(Stella)*; TREVOR HOWARD *(Chris Ford)*; OSCAR HOMOLKA *(Captain Van Dam)*; KIERON MOORE *(Kane)*; BERNARD LEE *(Wadlow)*; BEATRIX LEHMAN *(Housekeeper)*; NOEL PURCELL *(Hotel Porter)*; BRYAN FORBES *(Weaver)*; SIDNEY VIVIAN *(Grogan)*; RUPERT DAVIES *(Baker)*; RUSSELL WATERS *(Sparks)*; IRENE HANDL *(Clerk)*; JOHN CRAWFORD *(American Captain)*; JAMESON CLARK *(English Captain)*.

CREDITS:

A Columbia Release; a Highroad (British) Presentation; a CAROL REED *Production; a* CARL FOREMAN *Picture;* CARL FOREMAN *(Producer)*; CAROL REED *(Director)*; CARL FOREMAN *(Screenplay); based on the novel* Stella *by* JAN DE HARTOG; OSWALD MORRIS *(Photographer)*; BERT BATES *(Art Director)*; MALCOLM ARNOLD *(Music)*; WILFRED SHINGLETON *(Production Manager)*; CECIL F. FORD *(Editor)* GERRY O'HARA *(Assistant Director)*; GEOFFREY DRAKE *(Camera Operator)*; ARTHUR IBBETSON *(Special Effects)*; WILLIS COOK *(Sound)*; PETER HANDFORD *and* W. MILNER *(Makeup)*; DAVE AYLOTT *(Hairstyles)*; BARBARA RITCHIE *(Assistant Editor)*; VALERIE LESLIE *(Wardrobe Designer)*; BEATRICE DAWSON *(Wardrobe)*; BILL WALSH *and* EILEEN WELCH *(Technical Advisors)*; CAPTAIN J. BROOME, R.N., COMMANDER P. PEAKE, R.N., COMMANDER N. HANTER, R.N., *and* COMMANDER M. PAYNTER, R.N. *(Consultants); Filmed at Associated British Studios, Elstree, England; Cinema-Scope.*

Opened at Odeon and Fine Arts Theaters, New York, July 1, 1958. Running time, 125 minutes.

THE PICTURE:

When this somewhat tedious and slyly prurient drama was released in 1958, a number of critics made a lot of noise about its alleged "symbolism," "profundity," "wit," "suspense," "interplay of human and natural forces," and so on, but to this writer it has seemed after several viewings over the past fifteen years, to be just another tired movie sex-ploy, however well mounted.

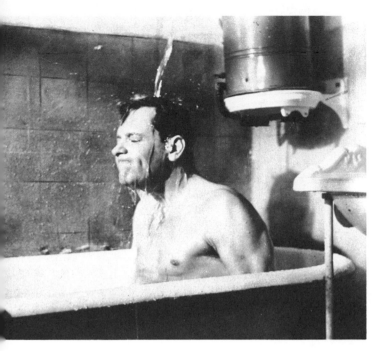

It gives the distinct impression that its rather outré and unconventional romantic hinge was its chief appeal to producers, and thus, they assumed, to 1958 audiences. Jan de Hartog, in his novel *Stella*, on which this film was based, was a conscientious literary craftsman who tried to say something meaningful about human relationships, the contrariness of fate, the delicate and tenuous threads by which love establishes contact with reality. Some of this is retained in the movie, to be sure; the sea-action scenes are well-staged and photographed with some artistry, and Holden and Miss Loren do their level best to inject the maximum sincerity and depth into their on-screen love relationship. But the writer is still left with the uncomfortable feeling that sex pure and simple was the chief appeal of this movie in the eyes of its makers—and that they were willing to put up with a certain amount of stylistic and philosophic window-dressing in order to sell what they regarded as the prime element. The story gives away the game. It seems that Miss Loren is a lady who has gone

With Sophia Loren

187

along with a strange rite indeed—that of "the key." This key idea was originated by a sea captain who, concerned about his possible demise in the dangerous work of commanding a rescue tug for crippled convoy freighters (the time is 1941), tried to insure his lady-love Loren's future by bequeathing a duplicate key to their flat to each succeeding tug captain. When he dies, Loren finds herself "entertaining" one key-owner after another (each with unfailing regularity had thoughtfully passed the dupe on to the next one). Trevor Howard, number three, passes it on to William Holden, number four, an American in Canadian service, then obliges the plot by getting killed along with his prede-cessors, thus clearing the way for some romantic profile-to-profile smooching for the Holden-Loren combine, who proceed to demonstrate at interminable length that Love Is Indeed a Many-Splendored Thing. Holden finally decides he loves Loren so much that he hands her the duplicate key to indicate that he is to be the last (*that* must have come as a relief to her after all that prior activity). Loren proceeds to register deep joy that all that is behind her. But alas, it is not to be, for Holden, fearful that he too will pass into the land of shades, slips his key to handsome Kieron Moore, still another sea captain on the lookout for shore-leave con-solation. When Loren is confronted with this new

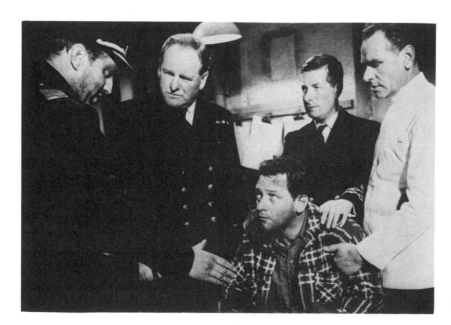

William Holden

*With Kieron Moore and
Trevor Howard*

With Sophia Loren

matinee-profile complete with key, she feels that Holden has betrayed their love. But our hero has not died at sea after all—he makes it back to shore eventually, and to their flat. Loren, however, fed up at last with revolving-door amour, no matter how tragically romantic the frosting, informs him she has had it. Does she forgive him? Do they get together? Do you care by now? We didn't. Reed's direction is best in the ocean scenes—at least he has something adult and palpable to work with there; in the more "intimate" scenes the likes of George

Cukor and Robert Z. Leonard would have run rings around him. The CinemaScope photography is okay (the picture was filmed in England), the rescue work by the tugs not without its share of excitement and drama—the rest is fundamentally twaddle. Whatever Holden himself may have thought of the picture, he did manage to insure still another advantageous financial deal for his participation in the proceedings, so it must have left a good taste in his mouth for this reason at least. A bevy of fine English supporting actors, incidentally, make some of the business look more meaningful than it is.

REVIEWS:

Time:

On the surface the film seems little different from a hundred other stories of men in war and women in love—except perhaps in the finesse of the witty and suspenseful writing and editing. But just beneath the surface can be glimpsed the glinting corpus of a hero myth—the story of the fight with a dragon, the release of a captive, the awakening of a sleeping beauty ... all this is beautifully expressed in the film—a language of symbol: the key, the wedding ring, the marriage with death, the sea, the enemy, the fight, the stairs, the tree of life ... one of the year's most strongly affecting pictures.

Saturday Review:

One of the best films of its kind in recent years. All great action pictures—and *The Key* is fundamentally that—have been characterized by the interplay of human and natural forces. [Reed] has managed to introduce natural forces into his story and make them serve his own ends.... William Holden's performance is one of the best yet of his artistically accelerating career. Miss Loren is alternately warm and wistful, but dominating all else is the masterly direction of Sir Carol Reed.

Rich in *Variety:*

Holden is heroic, edgy, tender and understanding—one of his best all-round showings.

Paul Beckley in the *New York Herald Tribune:*

One of the really excellent examples of movie storytelling, and what's more, it does not temper either unpleasantness or unconventionality. [The film has] a distinct odor of reality ... without making any apology to morality, the situation is handled with delicacy and not a breath of lasciviousness for its own sake ... in many ways a gentle film with very great respect for the feelings of men. [The stars] have given their roles a penetrating reality under the superb direction of Carol Reed.

Bosley Crowther in *The New York Times:*

A thoroughly brilliant blending of vivid war action and generally poignant romance. Carol Reed has got the color, excitement and technique of the work of rescue

Discussing a scene with director Sir Carol Reed, Sophia Loren, and writer Carl Foreman

With Sophia Loren

tugs in the Western approaches as keenly as the action of destroyers was got in Noel Coward's *In Which We Serve*. From his actors Mr. Reed has got the best. Mr. Holden is both cynical and sensitive. Miss Loren is affectingly distant yet quickly tender.

The Horse Soldiers

1959   United Artists

CAST:

JOHN WAYNE *(Colonel Marlowe);* WILLIAM HOLDEN *(Major Kendall);* CONSTANCE TOWERS *(Hannah);* ALTHEA GIBSON *(Lukey);* HOOT GIBSON *(Brown);* ANNA LEE *(Mrs. Buford);* RUSSELL SIMPSON *(Sheriff);* STAN JONES *(General U.S. Grant);* CARLETON YOUNG *(Colonel Miles);* BASIL RUYSDAEL *(Boys' School Commandant); and* HANK WORDEN, WILLIAM LESLIE, KEN CURTIS, BING RUSSELL, *and* O. Z. WHITEHEAD.

CREDITS:

A United Artists Release; a MAHIN–RACKIN *Production for the Mirisch Company;* JOHN LEE MAHIN *and* MARTIN RACKIN *(Producers);* JOHN FORD *(Director);* JOHN LEE MAHIN *and* MARTIN RACKIN *(Screenplay); based on the novel by* HAROLD SINCLAIR; WILLIAM CLOTHIER *(Photographer);* DAVID BUTTOLPH *(Music);* FRANK HOTALING *(Art Director);* ALLEN K. WOOD *(Production Manager);* WINGATE SMITH *and* RAY GOSNELL, JR. *(Assistant Directors);* JACK SOLOMON *(Sound);* JACK MURRAY *(Editor);* FRANK BRETSON *and* ANN PECK *(Wardrobe);* AUGIE LOHMAN *(Special Effects);* WEBB OVERLANDER *(Makeup); "I Left My Love" (song)—Music and Lyrics by* STAN JONES; *Filmed on location in Louisiana and Mississippi; Color by DeLuxe.*

Opened at the Astor Theater, New York, June 26, 1959. Running time, 119 minutes.

THE PICTURE:

There is a lot of John Ford–style excitement and human interest in this story of a Union cavalry raid through Southern territory in 1863. The novel by Harold Sinclair was based on a real-life incident of the Civil War. Holden and Ford, in their first pairing, each collected a hefty $750,000 salary, according to reports of the time, and perhaps pleasant meditations on all that nice green stuff helped them perform their assignments with the consummate force, intensity, and expert teamwork that they display here. Constance Towers, too, registers a vital presence as the Southern belle they encounter, and all the supporting cast are cleverly enlisted by ringmaster Ford into the required spirit of the thing. Ford got in a lot of good old-fashioned sentiment, caught within appropriate margins of restraint,

191

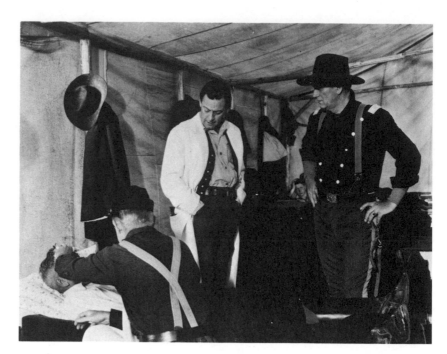

With John Wayne

and the action sequences were staged in the finest Ford tradition, proving all that could be desired. As to the basic story, since the Civil War is going against the North, General Grant (Stan Jones), who has been trying to take the Confederate fortress of Vicksburg for months without success, realizes the necessity of cutting off that city's supply sources. Wayne is assigned to take his several cavalry regiments for hundreds of miles into the Confederacy, the objective being the destruction of the supply nerve-center and railroad depot of Newton Station, Mississippi. Also in the regiment is Surgeon Major Kendall (Holden). As Wayne hates all medics because of his wife's death during unnecessary surgery, he and Holden square off for bickering combat almost immediately. They put up at a plantation whose high-spirited belle, Miss Towers, learns of their plans, so they are forced to take her with them to preserve security. A rabid Southern patriot, Towers gives the boys an

With John Wayne, Hank Worden,
Constance Towers, and Ken Curtis

initial hard time, making abortive escape attempts and what-not. Once Newton Station is destroyed, Wayne and Company head for safety at Union-held Baton Rouge, skirmishing with Confederate forces en route and sustaining bloody casualties. Wayne and Towers develop a romance (Holden is kept on the sidelines romancewise in this film) that climaxes when Towers nurses Wayne's wounded leg, and Wayne gradually comes to respect Holden's integrity and medical competence. The Confederates are hot in pursuit by this time, so when the party reaches a crucial bridge, Wayne crosses it with his remaining able-bodied men, then has it blown up, leaving on the other side of the stream the girl he now loves (with whom he hopes to be reunited after the war) and the sturdy Holden, who has decided to attend wounded Union soldiers in a Southern prison camp if need be. Among the more affecting scenes is that in which a gruffly compassionate Wayne comforts a dying young soldier and the one in which he registers his love for Miss Towers. There is also a compelling sequence, pure John Ford, in which a group of teenage cadets march out from a Southern military academy to take on the enemy, which scorns to battle boys and pulls a retreat, leaving the kids cheering. There is an unassuming, honest, underplayed integrity in the picture's direction and acting, the photography at times achieves an almost Matthew Brady verisimilitude, and the story courses along with relative smoothness. *The Horse Soldiers* can fairly be numbered among the more successful films of the great John Ford's later period.

REVIEWS:

Arthur Knight in *Saturday Review:*

Its action scenes, as directed by the veteran John Ford, tingle with an excitement all too rare upon the screen these days. There is visual beauty in its incessant shots of cavalry on the march. And the conflict between Marlowe and his Surgeon Major is projected with a surprisingly convincing intensity by John Wayne and William Holden. Not that either will win any Academy awards for their impersonations. But Ford knows how to handle his people, knows how to capture on cellu-

With Constance Towers, Hank Worden, Ken Curtis, and John Wayne

William Holden at right

loid those aspects of their own personalities most pertinent to the roles they may be playing. Best of all, the script makes no effort to blunt the issues over which the war was fought, nor does it pretend that war is a glorious pastime.

Paul V. Beckley in the *New York Herald Tribune:*
A flying slash and gallop (and essentially romantic) race through one of the stirring cavalry episodes of the Civil War.... In a way it has the spirit of a Western rather than historical drama, though some of its details

The boys pose for the birdie

With Althea Gibson, Constance Towers, and John Wayne

pinch very close to the reality of warfare . . . under the surface jingle of the main story line, the picture has a fine, authentic and always stirring wealth of incident.

Time:

It's all good clean fun, especially for customers who like John Wayne and don't care much about Grierson's Raid. For those who do not like Wayne, there's William Holden, who comes along for the ride as a military surgeon, and prescribes penicillin, or something mighty like it, a good eighty years before it was discovered.

Bosley Crowther in *The New York Times:*

Pretty much a conventional story involving a cavalry raid . . . but this is made supremely graphic and exciting by the touch of Mr. Ford and, what is more, some of it has the look of history seen through the mists of the years . . . and there is one sequence—showing the youngsters of a military school being called out to oppose the intruders—that has a fine authentic look and ring. It is recollective of the incident in which the uniformed cadets of the Virginia Miiltary Institute fought at the Battle of Newmarket.

Learning the fine art of firearms

195

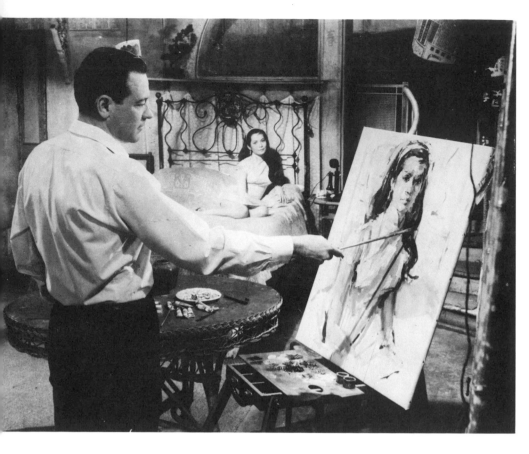

With Nancy Kwan

The World of Suzie Wong

1960   Paramount

CAST:

WILLIAM HOLDEN *(Robert Lomax)* NANCY KWAN *(Suzie Wong);* SYLVIA SYMS *(Kay O'Neill);* MICHAEL WILDING *(Ben);* LAURENCE NAISMITH *(Mr. O'Neill);* JACQUELINE CHAN *(Gwenny Lee);* ANDY HO *(Ah Tong);* BERNARD CRIBBINS *(Otis);* YVONNE SHIMA *(Minnie Ho);* LIER HWANG *(Wednesday Lu);* LIONEL BLAIR *(Dancing Sailor);* ROBERT LEE *(Barman);* RONALD ENG *(Waiter);* CALVIN HSAI *(Susie's Baby).*

CREDITS:

A RAY STARK *Production for Paramount Pictures.* RAY STARK *(Producer);* RICHARD QUINE *(Director);* JOHN PATRICK *(Screenplay); based on the novel by* RICHARD MASON *and the play by* PAUL OSBORN; GEOFFREY UNSWORTH *(Photographer);* JOHN BOX *(Art Director);* GEORGE DUNING *(Music);* BERT BATES *(Editor);* RAY BAKER *(Sound);* GUS AGOSTI *(Assistant Director); Title*

song by JIMMY VAN HEUSEN *and* SAMMY CAHN; *Location scenes filmed in Hong Kong; Interiors filmed in England; Color by Technicolor.*

Opened at Radio City Music Hall, New York, November 10, 1960. Running time, 129 minutes.

THE PICTURE:

The World of Suzie Wong opened to a critical chorus of ridicule and disparagement that must have roundly astonished its producers, and probably Holden, who had doubtless imagined he was head man in a charming interracial romance. The original had been a decent-enough little stage play about a young American artist and a Hong Kong prostitute, and as such was accepted on its own essentially-limited merits. However, when blown up by Hollywood to Brobdingnagian

196

With Nancy Kwan

cinematics, replete with Hong Kong exterior locations, Technicolor, CinemaScope, an inflated, phony screenplay, and totally unrealistic situations, the result was distinctly negative. The film has been seen recently on TV, and in some of its facets it seems rather better than the forthrightly harsh 1960 reviews would indicate, but the essentially spurious elements still are there. Holden at 42 was obviously much too old for his role. Nancy Kwan was pretty, but much too candified and antiseptic for a supposed Hong Kong whore. In fact, the situations, general ambience, and dialogue are all ersatz as can be. And as *Time* noted, the true facts of Asiatic prostitution, with its disease, high mortality rate, and unbelievably sordid conditions, made a cruel jest of this pretty Technicolored tale. Other critics noted that there were some good travelogue elements in the Hong Kong scenery. The story has Holden, an American architect who has decided to take a year's sabbatical to try painting, coming to Hong Kong. Here he encounters the prostitute, Miss Kwan, who is portrayed rather ridiculously by the writers as a dreamy type who imagines she comes from wealth and social prominence, and who plies her essentially sordid trade in a welter of mischievous fantasy. Kwan, attracted to Holden, offers to be

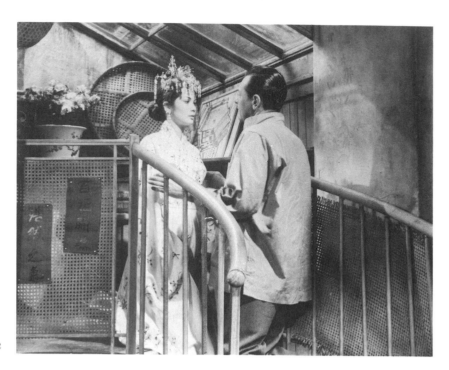

With Nancy Kwan

his "steady girlfriend," but the world-weary Holden (who incidentally looked mighty puffy around the eyes for a man of forty-two) informs her that he has had enough of love and wants only to paint. Paint he does, and Miss Kwan, deputized as a model, appears in his work in a variety of poses (from what we saw of the paintings, Holden should have stuck with his architecture). Shortly he is pursued by Sylvia Syms, daughter of an English banker, who helps him get his paintings sold in London. Syms wants to marry him, and is repelled by his involvement with Kwan, whom she snubs.

Meanwhile Kwan, who still plies her trade, is dropped abruptly by a middle-aged womanizer (Michael Wilding). A compassionate Holden suddenly realizes he loves her and takes her as his mistress. But she has a way of disappearing for long stretches of the day; a suspicious Holden follows her and learns she has had a baby whom she regularly visits. Holden is low on money, and Kwan wants to "go back to work" to support them. This piques his pride and he throws her out. Later, repentant, he looks for her and learns that the house where her baby lived had collapsed in a rainy-

With Sylvia Sims, Michael Wilding, and Nancy Kwan

season landslide. As Holden watches, the bereft young mother conducts traditional Chinese services for the dead infant; now he *really* loves her, he feels, and he proposes marriage. All of which, as most critics insisted, was totally sentimental, unbelievable, and alien to the true facts of the environment.

REVIEWS:

Bosley Crowther in *The New York Times:*

The glowingest commercial for love conquering every-thing, including the taint of prostitution, these old eyes have ever seen. Nothing, including social stigma, can keep Western boy and Eastern girl from walking off into the sunset . . . whether this beautiful concept of an American would-be painter's falling in love with a yum-yum girl in Hong Kong may be taken as a likely document of what might reasonably happen in that area is something else again . . . a new girl named Nancy Kwan plays [the prostitute] so blithely and innocently that even the ladies should love her. She and

With Nancy Kwan

*With Calvin Hsia and
Nancy Kwan*

With Calvin Hsia

the scenery are the best things in the film. William Holden is passably attractive, though he looks a bit worn for such moonshining and the script makes him seem a cautious chump.

Variety:

Scenarist John Patrick's attempt to enhance the romance by laying in some additional social significance is, for the most part, abortive. His little glimpses into Western prejudice do not quite ring true with three-dimensional insight...there are several passages of sheer travelogue, worthwhile glimpses of culture-in-action. Audiences unfamiliar with the city will marvel at them....Holden gives a first-class performance, restrained and sincere. Miss Kwan [is] a most agreeable-looking creature.

Paul V. Beckley in the *New York Herald Tribune:*

This story would not be the easiest kind of thing to make over into a family-type picture in any case. Holden's stoic puritan would give any actor pause. And it is a credit to Miss Kwan's account that she can carry off as well as she does the appalling archness of the dialogue she's been handed...there are good shots of Hong Kong. But the story is always with you, getting itself into repeated jams of nonsense.

Time:

Literally, the picture is a mad chow mein of Chinese-laundry English. Dramatically, it is just one long touristic stagger through the better bars and restaurants of Hong Kong. The direction is vague, and the principals are rigidly confined in miscasts. Actor Holden looks more like an aging bellboy than an artist...actress Kwan seems more Piccadilly than Wanchai. And the film's sentimental, sanitized conception of the Oriental prostitute as a sort of rising young calendar girl...will seem a cruel jest to the undernourished minions of Asia's vast sex industry, many of them dead of disease or exhaustion long before they reach the heroine's comparatively advanced age of 21.

Lionel Blair and Nancy Kwan

Satan Never Sleeps

1962   20th Century-Fox

CAST:

WILLIAM HOLDEN *(Father O'Banion);* CLIFTON WEBB *(Father Bovard);* FRANCE NUYEN *(Siu Lan);* ATHENE SEYLER *(Sister Agnes);* MARTIN BENSON *(Kuznietsky);* EDITH SHARPE *(Sister Theresa);* ROBERT LEE *(Chung Ren);* WEAVER LEE *(Ho San);* MARIE YONG *(Ho San's Mother);* ANDY HO *(Ho San's Father);* LIN CHEN *(Sister Mary);* ANTHONY CHINN *(Ho San's Driver).*

CREDITS:

LEO MCCAREY *(Producer and Director);* CLAUDE BINYON *and* LEO MCCAREY *(Screenplay); based on the novel* The China Story *by* PEARL S. BUCK; OSWALD MORRIS *(Photographer);* RICHARD RODNEY BENNETT *(Music);* MUIR MATHIESON *(Music Conductor); Title song "Satan Never Sleeps" by* HARRY WARREN, HAROLD ADAMSON *and* LEO MCCAREY, *sung by* TIMI YURO; TOM MORAHAN *(Production Designer);* JIM MORAHAN *and* JOHN HOESLI *(Art Directors);* JACK STEPHENS *(Set Decorator);* GORDON PILKINGTON *(Editor);* JOHN BRAMALL *(Sound);* ARTHUR NEWMAN *(Wardrobe);* GEORGE FROST *(Makeup)* BILL GRIFFITHS *(Hairstyles);* CECIL F. FORD *(Asso-*

ciate Producer); JACK SWINBURNE *(Production Manager);* DAVID ORTON *(Assistant Director); Filmed in England and Wales; CinemaScope; Color by Deluxe.*

Opened at the Paramount and the 72nd Street Playhouse, New York, February 22, 1962. Running time, 126 minutes.

THE PICTURE:

Holden never looked more tired, haggard, dispirited, and generally listless (at least up to 1962) than he did in this tasteless and flat rehash of the *Going My Way* theme. (He must have realized he was in a turkey after the first few scenes). Bing Crosby and Barry Fitzgerald had a good thing going in the Paramount hit of 1944, in which they were two lovable priests coping with various human problems in a rectory. Leo McCarey had done well by this earlier confection, but he disregarded the well-known cinematic law that remakes as a rule are suspect in conception and disastrous in execution. *Satan Never Sleeps* was duly a disaster. This time

McCarey took a Pearl Buck novel, *The China Story*, set the action in the China of 1949, got Holden and Clifton Webb dolled up in cassocks and Roman collars, and with a script that aped the earlier picture in ambience if not in plot, let these unlikely reincarnations of Bing and Barry run amuck amid the Chinese. It didn't work for a number of reasons. By 1962 Mc-Carey was frankly tired; his best days as a creative director were behind him. Holden just wasn't the type to play a priest, though he may have imagined he was, and Clifton Webb's hypersophisticated, delicious decadence, more suited to a martini glass than a chalice, was as amenable to a missionary characterization as Merv Griffin playing Winston Churchill. France Nuyen was along for the ride as a native girl with a yen for Holden, who keeps begging Satan to get behind him, especially when Nuyen starts peeking in his bedroom window and asking him if she can console him in any way (a piece of rampant vulgarity that the 1962 critics did not spare). Oh yes, the two good priests are constantly being harassed by the Communists under Colonel Weaver Lee (played as cartoon-strip characters) who finally get around to desecrating the chapel and destroying the dispensary, as you just knew they would. Holden is then strapped to a chair and given a demonstration by Lee of what he has been missing in the bedroom, forced as he is to watch Lee rape Nuyen. Nuyen has a baby (I had an old aunt who saw every 1930s-style movie ever made and who once said, "Lord, if I hear a woman say, 'I'm going to have a baby,' once more in a movie, I will drop down in a colorful fit then and there!") As of 1962, Nuyen was still doing it. Though the rapist is proud of his parenthood when baby arrives, and struts about displaying it, he still gives the mission a hard time. But the villagers revolt, and the Communist overlords order all Christians to be killed, including Lee's parents. Then the Colonel sees the light, and goes all-out anti-communist. Then he tries to smuggle the woman, the baby, and the priests out of the danger area. When their escape is threatened by a Communist helicopter out to get Lee, it is Webb, of course, who performs the last-minute heroics by putting on the colonel's cap and coat and driving off in his car. The helicopter riddles the hapless old cleric with bullets while the others escape. In one of the more bathetic endings of 1962 or any year, Holden marries the ex-Red and Nuyen, and baptizes the baby, with Webb presumably looking down benevolently from wherever it is good old priests go. The critics roasted the film in no uncertain terms, castigating the treatment of Chinese Communists as black-and-white caricature, the harping on the old-fashioned "human-interest" elements, and the cloying, cheap, falsely sentimental treat-

With France Nuyen

ment of religion and religious. Held up for especial ridicule was a scene that might have barely made it in 1944 but in 1962 seemed ludicrously cutesy-poo: Holden and Webb have hesitated in good conscience to have a rice wine nightcap because it is almost midnight and there *is* that communion fast before mass, but they solve the dilemma by going along with the time on Holden's watch which is slower than Webb's. Which gives you some idea.

REVIEWS:

Tube in *Variety:*

An unsatisfactory variation on *Going My Way.* With basically the same character premise he used to advan-

tage in his 1944 production, Leo McCarey has failed in *Satan Never Sleeps*. He has failed not necessarily because the idea of two lovable, whimsical priests has lost its edge and charm through repetition, but because he is here dealing not with the conflicts of young love and juvenile delinquency, but with grave and complicated matters of political and social ideologies on an international scale that do not lend themselves to light, cursory treatment and cannot gracefully be translated into comedy-melodrama. The modern film audience is not apt to accept a two-dimensional portrait of the

Communist as merely a bumbling, irrational arch-villain . . . Holden, Webb and Miss Nuyen make the most of their characters. Holden is a kind of leather-jacketed variation (how styles change) of Bing Crosby's sweat-shirted Father O'Malley, Webb a wry, caustic version of Barry Fitzgerald's Father Fitzgibbon. Miss Nuyen plays vivaciously. The Red villains are absurdly all black, with the exception of Weaver Lee, whose ultimate white-washing can be sensed throughout the film by any sharp, perspective viewer, at least partially a result of McCarey's rather obvious direction.

With France Nuyen

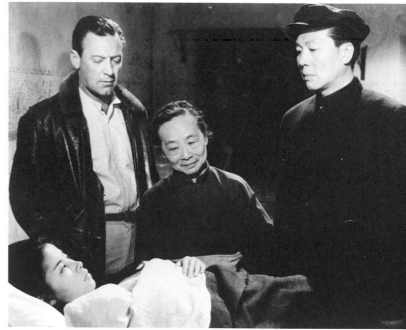

With France Nuyen, Marie Young, and Weaver Lee

Time:

God, in director Leo McCarey's movies, is always good —especially for business. McCarey's most famous religious pictures *(Going My Way, The Bells of St. Mary's)* were shrewdly aimed to please the millions of Roman Catholic moviegoers, and they managed to charm plenty of Protestants too. In this picture, after a run of unsuccessful shows, McCarey has once more called upon religion to perform a commercial miracle, but this time he appears to have used the Lord's name in vain. For all its superficial smirk of piety, McCarey's *Satan* is just a prurient, soft-soapy-and-holy-water version of the spicy story about the lonely missionary and the beautiful native girl.

A. H. Weiler in *The New York Times*:

Disturbingly reminiscent of *Going My Way*, [the film] is a lackluster imitation of that gem.... Mr. McCarey's direction, as well as the acting of the principals, is decidedly less than inspired ... France Nuyen, several times removed from the prostitute she played on stage in *The World of Suzie Wong*, is truly charming. William Holden is merely harried-looking. Clifton Webb is unusual only in that he is not wearing his usual moustache. Otherwise he is as austere and correct as a social leader. Although his cassock and collar become him, he seems out of place in clerical garb speaking re-

With France Nuyen and Clifton Webb

ligious lines. There is no doubt that the hearts of Mr. McCarey and Company are in the right places but [the film] has little heart in it. This Satan is a direct descendant of Madame Butterfly and soap opera.

Paul Beckley in the *New York Herald Tribune*:

As usual in this kind of picture, there is no particular spiritual content, merely the sham "humanizing" of priests by trivializing their behavior and thinking.

The Counterfeit Traitor

1962   Paramount

CAST:

WILLIAM HOLDEN (*Eric Erickson*); LILLI PALMER (*Marianne Mollendorf*); HUGH GRIFFITH (*Collins*); ERNST SCHRODER (*Baron Von Oldenbourg*); EVA DAHLBECK (*Ingrid Erickson*); ULF PALME (*Max Gumpel*); CARL RADDATZ (*Otto Holtz*); HELO GUTSCHWAGER (*Hans Holtz*); ERICA BEER (*Klara Holtz*); CHARLES REGNIER (*Wilhelm Kortner*); WERNER PETERS (*Bruno Ulrich*); WOLFGANG PREISS (*Colonel Nordoff*); JOCHEN BLUME (*Dr. Jacob Karp*); DIRK HANSEN (*Lieut. Nagler*); LUDWIG NAYBERT (*Stationmaster*); KLAUS KINSKI (*Kindler*); ERIK SCHUMANN (*Nazi Gunboat Officer*); GUNTER MEISSNER (*Priest*); STEFAN SCHNABEL (*Jaeger*); MARTIN BERLINER (*Porter*); PHIL BROWN (*Harold Murray*); PETER CAPELL (*Unger*); MAX BUCKSBAUM (*Fischer*); EJNER FEDERSPIEL (*Professor Christiansen*); EVA FIEBIG (*Frau Hecker*); HOLGER HAGEN (*Carl Bradley*); KAI HOLM (*Gunnar*); REINHARD KOLLDEHOFF (*Colonel Erdmann*); LOUIS MIEHE-RENARD (*Poul*); JENS OSTERHOLM (*Lars*); PAUL REICHARDT (*Fishing Boat Skipper*); BENDT ROTHE (*Mogens*); ALBERT RUEPRECHT (*Captain Barlach*); TED TAYLOR (*Monitor Man*); WERNER VAN DEEG (*Oil Refinery Manager*); GEORG VOELMMER (*Lieut. Bretz*); JOHN WITTIG (*Sven*).

CREDITS:

A PERLBERG–SEATON *Production*; WILLIAM PERLBERG (*Producer*); GEORGE SEATON (*Director and Writer*); *based on the book by* ALEXANDER KLEIN; JEAN BOURGOIN (*Photography*); ALFRED NEWMAN (*Music*); TAMBI LARSEN (*Art Director*); ALMA MACRORIE (*Editor*); HANS EBEL (*Sound*); EDITH HEAD (*Costumes*); NEVILLE SMALLWOOD (*Makeup*); THEODORE TAYLOR (*Assistant to the*

him a traitor. In Berlin he meets up with Lilli Palmer, a fellow spy who becomes his romantic interest, and later his mistress. Pretending that he wishes to build an oil refinery in Sweden, he is allowed by the Nazis to tour German oil plants, passing the information he collects on to Allied Intelligence. But the Gestapo learn that Palmer is working with the Allies, and she is imprisoned and executed, with Holden forced to witness the death from a cell aperture. Though heartbroken by developments, he dupes the Nazis into believing that he was unaware of her defection and is freed. He is later exposed by a member of the Hitler Youth, but succeeds in escaping via the German Underground into Denmark and thence to Sweden. The real-life Erickson retired in Sweden after the war. Upon the revelation of his true World War II role he was restored to honor. Holden's personal reviews for the film were good, as were Miss Palmer's. There was favorable comment on the exciting cinematics displayed and on Seaton's crisp writing and well-paced driection, though some observers thought the picture somewhat long.

Producer); ROBERT SNODY *(Production Manager);* TOM PEVSNER *(Assistant Director); Filmed in West Berlin, Hamburg, Copenhagen, and Stockholm; Color by Technicolor.*

Opened at the DeMille Theater, New York, April 17, 1962. Running time, 140 minutes.

THE PICTURE:

Holden's World War II spy melodrama, *The Counterfeit Traitor,* was one of the better-received film offerings of 1962. Based on the real-life exploits of one Eric Erickson, and sharply directed by George Seaton, who also wrote it, the film relates the harrowing adventures of an American-born Swedish citizen who trades in oil with the Nazis and gets himself on the Allied blacklist in the process. British Intelligence approaches him with an offer to clear his name at the war's conclusion if he will feed them information during his German trips. He ingratiates himself with Nazi officials, though his assumed stance alienates his wife and friends, who label

With Nazi soldiers

With Nazis

REVIEWS:

Hollis Alpert in *Saturday Review:*

William Holden is invariably pleasant to spend time with, and Lilli Palmer has always been a charmer. Get these people together on a film that involves a real-life spy risking his life among the wartime Nazis and the chances are you'll have something hard to resist. I see no reason to resist *The Counterfeit Traitor....* Mr. Seaton has captured a nice continental flavor by doing the film in German, Danish and Dutch locations, and has used actors of these nationalities to good advantage ... there is an urbane touch throughout, and more than usual depth of characterization (as well as depth of feeling) than is customary in the genre.

Gene in *Variety:*

Unlike so many glorifying-someone wartime retrospectives, this one has the ring of authenticity ... hard-hitting story values and staging ... all in all, it's a work of substance ... playing the principal part with remarkable effectiveness is William Holden. Miss Palmer is an accomplished performer and plays with sincerity. Hugh Griffith is properly coy and cunning as the British Intelligence major domo.

With Lilli Palmer

Time:

The picture is too long, but it is also incessantly exciting, occasionally witty... and in its expression of organized sadism comparatively subtle.

Paul V. Beckley in the *New York Herald Tribune:*
George Seaton has been admirably circumspect in avoiding any overstatement or any temptation to pitch forward into melodrama. On the contrary, every effort has been made to give the picture great authenticity and it is so far successful as to lend it at times the air of a documentary... the acting of both Mr. Holden and Miss Palmer is exceptional.

With Lilli Palmer

The Lion

1962   20th Century-Fox

CAST:

WILLIAM HOLDEN *(Robert Hayward)*; TREVOR HOWARD *(John Bullitt)*; CAPUCINE *(Christine)*; PAMELA FRANKLIN *(Tina)*; MAKARA KWAIHA RAMADHANI *(Bogo)*; ZAKEE *(Ol' Kalu)*; PAUL ODUOR *(Oriunga)*; SAMUEL OBIERO ROMBOH *(Kihoro)*; CHRISTOPHER AGUNDA *(Elder of Masai)*; *and* ZAMBA *the Lion*.

CREDITS:

SAMUEL G. ENGEL *(Producer)*; JACK CARDIFF *(Director)*; IRENE KAMP *and* LOUIS KAMP *(Screenplay)*; *based on the novel by* JOSEPH KESSEL; TED SCAIFE *(Photographer)*; MALCOLM ARNOLD *Music Composer and Conductor)*; ALAN WITHY *and* JOHN HOESL *(Art Directors)*; RUSSELL LLOYD *(Editor)*; DAVID HILDYARD, GORDON K. MCCALLUM *and* NORMAN SAVAGE *(Sound)*; BRIAN OWENSMITH *(Wardrobe)*; JOAN SMALLWOOD *(Hair Stylist)*; GEORGE FROST *(Makeup)*; CECIL F. FORD *(Associate Producer)*; DAVID W. ORTON *(Production Manager)*; TED STURGIS *(Assistant Director)*; *Location scenes filmed in Kenya and Uganda.*

Opened at the Victoria Theater, New York, December 21, 1962. Running time, 96 minutes.

THE PICTURE:

The story played a distinct second fiddle to the naturalistic wonders in *The Lion*, and that was as it should have been, for the location shots filmed in Kenya and Uganda were breathtaking indeed. The film is at its best when concentrating on the flora and fauna and animal life and occasional menacing excitement of the fabulous African continent. When the likes of William Holden, Capucine, and Trevor Howard get into it, matters slow down, and indeed all but peter out. This was one of Holden's more tired performances, the critics commenting on his listlessness and somehow-bemused manner. One gets the impression that in this as in other instances, he only did the picture to spend time in Africa, on which he was really hipped by 1962. Then also the burgeoning of his offscreen romance with the lovely Capucine may have accounted in part for his preoccupied manner. The rather silly and obstructive plot finds Holden, an American lawyer, arriving at the East African game preserve where supervisor Howard holds forth. It seems that Holden was once married to Howard's wife, Capucine, and their eleven-year-old daughter, Pamela Franklin, hardly knows her real dad. Capucine is worried because the kid is taking too readily to the promitive life of the veldt and moreover has raised from cubhood a full-grown lion who is her greatest friend. Hence the cross-the-seas summoning of Holden (who could have given his views in letters or asked his child for a visit in Connecticut, we should think). At any rate, father and daughter renew acquaintance. Then Holden puts his foot in it violating tribal customs by saving the life of a dying chief abandoned to the elements. The chief recovers, and denounces his son, who is ordered to prove his manhood by killing a lion. Of course the young tribesman singles out Franklin's pet. The girl sets the lion on the hapless native. When Holden, Capucine, and Howard arrive on the scene, Howard is forced to kill the lion after he has fatally wounded the tribesman. An enraged Franklin rejects Howard and turns to Holden. For that matter, Capucine decides to resume with Holden herself, and all three set out for the smog-traffic-supermarket wilds of Connecticut, While Howard, with what I suspected was a smug expression of good-riddance on his craggy face, returns to his game preserving or whatever

With Pamela Franklin

With Zamba the Lion and Capucine

211

With Pamela Franklin

he is doing in that African wild. As before noted, the natural beauty of Africa, and the compelling shots of its primitive wonders, take precedence over anything else, though Miss Franklin and the lion (a trained one from America) give good accounts of themselves. Oh yes, the lion's name is Zamba.

REVIEWS:

Leo Mishkin in the *New York Morning Telegraph:*
The moral is that it just doesn't do to have a full-grown lion as a playmate and a pet. Grownups won't under-

stand and they'll make you get rid of it or maybe take you some place else where you'll find more suitable companions . . . it's really that lion that carries the picture bearing his name, with all due respect to the humans taking part. Looks even more handsome than William Holden.

Bosley Crowther in *The New York Times:*
The fond dream of many a youngster to live on the African veldt and to be pals with wild animals may be vicariously fulfilled by a mere visit to see *The Lion.*

With Pamela Franklin and Capucine

212

For this picture abounds in handsome foliage, in color, of wild animals in Kenya . . . but the drama concocted for the movie is a distressing lot of twaddle that considerably gets in the way of the naturalist theme of the novel and the love affair of the youngster with the lion. William Holden, Capucine and Trevor Howard play their roles in a rather listless and shamefaced way, leaving most of the burden of being cheerful to little Miss Franklin and the lion. In view of the fact that the latter is shot and the little girl is shipped off to Connecticut at the end, to live with her reunited parents, this cannot be said to be an upbeat film.

Variety:

Holden is pleasantly charming and understanding, Capucine looks as coolly beautiful in the jungle as in a boudoir while Howard, at times looking fiercer than any of the animals, gives a powerful study of a rugged nononsense character. Native actors give colorful support.

Time:

Africa is for Africans. Connecticut is for people who can afford it. That's the moral of this movie, and it doesn't make much sense. But then the movie wasn't meant to make sense; it was meant to make money. It has one major star (William Holden), one good actor (Trevor Howard), one competent director (Jack Car-

With Trevor Howard and Capucine

diff, who did *Sons and Lovers*), infinitudes of the usual fauna, and some spectacular shots of Mount Kenya. It also has a portly, natty, sophisticated Hollywood lion named Zamba, who looks as though he came from F. A. O. Schwartz and waddles like a middle-aged millionaire stuffed with Chateaubriand and Trancopal. What's more, while on location in Kenya he nibbled daintily on breast of chicken and refused to associate with those poor, backward, underedeveloped African lions. Unfortunately the picture has a plot that attempts to solve—now really, fellows—a five-sided triangle. At the end, the hunter goes back to his wart hogs, and what's more he goes smiling. He seems to appreciate at last that there are boars—and bores.

With Trevor Howard and Capucine

Paris When It Sizzles

1964   Paramount

CAST:

WILLIAM HOLDEN (*Richard Benson*); AUDREY HEPBURN (*Gabrielle Simpson*); GREGOIRE ASLAN (*Police Inspector*); NOEL COWARD (*Alexander Meyerheimer*); RAMOND BUSSIERES (*Gangster*); CHRISTIAN DUVALLEX (*Maitre d' Hotel*); *Guest stars:* MARLENE DIETRICH, TONY CURTIS, MEL FERRER; *Singing voices of* FRED ASTAIRE *and* FRANK SINATRA.

CREDITS:

RICHARD QUINE *and* GEORGE AXELROD (*Producers*); RICHARD QUINE (*Director*); GEORGE AXELROD (*Screenplay*); *based on a story by* JULIEN DUVIVIER *and* HENRI JEANSON; CHARLES LANG, JR. (*Photography*); NELSON RIDDLE (*Music*); PAUL K. LERPAL (*Special Photographic Effects*); JEAN D'EAUBONNE (*Art Director*); GABRIEL BECHIR (*Editor*); ARCHIE MARSHEK (*Sound*); JO DE BRETAGNE *and* CHARLES GRENZBACH (*Sound*); ARTHUR MORTON (*Orchestrations*); HUBERT DE GIVENCHY (*Miss Hepburn's wardrobe and perfume*); FRANK MC COY (*Makeup*); CARTER DE HAVEN *and* JOHN R. COONAN (*Associate Producers*); PAUL FEYDER (*Assistant Director*); *Filmed in Paris; Color by Technicolor.*

Opened at the Paramount, Trans-Lux, and neighborhood theaters, April 8, 1964. Running time, 110 minutes.

THE PICTURE:

Paired for the second time with Audrey Hepburn, Holden developed an idea that he might give Cary Grant a run for his money (or he may have been persuaded to undertake such a foolhardy contest by his associates), but all he succeeded in proving with this film was that as Holden he could be Grade A (in better vehicles than this, however) but as Grant he was strictly a Grade C imitation. Based on a 1955 French release, *Henriette*, which Julien Duvivier had produced and directed with Hildegarde Neff and Michel Auclair, this farce-fantasy, or whatever it was, proved inferior even to an original which wasn't so hot in its own right. The film, which gossamer-gamin Hepburn did her best to salvage (unsuccessfully) via her unique personality, garnered some of the worst reviews of 1964 or any year, with terms like "embarrassingly unfunny," "trumped-up," "floundering," and "heavy-handed" proliferating in the copy. Shot in Paris in "lavish" Technicolor, the film contained credits that aroused particular amusement among the reviewers, with mention of Miss Hepburn's wardrobe *and perfume* by De Givenchy, giving rise to the crack that the perfume couldn't be smelt but the picture could. The plot, if you care by now, starts off with film producer Noel Coward (described by one reviewer as "repellent") waxing angry because scriptwriter Holden is dawdling on his screenplay for the new Coward masterpiece *The Girl Who Stole The Eiffel Tower*. When Coward serves peremptory notice that he has forty-eight hours in which to complete his masterpiece, Holden drafts secretary Hepburn to assist his muse. They proceed to move into a frantic fantasy-world of screenwriting, incorporating elements of romance, comedy, Western action, spy stuff, musicals, and anything else that could conceivably go into a picture. They act out each scene, and find themselves gradually becoming the protagonists of their fan-

With Audrey Hepburn

With Audrey Hepburn

tasies. Now and then they settle down to earth for meals, story revisions—and reallife romantic dalliance. The deadline approaches, the script is still unfinished, but the pair find themselves deeply in love. There is a temporary parting as Holden tells Hepburn he doesn't think he's good enough for her, but when she leaves he is presently hot in pursuit, and love triumphs—along with the implied indication that a great movie will yet result. The material meant to be light is heavy-handed indeed, the acting is leaden in Holden's case and fluttering, albeit energetically desperate, in Miss Hepburn's. Director Richard Quine shows himself inept at handling such thinly poised farce. Perhaps no one could have.

REVIEWS:

Stanley Kauffmann in the *New Republic:*

[The film] is based on an old Duvivier opus called *Henriette,* which itself was deadly; the new script by George Axelrod embalms the original instead of reviving it.... The possibilities are limitless, which is precisely what is wrong. It takes the invention of a Sacha Guitry to justify and control such license. Axelrod simply flounders. His dialogue and Holden's gift for comedy amply deserve each other. Noel Coward is briefly on hand at his most repellent. And in the midst of this meager harvest is Miss Audrey Hepburn trying to make chaff out of corn.

Hollis Alpert in *Saturday Review:*

A feeble, lame, embarrassingly unfunny story it is. None of it, under Richard Quine's direction, has the slightest charm or humor. It's hard to determine which is worst: Axelrod's script or the various scripts he has Holden invent. Fatuous is perhaps the word that best describes the quality of the writing. One would hardly expect, then, that Miss Hepburn or Mr. Holden would be able to surmount the handicap of their basic material, and they do not. Their pretense of a light, kidding style is simply bad acting and (I guess) bad direction...a dreadfully expensive display of bad taste.

A. H. Weiler in *The New York Times:*

Miss Hepburn, sylph-like as ever, seems slightly bewildered by the trumped-up zaniness in which she is involved. Mr. Holden shows signs of strain and a decided lack of conviction long before this pseudo-merry chase ends. In their breathless efforts at making *Paris* fashionable, smart and "in," Mr. Axelrod and Mr. Quine and their stars are not really inventive or funny. Even though they work up a great head of steam, *Paris When It Sizzles* is not so hot.

Judith Crist in the *New York Herald Tribune:*

Miss Hepburn is, as always, very lovely to look at and so is Paris. Mr. Holden, however, is not Cary Grant, even though he tries and he tries and he tries. And *Paris When It Sizzles?* Strictly Hollywood—when it fizzles.

With Audrey Hepburn

The Seventh Dawn

1964   United Artists

CAST:

WILLIAM HOLDEN *(Ferris)*; SUSANNAH YORK *(Candace)*; CAPUCINE *(Dhana)*; TETSURO TAMBA *(Ng)*; MICHAEL GOODLIFFE *(Trumphey)*; ALLAN CUTHBERTSON *(Cavendish)*; MAURICE DENHAM *(Tarlton)*; SIDNEY TAFLER *(C.P.O.)*; BEULAH QUO *(Ah Ming)*; HUGH ROBINSON *(Judge)*; TONY PRICE *(Morley)*; GRIFFITHS ALUN *(Sedgwick)*; CHRISTOPHER ALLEN *(C.I.D.)*; YAP MOOK FUI *(Lim)*; DAVID KEITH *(Aide)*; JAMES MASSONG *(Malay Engineer)*; R. WILLIAM KOH *(General Osaki)*; ALLAN WONG *(Colonel Hsai)*; IBRAHIM BIN *(Captain Chey)*; NOEL CHOW *(Captain Kiat)*; HEW THIAN CHOY *(Lieutenant Nelson)*; DAVID WEINMAN *(Tamil Cyclist)*; GEORGE ZAKHARIAH *(Indian Unionist)*; SEOW *(Chinese Unionist)*; TONY CHENG *(Walter)*; KIP BAHADUN *(Japanese Prisoner)*.

CREDITS:

A Holdean Production; CHARLES K. FELDMAN *(Producer)*; KARL TUNBERG *(Co-Producer)*; LEWIS GILBERT *(Director)*; KARL TUNBERG *(Screenplay); based on the novel* The Durian Tree *by* MICHAEL KEON; FREDERICK YOUNG *(Photography)*; JOHN DARK *(Associate Producer)*; JOHN STOLL *(Production Designer)*; JOHN SHIRLEY *(Editor)*; HERBERT SMITH *(Art Director)*; RIZ ORTOLANI *(Music Composer and Conductor)*; CHRIS GREENHAM *(Sound Editor)*; HARRY GILLAM *(Sound Operator)*; CLIFF RICHARDSON *(Special Effects)*; JOSE MACAVIN *(Set Decorator)*; JACK CAUSEY *(Assistant Director)*; JOHN O'GORMAN *(Makeup)*; BASIL FENTON SMITH *and* RED LAW *(Sound)*; MORRIS AZA *(Production Manager)*; HYLDA GILBERT *(Costumes)*; BETTY ADAMSON

With Susannah York

(Wardrobe Supervisor); JOHN DAVIES *(Continuity);* HARRY ARBOUR *(Construction);* MAURICE BINDER *(Main Title Design); Color by Technicolor.*

Opened at the Astor Theater and other metropolitan theaters, September 2, 1964. Running time, 123 minutes.

THE PICTURE:

Another of those Malaysian action dramas filled with lovely Eurasians, scheming Communists, and intrepid heroics courtesy of Bill Holden, *The Seventh Dawn* derived its principal interest from the by then widely publicized romance between Capucine and Holden, which had reportedly begun two years before during the shooting of *The Lion* in Kenya. Be that as it may, some critics noted that they seemed a strangely cool and spiritless pair on screen (possibly they elected to underplay). Susannah York is on hand to supply triangular love interest, and actor Tetsuro Tamba, who plays Holden's former fellow-guerrilla against the Japanese, provides the menace. Reviewers tended to regard the whole business as so-so movie fare, though there were kind words for the scenery and the lively action stuff revved up on occasion by director Lewis Gilbert. But there was notable impatience with the tiresomely involved plot mechanics, and the clichés abounded, giving the film at times the look of a parody of any fifteen 1938 action movies. The story, boiled down to its simplest essentials, dealt with the divergent paths of buddies Holden and Tamba after the war.

With Tetsuro Tamba

Holden starts a plantation in Malaya; Tamba goes to Moscow for Communist indoctrination. Their onetime guerrilla associate, Capucine, also remains in Malaya after the war. Holden, in love with Capucine and loved by Susannah York, gets caught in the triple squeeze of 1953 between Malaysians, British, and Communists. Tamba returns to terrorize the plantations with his Communist band, sparing only his former friend Hol-

With Tetsuro Tamba, Susannah York, and Capucine

den's land. The British ask Holden to betray Tamba, but he reneges on this, as does Capucine. Capucine is framed when grenades planted by Tamba are found in her bicycle. She is set for execution. Holden and Miss York determine to save her. York offers herself to Tamba as a hostage, and Tamba holds her while announcing that she will be killed if Capucine is not released. Realizing that their old friendship has terminated, Holden goes after Tamba, rescues York, and routs Tamba's men, but he is too late to save Capucine from execution. York then saves Holden's life by shooting Tamba when he and our hero get into a death struggle. With Capucine dead, Holden decides to leave Malaya. York offers to go with him, but he tells her to look for a younger man. Does all this sound reminiscent of many a movie plot of yore? We couldn't agree more.

REVIEWS:

Archer Winsten in the *New York Post:*

It's not a great film in any respect. It just has plenty of good looks where they count (Susannah York), scenery that resembles real jungle somewhere(heroes who are devil-may-care (Holden), a villain who is dedicated and honorable (Tetsuro Tamba) though a Communist, and the rat-tat-tat of machine gun fire, the frequent deaths of victims and almost anything else you could require for far-flung and far-fetched melodrama. A battalion of British actors give it the Pukka British air, and I'm happy to report that Bill Holden keeps them down single-handed. Its helps when you're the star and pretty much in control of the production. It is a picture that can be watched without too much pain, but not seriously.

Lawrence J. Quirk in *Screen Stars:*

If you like your William Holden brave, intrepid and resourceful, your Susannah York sexy, open-mouthed and deeply decolletaged, and your Capucine languorous, exotic and slightly mysterious a-la Garbo, this, friends, is the picture for you. The stars are more important than the plot, one of those standard Far-East-Communists-Versus-Free-Men yarns, but there is plenty of action, lots of romancing, and the acting is more than competent. Bill Holden at forty-six seems a trifle old for this kind of romantic action-drama.

Time:

Collectors of memorable movie clichés will find [the film] a treasure trove in a movie short on surprises.

With Susannah York

The most surprising thing is that Holden's widely-publicized off-screen romance with Capucine generates so little on-screen excitement. All too heedful of Hero Holden's tender regard for his co-star, the camera pores over both handsome profiles in a gallant but rather wearisome game of His and Hers. Mostly Hers.

With Susannah York

220

Alvarez Kelly

1966   Columbia

CAST:

WILLIAM HOLDEN *(Alvarez Kelly)*; RICHARD WIDMARK *(Colonel Tom Rossiter)*; JANICE RULE *(Liz Pickering)*; PATRICK O'NEAL *(Major Albert Stedman)*; VICTORIA SHAW *(Charity Warwick)*; ROGER C. CARMEL *(Captain Angus Fergson)*; RICHARD RUST *(Sergeant Hatcher)*; ARTHUR FRANZ *(Captain Towers)*; DONALD BARRY *(Lieutenant Farrow)*; DUKE HOBBIE *(John Beaurider)* HOWARD CAINE *(McIntyre)*; HARRY CAREY, JR. *(Colonel Peterson)*; MAURITZ HUGO *(Ely Harrison)*; G. B. ATWATER *(General Kautz)*; ROBERT MORGAN *(Captain Williams)*; PAUL LUKATHER *(Captain Webster)*; STEPHANIE HILL *(Mary Ann)*; INDUS ARTHUR *(Melinda)*; CLINT RITCHIE *(Union Lieutenant)*.

CREDITS:

SOL C. SIEGEL *(Producer)*; EDWARD DMYTRYK *(Director)*; FRANKLIN COEN *and* ELLIOTT ARNOLD *(Screenplay)*; *based on a story by* FRANKLIN COEN; JOSEPH MACDONALD *(Photography)*; JOHN GREEN *(Music)*; *Title song composed by* JOHN GREEN *and* JOHNNY MERCER; *Sung by the Brothers Four*; HAROLD F. KRESS *(Editor)*; WALTER M. SIMONDS *(Art Director)*; MORRIS HOFFMAN *(Set Decorations)*; DON RECORD *(Prologue and Main Title Design)*; BEN LANE *(Makeup)*; VIRGINIA JONES *(Hairstyles)*; CHARLES J. RICE *and* LAMBERT DAY *(Sound)*; LEE LUKATHER *(Production Manager)*; FRANK BAUR *(Assistant Director)*; *Location scenes filmed in and around Baton Rouge, Louisiana. Panavision. Eastman color by Pathé.*

Opened at neighborhood (showcase) theaters, New York, November 16, 1966. Running time, 116 minutes.

THE PICTURE:

After a two-year absence from the screen, Holden returned in late 1966 as the Mexican-Irish *Alvarez Kelly*, an unscrupulous Civil War cattleman who runs afoul of the Confederacy in his efforts to deliver beef to the Union Army. Reviews for this latest Holden effort were distinctly mixed, with one critic scoring the "uneven

With Victoria Shaw (left)

thesping" and "routine direction" while commending some "exciting action scenes" and "good production values." Another reviewer sniffed that the picture was "pasted up with more regard for the school-age viewer than Civil War historians," while still another consoled the producers with the observation that it "perked up beautifully in the ripely-detailed homestretch." In any event, the ambivalent critical reaction, plus the second-rate initial release in New York "neighborhood" theaters, indicated that the Holden prestige with critics and public had been somewhat dented—nor had that aforementioned twenty-six-month absence from cinemas helped the star's stock. The rather involved and not always suspenseful screenplay, based on a story by Franklin Coen and directed with so-so results by the usually able Edward Dmytryk, had cattleman Holden playing off the Union and Confederacy against each other. He starts off contracting with a Union Army officer (Patrick O'Neal) to deliver 5,000 head of cattle to feed Lincoln's army. Before he can profit from his endeavors he is betrayed by double-dealing Victoria Shaw, a Southern belle who offers him hospitality in her mansion, to Confederate officer Richard Widmark, who kidnaps Holden and forces him to teach the Southerners how to handle cattle. To keep Holden in line, Widmark shoots off one of his fingers, and warns him the other digits will follow if he doesn't do as told. Holden then encounters Janice Rule, Widmark's long-time fiancée, who is tired of waiting for marriage. To avenge his lost finger Holden engineers her elopement with a sea captain, Roger C. Carmel. When the cocky Widmark finds out about all this, his hatred of Holden knows no bounds, and he vows that Holden will die after he has helped the Confederates steal the Union cattle. All of which leads to a rousing finale, with the hard-bitten Widmark men stalking the woods and eventually overwhelming the enemy with a pounding,

With Indus Arthur

racing cattle herd. Holden, incidentally, manages to remain among the living, or did when last seen. Various slices of life are worked into the occasionally too leisurely 116-minute drama, including a rather superfluous—albeit colorful—brothel sequence, plus salty Kelly quotes about women, to wit: (about Miss Rule) "She's a female, not a crinoline saint" and "Cattle are like women; sometimes you have to be firm with them; sometimes gentle; and sometimes they need a slap on the rump." Widmark and Holden make a pair of fierce antagonists, though some critics averred that Holden seemed to have only part of his mind on his role and appeared to be sauntering through it most of the time. The story was reportedly based on a real-life incident during the Civil War.

With Stephanie Hill

REVIEWS:

Howard Thompson in *The New York Times:*
A good picture—nice and crisp and tough . . . trimly entertaining . . . and let's not forget Franklin Coen, the writer, for blueprinting a fresh idea and salting it with some tingling, unstereotyped behavior and gristly dialogue . . . while the middle section of the film kindles the festering two-man feud and considerable color and tension . . . it also dawdles. . . . Put down [the film] as a cynically cut but well-seasoned side of beef, at its best on the hoof.

With Richard Widmark

With Richard Widmark

The New York *Daily News:*

Grade school pep talk on the Civil War activities of a man who pulled off what Abraham Lincoln termed "the slickest piece of cattle stealing I ever heard of"... Holden can always manage to have the viewer pulling for him. The ingenuous actor still plays William Holden better than anyone else. Gruff and ready Widmark is a good match for Holden but no match for the Southern gentleman in the script so "honorable" he keeps his fiancée (Janice Rule) at arm's length for four years.

Murf in *Variety:*

Outdoor action sequences, including an exciting stampede, enliven a tame script, routinely directed and performed erratically.... Director Edward Dmytryk has achieved uneven response from his players, in part due to scripting which overdevelops some characters and situations, and underdevelops others. Dialog sometimes is excessive, and Dixie accents seem too cliché and not always consistent. Holden seems too relaxed and refined for a man who has herded cattle for thousands of miles, while Widmark's dedication to duty is often expressed in unruly temper, not cold firmness... the climactic stampede is a long-overdue excitement.

With Janice Rule and
Richard Widmark

Casino Royale

1967   Columbia

CAST:

PETER SELLERS *(Evelyn Tremble);* URSULA ANDRESS *(Vesper Lynd);* DAVID NIVEN *(Sir James Bond);* ORSON WELLES *(Le Chiffre);* JOANNA PETTET *(Mata Bond)* DALIAH LAVI *(The Detainer);* WOODY ALLEN *(Jimmy Bond);* WILLIAM HOLDEN *(Ransome);* CHARLES BOYER *(Le Grand);* JOHN HUSTON *(McTarry);* KURT KASZNAR *(Smernov);* GEORGE RAFT *(Himself);* JEAN-PAUL BELMONDO *(French Legionnaire);* TERENCE COOPER *(Cooper)* BARBARA BOUCHET *(Moneypenny);* ANGELA SCOULAR *(Buttercup);* GABRIELLE LICUDI *(Eliza);* TRACEY CRISP *(Heather);* JACKY BISSET *(Miss Goodthings);* ANNA QUAYLE *(Frau Hoffner);* DEREK NIMMO *(Hadley);* RONNIE CORBETT *(Polo);* COLIN GORDON *(Casino Director);* BERNARD CRIBBINS *(Taxi Driver);* TRACY REED *(Fang Leader);* DUNCAN MACRAE *(Inspector Mathis);* GRAHAM STARK *(Cashier);* RICHARD WATTIS *(British Army Officer);* PERCY HERBERT *1st Piper).*

CREDITS:

CHARLES K. FELDMAN *and* JERRY BRESLER *(Producers);* JOHN HUSTON, KENNETH HUGHES, VAL GUEST, ROBERT PARRISH, JOSEPH MC GRATH *(Directors);* WOLF MANKOWITZ, JOHN LAW, MICHAEL SAYERS *(Screenplay); suggested by the novel of* IAN FLEMING; JACK HILDYARD *(Photography);* JOHN WILCOX, NICHOLAS ROEG *(Additional Photography);* MICHAEL STRINGER *(Production Designer);* JOHN HOWELL, IVOR BEDDOES, LIONEL COUCH *(Art Direction);* TERENCE MORGAN *(Set Decoration);* BURT BACHARACH *(Music);* JOHN W. MITCHELL, SASH FISHER, BOB JONES, DICK LANGFORD *(Sound);* BILL LENNY *(Film Editor);* RICHARD TALMADGE, ANTHONY SQUIRE *(Second Unit Directors);* ROY BAIRD, JOHN STONEMAN, CARL MANNIN *(Assistant Directors); Panavision; Color by Technicolor.*

Opened at the Capitol and Cinema I theaters, New York, April 28, 1967. Running time, 131 minutes.

THE PICTURE:

Producers Charles K. Feldman and Jerry Bresler poured some $12 million, five directors, a number of writers, a pile of guest stars, and an army of technicians of all persuasions into a formless, undisciplined, something-for-everyone cinematic dud called *Casino Royale* based, and very loosely, on an Ian Fleming tome. The film opened in early 1967 and proved, according to most critics, a hopeless mishmash in which a host of talented people seemed either unable to bring their talents to fruition, were working with the wrong material, or were kept on screen long after their welcome had been worn out. Holden appeared, and most briefly, as one of a group of international agents who visit the original James Bond, played by David Niven, and attempt to enlist his services in fighting the nefarious SMERSH. The sequence, which appeared at the beginning of the film, was directed by John Huston, who also acted in it; several reviewers thought it the most creditable portion. The practically nonexistent plot deals with Bond's reemergence in the Secret Service where he combat's SMERSH's nefarious plans to wipe out most of the world's secret agents. To keep the enemy offbase, a plan is devised whereby such secret agents as Peter Sellers, Ursula Andress, Dahlia Lavi, and Terence Cooper assume the designation of Bond 007. SMERSH recruits an assortment of stunning females to entice Bond, with the result that a sort of antifemale league is established,

exemplified by Fake Bondite Cooper's conditioned immunization to distaff charms. One zany, illogical situation and inexplicable nonsequitur piles up on another. Sellers gets involved in gambling with superspy Orson Welles; there is an orgy in a Scottish castle where Deborah Kerr presides in a black lace negligee; a "spy school" in Berlin is surveyed; Sellers goes spectacularly transvestite in an array of gorgeous gowns; scantily clad women are lashed; various torture scenes are luridly introduced; and even flying saucers get into the act. Welles does some of his conjuring tricks before the footage has been exhausted, and the grand finale at the Casino Royale involves the French Foreign Legion, the French Police, Keystone Cops, the United States Cavalry, and Indians who parachute into the Casino. All of which should give some idea of *Casino Royale*. The 1967 critics and public were, to put it succinctly, not unduly impressed, the consensus of opinion being that it was all too much of a good thing—and too much of more than a few bad things into the bargain. Holden's now-you-see-him-now-you-don't flash bit added nothing to his stature, and some Holden aficionados wondered why he had bothered.

REVIEWS:

Judith Crist in the *New York World Journal Tribune:*
[The film] offers proof positive that the best of premises, talents and initial ideas can, like the biggest bal-

With John Huston, Charles Boyer,
David Niven, and Kurt Kasznar

loons, go phfft and collapse. And this latest (albeit non-Sean Connery and therefore offbeat) Bond balloon, alas, starts going phfft long before it's really off the ground, pricked by its own determination ... the movie's makers are so determined to be "different" that we are flooded with gadgets, gimmicks and sex mania, all rampant and explosive. Noise, incoherence, and sex play become the order of the film ... the dialogue is witless and unhampered by taste, and the interminable finale is a collection of clichés in a brawl involving the cavalry, parachuted Indians, split-second appearances by George Raft and Jean-Paul Belmondo, every variety of mayhem and Woody Allen burping radiation as a walking atom bomb. Everything goes up with a bang and [the film] goes phfft.

John Mahoney in the *Hollywood Reporter:*
Overlong, undisciplined, formless, confusing, misfiring and a threat to the coccyx. If those who delight in 131 minutes of consecutive non-sequitur can be relied upon,

this far-out, improvise-as-you-go spoof could well become a boxoffice hit. However, it is unlikely that many patrons will be satisfied or that that degree of success will recoup the money drained in production ... the most fully realized sequences are those directed by John Huston at the beginning of the film. Huston himself appears with William Holden, Charles Boyer and Kurt Kasznar as part of the international delegation hoping to lure Niven away from his Debussy and lion taming. Burt Bacharach's score is one of the most consistently good elements in the film.

Rich in *Variety:*
The picture has been devised as a three-ring circus entertainment rather than a film and it will be up to every cinemagoer to decide which bits of the comedy non-sequiturs provoke him to a giggle, a chuckle, a belly laff or a glum resistance to all the over-striving. [The guest stars] make only brief appearances and add little to the film, except as marquee bait.

With Cliff Robertson, Vince Edwards, and Carroll O'Connor

The Devil's Brigade

1968   United Artists

CAST:

WILLIAM HOLDEN *(Lieutenant Colonel Robert T. Frederick);* CLIFF ROBERTSON *(Major Alan Crown);* VINCE EDWARDS *(Major Cliff Bricker);* MICHAEL RENNIE *(Lieutenant General Mark Clark);* DANA ANDREWS *(Brigadier General Walter Naylor);* GRETCHEN WYLER *(A Lady of Joy);* ANDREW PRINE *(Private Theodore Ransom);* CLAUDE AKINS *(Rocky Rockman);* CARROLL O'CONNOR *(Major General Hunter);* RICHARD JAECKEL *(Omar Greco);* JACK WATSON *(Corporal Wilfred Peacock);* PAUL HORNUNG *(Lumberjack);* GENE FULLMER *(Bartender);* JEREMY SLATE *(Patrick O'Neal);* RICHARD DAWSON *(Hugh MacDonald);* TOM STERN *(Captain Cardwell);* TOM TROUPE *(Al Manella);* LUKE ASKEW *(Hubert Hixon);* BILL FLETCHER *(Bronc Guthrie);* JEAN-PAUL VIGNON *(Henri Laurent);* HARRY CAREY *(Captain Rose);* NORMAN ALDEN *(M.P. Lieutenant);* DON MCGOWEN *(Luke Phelan);* PATRIC KNOWLES *(Admiral Lord Louis Mountbatten);* DAVID PRITCHARD *(Corporal Coker);* PAUL BUSCH *(German Captain);* JAMES CRAIG *(American Officer).*

CREDITS:

A DAVID L. WOLPER *Production;* DAVID L. WOLPER *(Producer);* ANDREW V. MC LAGLEN *(Director);* WILLIAM ROBERTS *(Screenplay); based on the book by* ROBERT H. ANDERSON *and* COLONEL GEORGE WALTON; WILLIAM H. CLOTHIER *(Photographer);* ALEX NORTH *(Music Composer and Conductor);* HENRY BRANT *(Orchestration);* WILLIAM CARTWRIGHT *(Editor);* AL SWEENEY JR. *(Art Direction);* MORRIS HOFFMAN *(Set Decorations);* LOGAN FRAZEE *(Special Effects);* HAL NEEDHAM *(Stunt Supervisor);* AL OVERTON *and* CLEM PORTMAN *(Sound);* DON

With Carroll O'Connor and Michael Rennie

RECORD *(Titles)*; DONALD W. ROBERSON *(Makeup)*; THEODORE STRAUSS *and* JULIAN LUDWIG *(Associate Producers)*; CLARENCE EURIST *(Production Supervisor)*; HOWARD JOSLIN *(Production Manager)*; TERRY MORSE, JR., NEWT ARNOLD, *and* DENNIS DONNELLY *(Assistant Directors)*; *Partially filmed in Italy; Panavision; Color by Deluxe.*

Opened at the Astor, 86th Street East, and 34th Street East Theaters, May 22, 1968. Running time, 131 minutes.

THE PICTURE:

The Devil's Brigade, for all its energetic heroics under the busy direction of Andrew McLaglen, weathered a particularly fierce onslaught of critical opprobrium upon its release in 1968. It was flayed in more than one quarter as a second-rate, perfunctory, mechanical

With Cliff Robertson and Vince Edwards

230

With Cliff Robertson and Vince Edwards

imitation of *The Dirty Dozen*, and its interminable clichés were noted one by one, with a particularly acidulous critic stating that by that time World War II rehash movies might well be coming down with an epidemic of combat fatigue. Holden is forceful enough in his role, though his usual stances, attitudes, and expressions in such parts are paraded as always, sometimes to a monotonous degree. The other actors give him competent support in this tale of a commando force recruited for anti-Nazi raids in Norway. The Allies proceed to create a Special Service force that hopefully will engage and divert large groups of Nazi forces. The group commanded by Holden is made up of efficient, well-trained Canadian forces led by Cliff Robertson, combined incongruously with recalcitrant GI misfits. Holden finds himself refereeing incessant conflicts between the Amer-

icans under Vince Edwards and the Canadians under Robertson. The threatened disruption of the combined forces is averted when Holden shrewdly utilizes their mutual competitiveness to weld together an efficient overall fighting unit. After individual testings of mettle and a free-for-all tavern brawl, the Canadians and the Americans find a camaraderie developing between them, as well as a warm mutual respect. Just as Holden finds his force has been honed to fighting trim, with esprit de corps at an alltime peak, he is told to his profound disappointment that the Norway operation has been canceled by higher-ups. After an appeal to Washington, where he impresses tough general Carroll O'Connor with his confidence and enterprise, Holden wins for his men an equally hazardous assignment: patrolling German lines in the mountains of Italy. The force

With Cliff Robertson (left)

captures an enemy village, then is assigned the particularly difficult task of scaling an almost impassable mountain to knock out German positions. The men scale the precipitous terrain but sustain grievous losses, among them Robertson. But the eventual victory is so striking that it earns them the designation "The Devil's Brigade" and a bevy of commendations—though Holden sadly contemplates the human toll.

REVIEWS:

Murf in *Variety:*

An uneven combination of the worst of *The Dirty Dozen* and the best of *What Price Glory.* The irony here is that the story actually happened, as opposed to the somewhat fictitious plot of *Dozen*... as a result, [the film] may strike some as an imitation, which it isn't... it seems like many another programmer trying to portray the vulgar nobility of men at war. The marquee allure of William Holden, Cliff Robertson and Vince Edwards, strong production values and a few good performances will maintain some audience interest.

Judith Crist in *New York* Magazine:

One can, as in the case of *The Dirty Dozen,* even see a logical truth in the proposition that it takes a psychopath to indulge in the psychopathic activity of war with feeling and gusto. Further, the commando-wartime aspect permits us to see human flesh desecrated by more than shot and shell; what marvelous closeups we can get of garroting, of bashing, of sinking knife and shiv into meat and of the freshets of red stuff thereby released!

Vincent Canby in *The New York Times:*

There is hardly a character, a situation or a line of dialogue that has not served a useful purpose in some earlier movie or television show. Now with the passage of time, the characters, the situations and the lines have begun to look very tired and very empty, like William Holden's eyes ... the film is the first theatrical feature to be produced by David L. Wolper, who has made a number of competent television documentaries on war and other topics. Something a little less condescending might have been expected of him, especially since the story is based on fact.

Time:

As a mainstream tough-and-rumble military movie, [the film]—which is based on actual events—offers few new sights or insights. After nearly three decades of World War II films, it is hardly surprising that Hollywood is beginning to suffer from combat fatigue.

With Cliff Robertson and Vince Edwards

234

The Wild Bunch

1969   Warners-7 Arts

CAST:

WILLIAM HOLDEN *(Pike Bishop)*; ERNEST BORGNINE *(Dutch Engstrom)*; ROBERT RYAN *(Deke Thornton)*; EDMOND O'BRIEN *(Sykes)*; WARREN OATES *(Lyle Gorch)*; JAIME SANCHEZ *(Angel)*; BEN JOHNSON *(Tector Gorch)*; EMILIO FERNANDEZ *(Mapache)*; STROTHER MARTIN *(Coffer)*; L. Q. JONES *(T. C.)*; PAT HARRINGTON *(Albert Dekker)*; BO HOPKINS *(Crazy Lee)*; DUB TAYLOR *(Mayor WAINSCOAT)*; JORGE RUSSEK *(Lt. Zamora)*; ALFONSO ARROU *(Herrera)*; CHANO URUETA *(Don Jose)*; SONIA AMELIO *(Teresa)*; AURORA CLAVEL *(Aurora)*; ELSA CARDENAS *(Elsa)*; FERNANDO WAGNER *(German Army Officer)*; *and* PAUL HARPER, CONSTANCE WHITE, *and* LILIA RICHARDS.

CREDITS:

PHIL FELDMAN *(Producer)*; SAM PECKINPAH *(Director)*; *based on a story by* WALON GREEN *and* ROY N. SICKNER; LUCIEN BALLARD *(Photographer)*; JERRY FIELDING *(Music)*; SONNY BURKE *(Music Supervision)*; EDWARD CARRERE *(Art Director)*; LOUIS LOMBARDO *(Editor)*; BUD HULBURD *(Special Effects)*; ROBERT J. MILLER *(Sound)*; GORDON DAWSON *(Wardrobe)*; AL GREENWAY *(Makeup)* ROY N. SICKNER *(Associate Producer)*; WILLIAM FARALLA *(Production Manager)*; CLIFF COLEMAN *and* FRED GAMMON *(Assistant Directors)*; Filmed in Mexico; Panavision 70; Technicolor.

Opened at the Trans-Lux East and West theaters, New York, June 25, 1969. Running time, 140 minutes.

THE PICTURE:

The Wild Bunch turned out to be one of the most controversial pictures of 1969 or any year, its almost pathologically extreme violence and bloody excess commanding on the one hand a gushing admiration from some critics that amounted almost to the masochistic, and on the other an expression from more responsible, objective reviewers of deep disgust with the theme and content. Holden himself drew some critical barbs when he unwisely stated in an interview that violence

With Ernest Borgnine

was cathartic and purgative, and in effect proved a deterrent to actual bloodletting, at which words more than one film commentator scoffed. It was noted that Holden's lined and puffy face at fifty-one had become almost unrecognizable, but he was credited for an energetic performance in a picture many felt should never have been made—or at least not made in that particular manner. Director Sam Peckinpah came in for his share of brickbats, seeming as he did to glory in death, gore, and negatives of all kinds and persuasions, or as one reviewer commented to her escort at a preview, "his sex life must be quite interesting the way he directs." The height of critical masochism or purgation or displacement or sublimation (or *something*) was reached when a reviewer used the word beautiful to describe Peckinpah's lovingly choreographed killings and bloodlettings, which continually spot the surface of *The Wild Bunch* like rampant adolescent acne. Edmond O'Brien, Ernest Borgnine, Robert Ryan, and other talented actors drew their share of praise (along with honest wonderment at this prodigally scandalous *waste* of their talents) in this story, set in 1913, of an outlaw gang of

With Ernest Borgnine, Warren Oates,
and Ben Johnson (right)

the almost extinct Old West, one of a breed that was being driven into oblivion by the onrush of civilization and more sophisticated and thorough public policing techniques. One of these residual gangs, led by Holden, tries to rob a railway office in a Texas border town. They are ambushed by bounty hunters led by Ryan. Once Ryan and Holden had been saddle buddies; now Ryan is employed by the railway to capture Holden's "wild bunch." Holden and his men escape into Mexico after one of the wild scenes of carnage that recur often in the film, and have a rendezvous with a gone-to-seed old gunman, Edmond O'Brien. The gang discovers that the railway bags contain only washers rather than the money they expect. Next the gang makes a deal with Mexican bandits to rob an Army munitions train and sell its rifles to the bandits. Holden outwits Ryan's bounty hunters to rob the train on schedule. Knowing that the Mexicans will try to get the guns without paying, Holden devises a stratagem whereby the money is collected in small parcels. When one of their number is

With Ernest Borgnine and
Ben Johnson

With Ernest Borgnine

Robert Ryan

seized by the bandits, group loyalty demands that they obtain his release, but during a drunken celebration the chief of the bandits slashes the boy's throat with a knife. Holden then kills the chief. He and "the wild bunch" find themselves taking on some two hundred Mexicans. All of the Holden gang are slain, in a scene of gory mayhem that his given Mr. Peckinpah his famous—or notorious—directorial trademark. Later Ryan and his bounty hunters arrive, but most of them are also dispatched by the bloodthirsty Mexicans. The only survivors of all this carnage are Ryan and O'Brien, who presumably team up for one last stand against the onrush of law-and-order civilization. It is presumed that theirs will be an equally grim fate.

REVIEWS:

Judith Crist in *New York* Magazine:
The film winds up with a shootdown that is the bloodiest and most sickening display of slaughter that I can ever recall in a theatrical film, and quotes attributed to Mr. Holden that this sort of ultra-violence is a healthy purgative for viewers is just about as sick.

Charles Champlin in the *Los Angeles Times:*
William Holden [gives] an excellent performance, betten than any he has given in years.

Vincent Canby in *The New York Times:*
The first truly interesting American-made Western in

years. . . . Borrowing a device from *Bonnie and Clyde,* Packinpah suddenly reduces the camera speed to slow motion, which at first heightens the horror of mindless slaughter and then—and this is what really carries horror—makes it beautiful, almost abstract, and finally into terrible parody . . . after years of giving bored performances in boring movies, William Holden comes back gallantly.

Penelope Gilliatt in *The New Yorker:*
Worth ten times the puff ethical theses of films like, say, *Judgment at Nuremberg.* [Written] with ten times more perception than the dialogue in most of the studiously high-class movies made here . . . it is like listening to characters in Ibsen: when we see them they are a long way into their lives together.

Stanley Kauffmann in the *New Republic:*
The best Western I can remember since Brando's *One-eyed Jacks.* Peckinpah is such a gifted director that I don't see how one can avoid using the word "beautiful" about his work. [There is] a kinetic beauty in the very violence that his film lives and revels in. . . . The violence *is* the film. Those who have complained that there's too much of it might as well complain that there's too much punching in a prizefight. [Peckinpah] has found a medium that perfectly accommodates his passion. He likes killing and he does it very well.

238

With Virna Lisi and Brook Fuller

The Christmas Tree

1969   Walter Reade–Continental

CAST:

WILLIAM HOLDEN *(Laurent)*; VIRNI LISI *(Catherine)*; ANDRE BOURVIL *(Verdun)*; BROOK FULLER *(Pascal)*; MADELEINE DAMIEN *(Marinette)*; FRIEDRICH LEDEBUR *(Vernet)*; MARIO FELICIANI *(The Doctor)*.

CREDITS:

A Co-Production of Corona Films (Paris) and Jupiter Films (Rome); Released in the United States by the WALTER READE *Organization through Continental Distributing;* ROBERT DORFMANN *(Producer);* TERENCE YOUNG *(Director and Writer); based on the novel* L'Arbre de Noel *by* MICHEL BATAILLE; BERNARD FARREL *(Second Unit Director);* HENRI ALEKAN *(Photographer);* RAYMOND PICON-BORREL *(Second Unit Photographer);* GEORGES AURIC *(Music);* JEAN ANDRE *(Production Designer);* TONY ROMAN, ROBERT ANDRE *and* EUGENE ROMAN *(Art Directors);* FERNAND BERNARDI *and* ROBERT TURLURE *(Set Decorators);* JOHNNY DWYRE *(Editor);* KARL BAUMGARTNER *and* DANIEL BRAUNSCHWEIG *(Special Effects);* WILLIAM R. SIVEL *(Sound);* TANINE AUTRE *(Costumes);* MARIE-MADELEINE PARIS *(Makeup);* ALAIN SCEMAMA *(Hairstyles);* GEORGES VALON *(Production Supervisor);* PAUL FEYDER *(Assistant Director); Filmed on location in Nice and Corsica; interiors at Studio Boulogne, Paris; Eastman Color; U.S. Print by Movielab.*

Opened at Radio City Music Hall, New York, September 25, 1969. Runnnig time, 110 minutes.

THE PICTURE:

Terence Young then wrote and directed a film for Holden, and shot it in Paris, Nice, and Corsica. Holden's

of radiation poisoning, it got a somewhat mixed reaction from the critics, with such as Judith Crist calling it "an obscenity"—after which she added, "There won't be a dry eye—or a full stomach—in the house." Mrs. Crist pressed home the point that dealing with nuclear contamination on such a personal, sentimental level was essentially a vulgarity while other critics stressed that "the weep's the thing," and felt it would appeal to distaff audiences. Though Holden's and Young's intentions were of the best, the whole thing failed to jell, and it is not one of Holden's memorable features. The direction was adjudged to be wavering, the performances listless, and the overall staging awkward. The film was said to be suggested by the Palomares incident—the accidental dropping from a U.S. plane of an H-bomb off the coast of Spain. The plot in detail? A wealthy French-American widower (Holden) and his eleven-year-old son Pascal (Brook Fuller) are fishing near a beach when an atomic-weapon-carrying plane explodes overhead. Young Fuller contracts radiation poisoning, which leads to leukemia. (Holden escapes because he was swimming underwater). Holden learns that his son has only a few months to live and takes him to his French country home. Also on hand are Holden's girlfriend Catherine (Virna Lisi) and his old war buddy Verdun (Bourvil). Sadly they set in for the protracted death watch, with the grieving father indulging such whims as the boy's desire for pet wolves, which Holden and Bourvil steal from a Paris zoo and help the boy train. Christmas eve comes, and the father returns from shopping to find his boy dead beneath his Christmas tree, his presents opened and his wolves on guard. The boy leaves his father, as a present, an affecting plaque in which he wishes the survivors the best. As the plot indicates, there is much contrivance of the kind

choice of *The Christmas Tree* as his next was thought to be one of his reactions to the criticism of his purported remarks about *The Wild Bunch,* for which he was castigated publicly for seeming to condone violence as a cathartic element in films. A sentimental, highly contrived tale about a father who watches his boy die

With Brook Fuller and Bourvil

240

With Brook Fuller

the critics deplored. The idea of stealing wolves from a zoo is far-fetched, the Christmas tree gimmick is much too much, and assorted shots of Holden staring skyward as if anticipating more nuclear horrors, seem forced. Though the film was given some credit for worthy aims, attempting as it did to say something about life, death, and the human capacity for wanton destruction, its gimmicks, cloying quality, and awkward concept canceled out whatever assets it had.

REVIEWS:

Joseph Gelmis in *Newsday:*
Holden's interpretation of the father is totally unlike the tough, cynical parts with which he has been identified for the past decade or so. He's anguished and tender and altogether brilliant.

Lawrence J. Quirk in *Screen Slants:*
While it is nice to see a picture that doesn't fear sentiment in these most unsentimental sixties, I am afraid that this is a case of too much of a good thing, and what should be moving is more often bathetic and contrived. Mr. Holden's desire to vary his pace and fare is commendable but in this case misplaced. Indeed he seems none too relaxed throughout, as if he subconsciously knows he has picked a loser.

Kevin Thomas in the *Los Angeles Times:*
Holden is his familiar, if older, suave self, and Brook Fuller, though somewhat the kid actor type, is convincingly the precocious son of a detached, middle-aged father. . . . Virna Lisi is just the sort of chic beauty the affluent, still attractive Holden would capture, and French character star Bourvil lends the film great warmth and substance as a lovable family retainer.

William Wolf in *Cue:*
[The Film] treats a scorching problem with a mere evasive whimper . . . only the most hardened moviegoer will be able to avoid that ultimate lump in the throat. However, by not dealing head-on with the forces responsible, the film really has nowhere to go.

Whit in *Variety:*
A story that might be taken out of today's headlines, legitimately premised and boasting a cast which does yeomen service to Terence Young's potent direction of his own powerful screenplay . . . one of the most understanding portrayals of [Holden's] career.

With Brook Fuller

241

With Ryan O'Neal

Wild Rovers

1971   Metro-Goldwyn-Mayer

CAST:

WILLIAM HOLDEN *(Ross Bodine)*; RYAN O'NEAL *(Frank Post)*; KARL MALDEN *(Walter Buckman)*; LYNN CARLIN *(Sada Billings)*; TOM SKERRITT *(John Buckman)*; JOE DON BAKER *(Paul Buckman)*; JAMES OLSON *(Joe Billings)*; LEORA DANA *(Neil Buckman)*; MOSES GUNN *(Ben)*; VICTOR FRENCH *(Sheriff)*; RACHEL ROBERTS *(Maybell)*; CHARLES GRAY *(Hereford)*; SAM GILMAN *(Hansen)*; WILLIAM BRYANT *(Cap Swilling)*; JACK GARNER *(Bodine's Girl)*; CAITLIN WILES *(Sada's Mother)*; MARY JACKSON *(Ruff)*; WILLIAM LUCKING *(Gambler)*; ED BAKEY *(Tucson Sheriff)*; TED GEHRING *(Palace Bartender)*; ALAN CARNEY *(Cassidy)*; ED LONG *(Palace Tenor)*; PATRICK SULLIVAN BURKE *(Leaky)*; LEE DE BROUX *(Mack)*; HAL LYNCH *(Sheepman)*; RED MORGAN *(Sheepman)*; BENNIE DOBBINS *(Bathhouse Attendant)*; BOB BECK *(Attendant's Son)*; GEOFFREY EDWARDS *(Piano Player)*; STUDS TANNEY *(Canteen Bartender)*; BRUNO DE SOTA *(Deputy)*.

CREDITS:

A BLAKE EDWARDS *Film*; BLAKE EDWARDS *and* KEN WALES *(Producers)*; BLAKE EDWARDS *(Director and Writer)*; DICK CROCKETT *(Second Unit Director)*; PHILIP LATHROP *(Photography)*; FRANK STANLEY *(Second Unit Photography)*; JERRY GOLDSMITH *(Music)*; "Wild Rover" *(song; lyrics by* ERNIE SHELDON; *music by* JERRY GOLDSMITH; *sung by* SHEB WOOLEY); GEORGE W. DAVIS *and* ADDISON HEHR *(Art Directors)*; JOHN F. BURNETT *(Editor)*; ROBERT BENTON *and* REG ALLEN *(Set Decorations)*; BRUCE WRIGHT *and* HARRY W. TETRICK *(Sound)*; JACK BEAR *(Costumes)*; TOM TUTTLE *(Makeup)*; CHERIE *(Hairstyles)*; ALAN CALLOW *(Assistant Director)*; RIDGEWAY CALLOW *(Production Manager)*; *Filmed in Arizona and Utah; Metrocolor; Panavision.*

Opened at Astor, Juliet 2, and 34th Street East theaters, June 23, 1971. Running time, 106 minutes.

THE PICTURE:

The consensus on *Wild Rovers* seemed to be that Blake Edwards was not cut out to handle Westerns, his talents being of a more psychologically introspective and thematically elegant stripe; that William Holden was working his Western stereotype to death; and that Ryan O'Neal's was a small but distinctive talent that could

With Ryan O'Neal

243

not sustain ill-advised direction and a meaningless, listless script (an original by Edwards). The story line and general treatment give rise to the suspicion that Edwards had an authentic, clear-spirited original inspiration but self-consciously and self-protectively tricked it up and obscured its point, possibly because he distrusted (or feared) his own inspiration, and was more interested in pleasing the twelve-year-old mind in a commercialistic copout than in following Emerson's principle of self-realization. *Wild Rovers* is certainly an irritating film—irritating in its pointlessness, in its proliferation of blind-alley allusions, in its empty symbol-

isms and silly abstractions-that-are-not-abstractions—a true "existentialist" movie. The original version had run 130 minutes, but when the reaction to the interminable atmospheric stuff and the downbeat theme was registered sharply and vociferously at a preview, the picture was cut to its 106-minute release length—not that any real or meaningful improvement resulted. For some unaccountable reason, the theme has been compared with O'Neal's 1970 film, *Love Story*, in the sense, we suppose, that Ali MacGraw had died while he agonized over her, while in *Wild Rovers he* dies while Holden agonizes over *him*. This is a silly comparison,

With Ryan O'Neal

With Ryan O'Neal

With Ryan O'Neal

since the plots are essentially dissimilar, unless the point is stretched that the man of fifty and the boy of twenty-five, two companions in outlawry who eventually find death in the vast open spaces, indulged an intense, albeit platonic, form of camaraderie-love. The plot, what there was of it, dealt with two buddies in the 1880s West who work on Karl Malden's ranch. For no reason that remotely makes sense, they decide that they will rob a bank together in the muddled belief that this will prove an open-sesame to a less drab, more adventurous life. This brings about the inevitable pursuit by a posse that includes Malden's two sons. Malden demands that the search be continued even beyond the sheriff's territorial jurisdiction, in line with his feeling that justice is due the men because it will discourage other outlawry. There are scenes (during the flight) in a smalltown bordello and bar that are as pointless as their wanderings here and there, and a pictorially handsome but thematically vague sequence in which Holden lassoes a wild horse while his young partner happily cavorts in the snow. O'Neal is then seriously wounded

in a shootout and the pair flee town. Meanwhile the original posse has dwindled to Malden's two sons, who persist in their search for the "wild rovers" even though they get news of their father's death in a range war. Holden realizes that O'Neal is dying of his wound. The young man passes away quietly as Holden sits by him drawing rosy pictures of their future life together in Mexico. Holden buries his pal and rides on until the two-man posse finally reaches and kills *him*. Make of all that what you will.

REVIEWS:

Charles Champlin in *The Los Angeles Times:*

An existentialist Western which will not do much for existentialism, the Western or the boxoffice . . . Edwards has turned out another handsomely mounted and excellently photographed movie, and he has extracted good if impersonal performances from William Holden and Ryan O'Neal. But Edwards has also come up with a strangely flaccid and listless story which somehow never works either as make-believe or might-have-been

With Ryan O'Neal

and whose characters are never able to engage the sympathy and interest of the audience . . . there seems at last no real point in tagging along with this tame and colorless twosome. Fatalism can be fatal.

The *Village Voice:*

Despite the behavioral blandness in Ryan O'Neal's performance, *Wild Rovers* is well served by the iconography of its stars: Holden's craggy, lined face indicating a depth of feeling simply in terms of years lived, memories accumulated; O'Neal's baby-smooth face and limited range of expression searching for the kind of depth indicated by Holden's lines. The film then becomes a kind of odyssey in search of memory, the creation of a past that can scatter away the darkness of the present.

The *Washington Post:*

The movie is just about everything a Western shouldn't

be—slow-moving, uneventful, vague, colorless, emotionless. . . . Holden's character remains a tiresome old codger-in-the-making, weighed down with the kind of homely-philosophizin' dialogue that blunders in one ear and right out the other, unwanted and unheeded. . . . O'Neal happens to look cherubic, but to the minute degree his character is developed at all, he's not even likable. [The film] shows every sign of being dead from the start, done in by fundamental lack of feeling and facility on Edwards' part . . . since there is no particular motive or justification for anything that happens and so little character to identify with, one is never involved in the action or stirred by the violent interludes and climaxes which feel trumped-up, just a temporary relief from boredom, rather than climactic.

The Revengers

1972   National General Pictures

CAST:

WILLIAM HOLDEN (*John Benedict*); SUSAN HAYWARD (*Elizabeth*); ERNEST BORGNINE (*Hoop*); WOODY STRODE (*Job*); ROGER HANIN (*Quiberon*); RENE KOLDEHOFF (*Zweig*); JORGE LUKE (*Chamaco*); JORGE MARTINEZ DE HOYOS (*Cholo*); ARTHUR HUNNICUTT (*Free State*); WARREN VANDERS (*Tarp*); LARRY PENNELL (*Arny*); JOHN KELLY (*Whitcomb*); SCOTT HOLDEN (*Lieutenant*); JAMES DAUGHTON (*Morgan*); LORRAINE CHANEL (*Mrs. Benedict*); RAUL PRIETO (*Warden*).

CREDITS:

MARTIN RACKIN (*Producer*); DANIEL MANN (*Director*); WENDELL MAYES (*Screenplay*); *from a story by* STEVEN W. CARABATSOS; GABRIEL TORRES (*Photography*) PINO CALVI (*Music*); JORGE FERNANDEZ (*Art Director*); WALTER HANNEMANN *and* JUAN JOSE MARINO (*Editors*); JESUS GONZALEZ GANCY *and* ANGEL TREJO (*Sound*); ROBERT GOLDSTEIN *and* FELIPE PALOMINO (*Assistant Directors*); *Filmed in Mexico; Panavision, Deluxe Color.*

Opened at showcase theaters, New York, June 21, 1972. Running time, 107 minutes.

THE PICTURE:

Holden is wasted in this pedestrian Western which came into New York in June, 1972, and made a relatively quick departure. No wonder, for it has all been

With Susan Hayward

done before, indeed many times too often. Holden plays a Civil War veteran and Colorado rancher who returns from a hunting trip to find his wife and four children have been massacred by a band of Comanches headed by a white renegade. Holden proceeds to plot pursuit and revenge in the usual style. He recruits six condemned men from a Mexican prison to help him. They trek into the Mexican wilderness, and much footage is given to his tense relationships with the men, who prove dangerous and unpredictable. One of them shoots him. Susan Hayward appears out of nowhere as a variety of frontier nurse ensconced on an isolated potato farm; she nurses Holden back to health, and a romance of sorts develops. But it becomes obvious that Holden won't settle down with Susan until he has gotten the varmint who destroyed his loved ones, and soon he is off to the chase again. The action then involves Holden's incarceration in a Mexican prison, his rescue by members of his ambivalent rogues' contingent, and their eventual alliance with an Army contingent besieged by Indians. The Indians are licked, the murderer turns up as a prisoner on the Army post, Holden reaches a belated decision—that revenge isn't worth the spiritual cost—and rides off, presumably to Miss Hayward, with the parting felicitations of his semiredeemed gang. Scott Holden has a role in his dad's film, playing an Army lieutenant. There are a number of good actors along for the ride, including Ernest Borgnine and Woody

With James Daughton

249

With Raul Prieto (right)

Strode. Daniel Mann tries to inject excitement and variety, but everyone has been thataway before, and it all has a tired look. Holden performs creditably enough, though the weight of his fifty-four years seems to slow him up at times. Nor is there as much action as is customary in this genre. Miss Hayward is altogether superfluous in a role limited in footage and characterization. It was her first screen appearance with Holden since *Young and Willing* thirty years before. They posed together looking at a still of themselves in the earlier film, and reminisced about old times and former associates.

REVIEWS:

Whit in *Variety:*

Blessed with a natural boxoffice title [the film] meets the demands of screen westerns as a shooting gallery, but storywise, despite a premise that could have elevated feature into a slick actioner, plunges into a slough of indecisive writing in need of 15 to 20 minutes shear-

With Ernest Borgnine, Roger Hanin, Woody Strode, Jorge Luke, Rene Koldehoff, and Jorge Martinez De Hoyos

With Roger Hanin, Jorge Luke, Rene Holdehoff, Jorge Martinez De Hoyos, Ernest Borgnine, and Woody Strode

ing. Starting out strongly . . . expected gutsy action fails to generate much suspense or highlights. . . . Holden handles himself well enough although there are occasions when his reaction to circumstances lacks conviction . . . Scott Holden—his son—does a nice job as a cavalry lieutenant . . . Daniel Mann's direction was partially stymied by script deficiencies but managed fast action at times.

William Wolf in *Cue:*

One wonders what prompts an actor like William Holden to take a part like this. The screenplay . . . is drab and predictably routine. [Susan Hayward's] Irish brogue as unconvincing as everything else. Eventually [Holden] realizes that a thirst for vengeance eats a man up for no good purpose. It's an old idea but nothing new or compelling is done with it. Director Daniel Mann does about what one might expect, and Holden plods along looking stoic.

Howard Thompson in *The New York Times:*

A good, blunt Western like *The Revengers* is easy to take on its own terms. . . . This is a workmanlike movie, snugly directed by Daniel Mann, with a solid, craggy and dusty sweep of Mexican background. And the scroungy, amusingly ribald dialogue by Wendell Mayes is handled with tough relish by Holden and his abettors. . . . Curiously the film sacrifices wallop for laconic bite, as the men gallop back and forth in the testy camaraderie that is its main appeal. The revenge theme is more or less shelved, as it emphatically was not in that Gregory Peck Western *The Bravados.* Furthermore, the story shoehorns into the middle a brief, tender vignette involving a wounded Holden and a frontier nurse, played by Susan Hayward. Miss Hayward is a fine, honest actress but entirely incredible as this gentle altruist who sheds wisdom way out in the middle of nowhere. In any case, when Holden finally nabs his original quarry, after a rousing Indian foray, it seems anticlimactic. And if I hadn't heard Holden's final dialogue sign-off, like a cop-out prairie poet, I wouldn't have believed it. Even so, *The Revengers* is an entertaining, leathery compromise.

With Ernest Borgnine, Rene Koldehoff, and Roger Hanin

Breezy

1973   Universal

CAST:

WILLIAM HOLDEN *(Frank Harmon)*; KAY LENZ *(Breezy)*; DENNIS OLIVIERI *(Bruno)*; MARJ DUSAY *(Betty Tobin)*; EUGENE PETERSON *(Charlie)*; JOAN HOTCHKISS *(Paula)*; ROGER C. CARMEL *(Bob)*; SHELLEY MORRISON *(Nancy)*; JAMIE SMITH JACKSON *(Marcy)*; SCOTT HOLDEN *(Veterinarian)*.

CREDITS:

A Universal/Malpaso Production. CLINT EASTWOOD *(Director)*; ROBERT DALEY *(Producer)*; JO HEIMS *(Associate Producer and Screenwriter)*; *Original Screenplay by* JO HEIMS; FRANK STANLEY *(Photographer)*; ALEXANDER GOLITZEN *(Art Director)*; DON ROBERTS *(Unit Production Manager)*; JAMES ALEXANDER *(Sound)*; FERRIS WEBSTER *(Film Editor)*.

THE PICTURE:

Holden's 1973 release, *Breezy*, is a love story about a fifty-year-old man, divorced and disillusioned, who falls in love slowly but surely with a life-loving, vibrant girl of seventeen (Kay Lenz). Caught previously in a listless "uninvolvement," Holden had carried on friendships, including one with Marj Dusay, whose feeling for him he cannot return. She finally marries someone else. He encounters Breezy near his house after she has spent the night with a hippie friend (Dennis Olivieri) and he agrees to give her a lift in his car. They get to know each other, and Holden finally warms to her youthful high spirits. He comes to realize that another deep and meaningful love relationship is yet possible for him, and they have an affair.

But matters grow complicated when his mature

With Kay Lenz

With Marj Dusay

friends express their disapproval, and Frank (Holden), aware of the thirty-three-year-difference in their respective ages, and feeling that Breezy should be seeking a more natural and lasting happiness with friends her own age, decides to give her up. But the mutual attraction is too strong, and though Holden feels that at best they will have a year or two together, they decide that a brief period of complete happiness is infinitely preferable to no happiness at all. Scott Holden, who appeared with his father in *The Revengers*, portrays a veterinarian who saves the life of an injured dog adopted by Holden and Miss Lenz, who names it "Sir Love-a-Lot."

Breezy marks actor Clint Eastwood's third picture as a director, his first two being *Play Misty For Me* and *High Plains Drifter*. The film was shot in various spots around Los Angeles, Eastwood being a firm believer in location filming. Actual sites called for in the script were used, with Eastwood and his staff scouting unusual locations. Among those used were Laurel Canyon, Lookout Mountain, Topanga Canyon, Plummer Park, Griffith Park and Hollywood and Ventura Boulevards. Kay Lenz, nineteen, Holden's young co-star, makes her film debut in *Breezy*. She had acted under the name of Kay Ann Kemper on TV's *The Monroes*, *Ironside* and other shows, but switched back to her real name for this picture. Many of Holden's admirers have welcomed his switch from violent period westerns to this intimate contemporary romance.

With Kay Lenz